Distinguished Dissertations

Springer
London
Berlin
Heidelberg
New York
Barcelona
Budapest
Hong Kong
Milan
Paris
Santa Clara
Singapore
Tokyo

Other titles published in this Series:

Extensional Constructs in Intensional Type Theory
Martin Hofmann

Hardware Evolution: Automatic Design of Electronic Circuits in Reconfigurable Hardware by Artificial Evolution
Adrian Thompson

Games and Full Abstraction for a Functional Metalanguage with Recursive Types
Guy McCusker

Search and Planning Under Incomplete Information: A Study Using Bridge Card Play
Ian Frank

John Harrison

Theorem Proving with the Real Numbers

Springer

John Harrison, PhD, MA
University of Cambridge Computer Laboratory, New Museums Site, Pembroke Street, Cambridge, CB2 3QG

Series Editor

C.J. van Rijsbergen

ISBN-13:978-1-4471-1593-9

British Library Cataloguing in Publication Data
Harrison, John Robert
Theorem proving with the real numbers. - (Distinguished dissertations)
1.Proof theory
I.Title
511.3
ISBN-13:978-1-4471-1593-9

Library of Congress Cataloging-in-Publication Data
Harrison, J. (John), 1966-
Theorem proving with the real numbers / John Harrison.
p. cm, -- (Distinguished dissertations)
ISBN-13:978-1-4471-1593-9 e-ISBN-13:978-1-4471-1591-5
DOI: 10.1007/978-1-4471-1591-5
1. Automatic theorem proving. I. Title. II. Series:
Distinguished dissertations (Springer-Verlag)
QA76.9.A96H37 1998
00.5.1'4--dc21 98-17946

Softcover reprint of the hardcover 1st edition 1998

Typesetting: Camera ready by author

34/3830-543210 Printed on acid-free paper

Preface

This book discusses the use of the real numbers in theorem proving. Typically, theorem provers only support a few 'discrete' datatypes such as the natural numbers. However the availability of the real numbers opens up many interesting and important application areas, such as the verification of floating point hardware and hybrid systems. It also allows the formalization of many more branches of classical mathematics, which is particularly relevant for attempts to inject more rigour into computer algebra systems.

Our work is conducted in a version of the HOL theorem prover. We describe the rigorous definitional construction of the real numbers, using a new version of Cantor's method, and the formalization of a significant portion of real analysis. We also describe an advanced derived decision procedure for the 'Tarski subset' of real algebra as well as some more modest but practically useful tools for automating explicit calculations and routine linear arithmetic reasoning.

Finally, we consider in more detail two interesting application areas. We discuss the desirability of combining the rigour of theorem provers with the power and convenience of computer algebra systems, and explain a method we have used in practice to achieve this. We then move on to the verification of floating point hardware. After a careful discussion of possible correctness specifications, we report on two case studies, one involving a transcendental function.

We aim to show that a theory of real numbers is useful in practice and interesting in theory, and that the 'LCF style' of theorem proving is well suited to the kind of work we describe. We hope also to convince the reader that the kind of mathematics needed for applications is well within the abilities of current theorem proving technology.

Preface to this edition

This book is a slightly revised version of my University of Cambridge PhD thesis, incorporating a few changes suggested by my examiners and one or two of my own. For publication, the opportunity has also been taken to correct a few small errors and to bring some references up to date. The most substantial changes are to the appendices. Appendix A has been expanded and updated to give a more thorough discussion of HOL Light's deductive system. Appendix B is new, and summarizes some recent work since the original thesis was written in Summer 1996.

I would like to thank my PhD examiners, Ursula Martin and Larry Paulson, for making the viva voce examination such a pleasant experience, and for suggesting that my thesis should be entered for the Distinguished Dissertation scheme.

Acknowledgements

I owe an immense debt of gratitude to Mike Gordon, whose supervision has been a perfect mixture of advice, encouragement and indulgence. His intellectual powers and enthusiasm for research, as well as his kindness and modesty, have provided an inspiring model. Many other people, especially members of the Hardware Verification and Automated Reasoning groups at the Computer Laboratory in Cambridge, have provided a friendly and stimulating environment. In particular Richard Boulton first interested me in these research topics, John Van Tassel and John Herbert did so much to help me get started during the early days, Tom Melham greatly deepened my appreciation of many issues in theorem proving and verification, Thomas Forster taught me a lot about logic and set theory, Larry Paulson often gave me valuable advice about theorem proving and formalization, Laurent Théry motivated much of the work in computer algebra, and Konrad Slind and Joseph Melia were a continual source of inspiration both intellectual and personal. In practical departments, I have been helped by Lewis and Paola in the library, by Margaret, Angela and Fay in administrative and financial matters, and by Edie, Cathy and others in catering. Thanks also to Piete Brookes, Martyn Johnson and Graham Titmus for help with the machines, networking, LaTeX and so forth.

My work was generously funded by the Engineering and Physical Sciences Research Council (formerly the Science and Engineering Research Council) and also by an award from the Isaac Newton Trust. Additional funding for visits to conferences was given by the European Commission, the University of Cambridge Computer Laboratory, Churchill College, the British Council, and the US Office of Naval Research. I am also grateful to those organizations that have invited me to visit and talk about my work; the resulting exchanges of ideas have always been productive. Thanks to those at Technische Universität München, Cornell University, Digital Equipment Corporation (Boston), Åbo Akademi, AT&T Bell Labs (New Jersey), Imperial College, INRIA Rocquencourt, and Warsaw University (Białystok branch) who looked after me so well.

The writing of the original thesis was completed while I was a member of Ralph Back's Programming Methodology Group at Åbo Akademi University, funded by the European Commission under the HCM scheme. Thanks to Jockum von Wright for inviting me there, and to him and all the others who made that time so enjoyable and stimulating, especially Jim Grundy and Sandi Bone for their hospitality. Finally, I'm deeply grateful to my parents for their support over the years, and of course to Tania, for showing me that there's more to life than theorem proving.

To my parents

Contents

1. Introduction

We briefly survey the field of computer theorem proving and emphasize the recent interest in using theorem provers for the verification of computer systems. We point out a significant hole in existing practice, where verification of many interesting systems cannot be performed for lack of mathematical infrastructure concerning the real numbers and classical 'continuous' mathematics. This motivates the remainder of the book where we show how to plug this gap, and illustrate the possibilities with some applications.

1.1 Symbolic computation

Early in their development, electronic computers were mainly applied to numerical tasks arising in various branches of science, especially engineering. They subsequently escaped from this intellectual ghetto and assumed their present ubiquity in all walks of life. Partly this was because technological advances made computers smaller, more reliable and less power-hungry, but an equally important factor was the ingenuity of programmers in applying computers to areas not previously envisaged. Many of these applications, like video games and word processing, break away from the scientific field completely. Two that stay within its purview are *computer algebra* and *computer theorem proving*.

Computer algebra systems are able to perform symbolic computations like factorizing polynomials, differentiating and integrating expressions, solving equations, and expanding functions in power series. These tasks are essentially routine, and hence quite easy to automate to a large extent. Their routine nature means that any mathematician should in principle be able to do them by hand, but it is a time-consuming and error-prone process. One may say that computer algebra systems are to higher mathematicians what simple pocket calculators are to schoolchildren. Their use is very common in all areas of science and applied mathematics.

Computer theorem proving also involves symbolic manipulations, but here the emphasis is on performing basic logical operations rather than high level mathematics. The twentieth century has seen an upsurge of interest in symbolic logic. This was envisaged by at least some of its developers, like Peano, as a practical language in which to express mathematical statements clearly and unambiguously. Others, like Hilbert, regarded formal logic merely as a theoretical device permitting *metamathematical* investigation of mathematical systems — all that mattered was that proofs could 'in principle' be written out completely formally. The enormous practical difficulties of actually rendering proofs in formal logic are illustrated by the size of the *Principia Mathematica* of Whitehead and Russell (1910). But just as it helps with tedious arithmetical and algebraic reasoning, the computer can help with the tedium of constructing formal proofs — or even automate the process completely.

1.2 Verification

In recent years theorem proving has received a new impetus, and it has come from just the explosion in the use of computers and the ingenuity of programmers which we discussed above. Because of the complexity of computer systems (software especially, but nowadays hardware is very complex too) it is increasingly difficult to make them work correctly. Their widespread use means that the economic consequences for a manufacturer of incorrectness can be very serious. An infamous example at the time of writing is the Pentium[1] floating point bug, which we shall discuss in more detail later. Moreover, computers have found their way into applications such as heart pacemakers, radiation therapy machines, nuclear reactor controllers, fly-by-wire aircraft and car engine management systems, where a failure could cause loss of life.

Traditional techniques for showing the validity of a design rely mainly on extensive test suites. It's usually impossible to verify designs exhaustively by such methods, simply because of the number of possible states, though some approaches, like those described by Kantrowitz and Noack (1995), use extremely sophisticated ways of picking useful test cases. The alternative is some kind of formal verification, which attempts to *prove* mathematically that a system meets its specification.

However, to be amenable to mathematical proof, both the specification of the system and the model of its actual behaviour need to be stated mathematically. It is impossible to *prove* that a given chip or program will function as intended.[2] Even given a proof that the formal model obeys the formal specification, there remain two gaps that cannot be closed by a mathematical treatment:

1. Between the formal model of the system's behaviour and its actual, real-world behaviour.
2. Between the formal specification of the system and the complex requirements (of the designer, customer etc.) in real life.

[1] Pentium is a registered trademark of Intel Corporation.

[2] For this reason some people find the use of the term 'verification' objectionable, but to us it seems no worse than referring to 'optimizing compilers'.

The former is of course common to all engineering disciplines, and most other applications of physical science.[3] We will have little to say about this gap, except to reiterate the point, made forcefully by Rushby (1991), that engineers involved in fabrication have made such progress that errors in this stage are much less of a problem than design errors which *are* amenable to mathematical treatment.

The second gap is rather interesting. The requirements for a complex system in real life may defy formalization. Sometimes this is on grounds of complexity, sometimes because they are inherently sociological or psychological. We want to write the specification in a language that is clear, unambiguous and amenable to mathematical treatment. The second and third requirements generally rule out the unrestricted use of natural language; the obvious alternative is the kind of formal logic that we have already touched on. However these formalisms tend to fall down on the first requirement: typically they are rather obscure even to those schooled in their intricacies.

1.3 Higher order logic

Many successful specification languages such as Z (Spivey 1988) are loosely based on formal logic, but augment it with powerful and flexible additional notation. However Z and its ilk were not designed for the purpose of verification, but for *specification alone.* This is by no means useless, since the process of writing out a specification formally can be enormously clarifying. But standards for these languages typically leave unsaid many details about their semantics (e.g. the use of partial functions and the exact nature of the underlying set or type theory). Instead, the use of classical higher order logic has been widely advocated. It is a conceptually simple formalism with a precise semantics, but by simple and secure extension allows the use of many familiar mathematical notations, and suffices for the development of much of classical mathematics.

The benefits of higher order logic in certain fields of verification have long been recognized — Ernst and Hookway (1976) were early advocates. For example, Huet and Lang (1978) show how the typical syntactic resources of higher order logic are useful for expressing program transformations in a generic way. More recently, the use of higher order logic has been advocated for hardware verification by Hanna and Daeche (1986), Gordon (1985) and Joyce (1991). Part of the reason is that higher order functions allow a very direct formalization of notions arising in hardware, e.g. signals as functions from natural numbers to booleans or reals to reals. Moreover, since higher

[3] Computer systems construction has more in common with engineering than with explanatory applications of physical science, in that a mismatch between the model and reality indicates that *reality is wrong* rather than pointing to a deficiency in the model: the primitive components are supposed to conform to the model!

order logic suffices for the development of numbers and other mathematical structures, it allows one to reason generically, e.g. prove properties of n-bit circuits for variable n. But there is also another important reason why a general mathematical framework like higher order logic or set theory is appealing.

Computer systems are often reasoned about using a variety of special formalisms, some quite mundane like propositional logic, some more sophisticated such as temporal logics and process calculi. A great advantage of higher order logic is that all these can be understood as a special syntax built on top of the basic logic, and subsumed under a simple and fundamental theory, rather than being separate and semantically incompatible.[4] Indeed Gordon (1996) reports that he was heavily influenced by the work of Moskowski (1986) on Interval Temporal Logic (ITL).

There has been a great deal of work done in this field, mostly mechanized in Gordon's HOL theorem prover which we consider below. The idea is not limited to hardware verification or to traditional logical formalisms. In a classic paper, Gordon (1989) showed how a simple imperative programming language could be semantically embedded in higher order logic in such a way that the classic Floyd-Hoare rules simply become derivable theorems. The same was done with a programming logic for a more advanced theory of program refinement by von Wright, Hekanaho, Luostarinen, and Långbacka (1993). (This fits naturally with the view, expressed for example by Dijkstra (1976), that a programming language should be thought of first and foremost as an algorithm-oriented system of mathematical notation, and only secondarily as something to be run on a machine.) Other formalisms embedded in HOL in this way include CCS (Nesi 1993), CSP (Camilleri 1990), TLA (von Wright 1991), UNITY (Andersen, Petersen, and Pettersson 1993) and Z (Bowen and Gordon 1995).[5]

These approaches ascribe a denotational semantics in terms of higher order logic, where the denotation function is extra-logical, essentially a syntactic sugaring. Boulton et al. (1993) describe similar approaches to formalizing the semantics of hardware description languages, and draw a contrast between this approach ('shallow embedding') and a more formal style of denotational semantics where the syntax of the embedded formalism and the semantic mapping are represented directly in the logic, rather than being external. A semantics for a fragment of the VHDL hardware description language in this latter style is given by Van Tassel (1993); there are several other recent examples of such 'deep embeddings'.

[4] Even without its practical and methodological utility, many find this attractive on philosophical grounds. For example there is an influential view, associated with Quine, that the presence of (perceived) non-extensional features of modal operators indicates that these should not be regarded as primitive, but should be further analyzed.

[5] An earlier and more substantial embedding of Z was undertaken by ICL Secure Systems.

1.4 Theorem proving vs. model checking

Whatever the formalism selected for a verification application, it is then necessary to relate the specification and implementation; that is, to perform some sort of mathematical proof. It is possible to do the proof by hand; however this is a tedious and error-prone process, all the more so because the proofs involved in verification tend to be much more intricate than those in (at least pure) mathematics. Mathematics emphasizes conceptual simplicity, abstraction and unification, whereas all too often verification involves detailed consideration of the nitty-gritty of integer overflow and suchlike. Melham (1993) discusses ways of achieving abstraction in verification applications, but even so the point stands. Therefore it is desirable to have the computer help, since it is good at performing intricate symbolic computations without making mistakes.

We can divide the major approaches into two streams, called 'model checking' and 'theorem proving'. These correspond very roughly to the traditional divide in logic between 'model theory' and 'proof theory'. In model theory one considers the underlying models of the formal statements and uses arbitrary mathematical resources in that study, whereas in proof theory one uses certain formal procedures for operating on the symbolic statements. Likewise, in theorem proving one uses some specific deductive system, whereas in model checking one typically uses ingenious methods of exhaustive enumeration of the finite set of possible models.[6] As an example of how exhaustive enumeration can be used, it is possible to decide whether two combinational digital logic circuits exhibit the same behaviour simply by examining all possible combinations of inputs. Such approaches have the benefit of being essentially automatic: one pushes a button and waits. However they also have two defects. First, theoretical decidability does not imply practical feasibility; it often happens that large examples are impossible. (Though using better algorithms, e.g. Binary Decision Diagrams (Bryant 1986) or a patented algorithm due to Stålmarck (1994), one can tackle surprisingly large examples.) Second, they usually require us to restrict the specification to use rather simple and low-level mathematical ideas, which militates against our wish to have a high-level, readable specification.

The 'theorem proving' alternative is to take up not only the formal language of the pioneers in symbolic logic, but also the formal proof systems

[6] The analogy is not completely accurate, and neither is the division between theorem proving and model checking completely clear-cut. For example, the statements derivable by any automated means form a recursively enumerable set, which abstractly is the defining property of a 'formal system'. And on the other hand, model checking is often understood in a more specific sense, e.g. to refer only to work, following the classic paper of Clarke and Emerson (1981), on determining whether a formula of propositional temporal logic is satisfied by a particular finite model. However there are important model-checking methods that keep time explicit and don't use temporal operators (Seger and Bryant 1995).

they developed. This means doing something much like a traditional mathematical proof, but analyzed down to a very small and formal logical core. In this way both the drawbacks of the model checking approach are avoided.

1.5 Automated vs. interactive theorem proving

The great disadvantage of theorem proving as compared with model checking is that decidability is usually lost. While in certain problem domains (e.g. propositional tautologies, linear arithmetic, certain algebraic operations), complete automation is possible, even validity in first order logic is not decidable; it may require arbitrarily long search. So attempts at complete automation seem likely to founder on quite simple problems. In fact, some impressive results have been achieved with automatic provers for first order logic (Argonne National Laboratories 1995), but these are still not problems of real practical significance. The NQTHM theorem prover (Boyer and Moore 1979) is more successful in practical cases; by restricting the logic, it becomes possible to offer some quite powerful automation. However it is still usually impossible for NQTHM to prove substantial theorems completely automatically; rather it is necessary to guide the prover through a carefully selected series of lemmas. Selection of these lemmas can demand intimate understanding of the theorem prover. There is also the problem of knowing what to do when the prover fails to prove the given theorem.

The main alternative is interactive theorem proving or 'proof checking'; here the user constructs the proof and the computer merely checks it, perhaps filling in small gaps, but generally acting as a humble clerical assistant. Two pioneering examples are Automath (de Bruijn 1980) and Mizar (Trybulec 1978). However these systems require rather detailed guidance, and performing the proof can be tedious for the user. For example, simple algebraic steps such as rearrangements under associative-commutative laws need to be justified by a detailed series of applications of those laws.

It seems, then, that there are reasons for dissatisfaction with both approaches, and the Edinburgh LCF project (Gordon, Milner, and Wadsworth 1979) attempted to combine their best features. In LCF-style systems, a repertoire of simple logical primitives is provided, which users may invoke manually. However these primitive inference rules are functions in the ML programming language[7] and users may write arbitrary ML programs that automate common inference patterns, and even mimic automatic proof procedures, breaking them down to the primitive inferences. For example, the HOL system (Gordon and Melham 1993) has derived rules for rewriting,

[7] ML for Meta Language; following Tarski (1936) and Carnap (1937) it has become customary in logic to draw a sharp distinction between the 'object language' under study and the 'metalanguage' used in that study. In just the same way, in a course in Russian given in English, Russian is the object language, English the metalanguage.

associative-commutative rearrangement, linear arithmetic, tautology checking, inductive definitions and free recursive type definitions, among others. Should users require application-specific proof procedures, they can implement them using the same methodology. In this way, LCF provides the controllability of a low-level proof checker with the power and convenience of an automatic theorem prover, and allows ordinary users to extend the system without compromising soundness. The main disadvantage is that such expansion might be too inefficient; but for reasons discussed by Harrison (1995b) this is not usually a serious problem. The two main reasons, which will be amply illustrated in what follows are: (1) sophisticated inference patterns can be expressed as object-level theorems and used efficiently, and (2) proof search and proof checking can be separated. Nevertheless, LCF provers are still some way behind the state of the art in finding optimal combinations of interaction and automation. Perhaps PVS (Owre, Rushby, and Shankar 1992) is the best of the present-day systems in this respect.

We have already remarked on how error-prone hand proofs are in the verification-oriented domains we consider. In fact the danger of mistakes in logical manipulations was recognized long ago by Hobbes (1651). In Chapter V of his *Leviathan*, which anticipates the later interest in mechanical calculi for deduction ('reasoning ... is but reckoning') he says:

> For as Arithmeticians teach to adde and subtract in *numbers* [...] The Logicians teach the same in consequences of words [...] And as in Arithmetique, unpractised men must, and Professors themselves may often erre, and cast up false; so also in any other subject of Reasoning the ablest, most attentive, and most practised men, may deceive themselves, and inferre false conclusions.

If a computer theorem prover is to represent an improvement on this sorry state of affairs, especially if used in a safety-critical application, then it should be reliable. Unfortunately, in view of the complexity of modern theorem proving systems, this can be difficult to guarantee.[8] LCF systems are strong in this respect: theorems only arise by the simple primitive inferences (this is enforced using the ML type system). Hence only the part of the code that implements these primitives is critical; bugs in derived inference rules may cause failures, but will not lead to false 'theorems'. It is also possible to record the trace of the proof and verify it using a simple (external) proof checker, if even further reassurance is needed. One can regard LCF as a soft-

[8] In May 1995, there was a public announcement that the 'Robbins conjecture' had been proved using the REVEAL theorem prover. This was subsequently traced to a bug in REVEAL, and the conjecture remained open until October 1996, when it was proved by McCune (1997), again using an equational reasoning program, EQP. The conjecture states that an algebraic structure with the same signature as a Boolean algebra, where the commutativity and associativity of $+$ and the law $n(n(x+y)+n(x+n(y))) = x$ are assumed, is in fact a Boolean algebra.

ware engineering methodology, giving a canonical technique for implementing other theorem proving procedures in a sound way.

In HOL, even the mathematical theories are developed by a rigorous process of definitional extension. The fact that various mathematical notions can be defined in ZF set theory ($(x, y) = \{\{x\}, \{x, y\}\}$, $n + 1 = \{0, \ldots, n\}$ etc.) is widely known. Higher order logic provides similar power; the definitions are less well-known, but no more obscure. It is usually easier to postulate the required notions and properties than to define and derive them; the advantages were likened by Russell (1919) to those of theft over honest toil.[9] But postulation does create the risk of introducing inconsistent axioms: this has happened several times in various theorem proving systems. So insisting on honest toil has its advantages too. This approach was pioneered in HOL; it was not present in the original LCF project, but it provides a natural fit. It means that both for the logical inference rules *and* the underlying axioms we are adopting a simple basis that can be seen to be correct once and for all. Now the only extension mechanisms (breaking inference rules down to primitives and defining new mathematical structures in terms of old ones) are guaranteed to preserve consistency, so all work in the system is consistent per construction. Of course this does not guarantee that the definitions capture the notions as intended, but that can never be guaranteed.

We should mention one apparent circularity: we are attempting to use systems like HOL to verify hardware and software, yet we are reliant on the correctness of the hardware and software underlying the system. We should not neglect the possibility of computer error, but too much scepticism will lead us into an ultimately barren regress in any field of knowledge.

1.6 The real numbers

We have seen that the more 'high level' a specification is, the smaller the gap is between it and the informal intentions of the designers and customers. This means that the specification formalism should at least be capable of expressing, and presumably proving things about, mathematical objects such as numbers. In particular, the work described here grew out of the conviction that for many applications, natural numbers, integers and rationals are not enough, and the real numbers are necessary. Applications that we have in mind include:

- Floating point hardware. Although such hardware deals with bitstrings constituting finite approximations to actual real numbers, a specification in those terms is much less readable. It's better to express the correctness of the hardware as an assertion about real numbers.

[9] Page 71. Russell wrote this book, a semi-popular version of 'The Principles of Mathematics', while imprisoned for his pacifist activities during WW1. This must have focused his mind on issues of criminality.

- Hybrid systems, i.e. those that incorporate both continuous and discrete components. Even if it is not desirable that the specification itself explicitly mention real numbers, the interaction of the system with the outside world will inevitably be expressed as some sort of differential equation, and the formal correctness proof must involve this domain.
- Computer algebra systems. We have already noted how useful they are, but they have the significant disadvantage that most of them often return incorrect answers, or answers that are conditional on some quite strong hypotheses. We would like to combine the power and ease of use of computer algebra systems with the rigour and precision of theorem provers.

In this book, we provide a survey of techniques for constructing the real numbers from simpler entities, and show how a particular choice has been completely formalized in the HOL theorem prover. We then discuss the formal development of a significant fragment of mathematical analysis, up to integration of functions of a single real variable. We show how it is possible to perform explicit calculations with the computable subset of the real numbers, again entirely inside the logic, and how certain logical decision procedures can be realized as LCF derived rules. We also give practical examples of how the resulting system can be applied to some of the above applications.

1.7 Concluding remarks

A brief description of the HOL logic is given in an appendix. These details are not necessary in order to understand this book, but it is worthwhile to show the deductive system explicitly, since we want to emphasize that from this foundation, all the existing HOL theories, and the development of real analysis we describe in this book, are derived by definitional extension. In a sense, the HOL mathematical development, of which this work represents the culmination, realizes at last the dreams of the logical pioneers.

We will often describe our work using the conventional mathematical notation. However we think it is appropriate to show explicit examples of HOL terms and theorems. We do this in different chapters to a varying extent, most of all in the chapter on formalized analysis, whose raison d'être is to illustrate how mathematics is expressed formally in HOL. Part of the objective is to emphasize that this book is not merely an abstract exercise; though it attempts to draw interesting general conclusions, it's solidly based on a core of practical work.[10] But we also hope to show that the syntax is by no means

[10] Similarly, we often give actual runtimes for some automatic proof procedures. All runtimes in this book are user CPU times in seconds for a version of HOL running in interpreted CAML Light version 0.71 on a Sparc 10. On a Pentium II machine current at time of writing, runtimes are typically about half those given here.

unreadable; one does not enter a completely different world when interacting with HOL. The ASCII version of the connectives are as follows:

$\bot$	F	Falsity
$\top$	T	Truth
$\neg$	~	Not
$\wedge$	/\	And
$\vee$	\/	Or
$\Rightarrow$	==>	Implies
$\Leftrightarrow$	=	If and only if
$\forall$	!	For all
$\exists$	?	There exists
$\exists!$	?!	There exists a unique
ε	@	Hilbert choice
λ	\	Lambda abstraction

(Readers unfamiliar with lambda abstractions or the Hilbert choice operator will find a brief explanation in Appendix A.) They bind according to their order in the above table, negation being strongest and the variable-binding operations weakest. Note that equality binds more weakly than the other binary connectives, even when it is used for term equality rather than 'if and only if'. HOL theorems are distinguished from arbitrary assertions that may or may not be true by prefixing them with the customary turnstile symbol `|-`. For example:

```
|- !x. x > 0 = (?y. x = y + 1)
```

is a HOL theorem asserting that every number x is greater than zero if and only if there is some number y of which x is the immediate successor. Most of the operations on natural and real numbers should look familiar even in their HOL ASCII representations. Many of them are explained at various points in the sequel, but to aid readers wishing to browse, here are some of the less obvious ones together with renderings in standard mathematical notation and English:

HOL	Standard	Meaning
`SUC(n)`	$n+1$	Successor operation on $\mathbb{N}$
`m EXP n`	m^n	Natural number exponentiation
`&`	*(none)*	Natural map $\mathbb{N} \to \mathbb{R}$
`--x`	$-x$	Unary negation of x
`inv(x)`	x^{-1}	Multiplicative inverse of x
`abs(x)`	$\lvert x \rvert$	Absolute value of x
`x pow n`	x^n	Real x raised to natural power n
`root n x`	$\sqrt[n]{x}$	Positive n^{th} root of x
`Sum(n,d) f`	$\Sigma_{i=n}^{n+d-1} f(i)$	Sum of d terms $f(i)$ starting with $f(n)$

To make things slightly easier to read, we sometimes reformat a little, and add or remove brackets for clarity. However these changes are fairly superficial. We hope to convince the reader that even such minimal measures are enough to render formal mathematics palatable, at least in fairly simple domains such as the ones we consider here. By contrast, many researchers devote a great deal of energy to improving the user interface, sometimes leaving less to devote to the fundamental business of actually proving theorems. We echo the slogan of Kreisel (1990): Experience, Not Only Doctrine (ENOD). Only by actually trying to formalize mathematics and perform verifications, even in systems that do not render it especially convenient, can we develop a balanced appreciation of the real needs, and make the next generation of systems genuinely easier to use.

2. Constructing the Real Numbers

True to the foundational approach we take, the real numbers are constructed rather than merely axiomatized. In this chapter we survey existing approaches and remark on their strengths and weaknesses before presenting in detail the construction we used. Our method is a rather unusual one which has not been published before. Originally presented as a trick involving 'nearly additive' functions, we show it in its proper light as a version of Cantor's method. Mechanization of the proofs involves a procedure to construct quotient types, which gives an example of the possibilities arising from HOL's programmability.

2.1 Properties of the real numbers

We can take a formal view that the reals are a set $\mathbb{R}$ together with two distinguished constants $0 \in \mathbb{R}$ and $1 \in \mathbb{R}$ and the operations $+ : \mathbb{R} \times \mathbb{R} \to \mathbb{R}$, $. : \mathbb{R} \times \mathbb{R} \to \mathbb{R}$, $- : \mathbb{R} \to \mathbb{R}$ and $inv : \mathbb{R} - \{0\} \to \mathbb{R}$ having all the 'ordered field' properties: [1]

$$\begin{array}{l}
1 \neq 0 \\
\forall x\ y.\ x + y = y + x \\
\forall x\ y\ z.\ x + (y + z) = (x + y) + z \\
\forall x.\ 0 + x = x \\
\forall x.\ (-x) + x = 0 \\
\forall x\ y.\ xy = yx \\
\forall x\ y\ z.\ x(yz) = (xy)z \\
\forall x.\ 1x = x \\
\forall x.\ x \neq 0 \Rightarrow x^{-1}x = 1 \\
\forall x\ y\ z.\ x(y + z) = xy + xz
\end{array}$$

[1] We use the more conventional notation xy for $x.y$ and x^{-1} for $inv(x)$. The use of such symbolism, including 0 and 1, is not intended to carry any connotations about what the symbols actually denote.

$$\forall x\, y.\, x = y \vee x < y \vee y < x$$
$$\forall x\, y\, z.\, x < y \wedge y < z \Rightarrow x < z$$
$$\forall x.\, x \not< x$$
$$\forall y\, z.\, y < z \Rightarrow \forall x.\, x + y < x + z$$
$$\forall x\, y.\, 0 < x \wedge 0 < y \Rightarrow 0 < xy$$

together with *completeness*. This is the property that sets the reals apart from the rationals, and can be stated in many equivalent forms. Perhaps the simplest is the *supremum property* which states that any nonempty set of reals that is bounded above has a least upper bound (supremum).

$$\begin{aligned}&\forall S.\, (\exists x.\, x \in S) \wedge (\exists M.\, \forall x \in S.\, x \leq M)\\ &\quad \Rightarrow \exists m.\, (\forall x \in S.\, x \leq m) \wedge \forall m'.\, (\forall x \in S.\, x \leq m') \Rightarrow m \leq m'\end{aligned}$$

(Here we can regard $x \leq y$ as an abbreviation for $x < y \vee x = y$.) For example, the two sets $\{x \in \mathbb{R} \mid x^2 \leq 2\}$ and $\{x \in \mathbb{R} \mid x^2 < 2\}$ *both* have a supremum of $\sqrt{2}$, although one of the sets contains $\sqrt{2}$, as a maximum element, and the other does not.

We could easily introduce a new type `real` together with the appropriate operations, and assert the above axioms. However this is contrary to the spirit of HOL as set out in the introduction, where all new types are explicitly constructed and all new operations explicitly defined, an approach that can be guaranteed not to introduce inconsistency. There are also philosophical objections, vehemently expressed by Abian (1981): the reals are normally thought of intuitively using a concrete picture such as decimal expansions, so it's artificial to start from an abstract set of axioms. We chose to construct the reals in HOL.

2.2 Uniqueness of the real numbers

As we shall see later, the above axioms are not all independent. However they are categorical, i.e. all structures satisfying them are isomorphic — see Burrill (1967), Cohen and Ehrlich (1963) or Stoll (1979) for example. This is assuming that the axioms are interpreted in set theory or higher order logic. The analogous first order axiomatization, using an axiom schema for the completeness property, is adequate for many purposes, but these axioms are inevitably not categorical: indeed the existence of non-Archimedean models is the starting point for nonstandard analysis (Robinson 1966). In fact the axioms are not even κ-categorical for any infinite κ, in contrast to a reasonable axiomatization of the *complex* field. However the first order real axioms are complete: we shall later exhibit an actual decision procedure for a slightly different axiomatization of the same theory.[2]

[2] This shows that the implication in the Łoś-Vaught test cannot be reversed.

All this assumes that the multiplicative inverse is a function from $\mathbb{R} - \{0\}$, not the full set $\mathbb{R}$. HOL's functions are all total, and it doesn't have a convenient means of defining subtypes. This means that it's easiest to make the multiplicative inverse a total function $\mathbb{R} \to \mathbb{R}$, giving us an additional choice over the value of 0^{-1}. In early versions of the theory, we made 0^{-1} arbitrary, i.e. $\varepsilon x.\, \bot$. However this isn't the same as real undefinedness, which propagates through expressions. In particular, since we take the standard definition of division, $x/y = xy^{-1}$, this means that $0/0 = 0$, since 0 times any real number is 0. Because of this, the idea of making the result arbitrary seemed artificial, so in the latest version, we have boldly defined $0^{-1} = 0$. This achieves considerable formal streamlining of theorems about inversion, allowing us to prove the following equations without any awkward sideconditions:

$$\begin{aligned} \forall x.\, (x^{-1})^{-1} &= x \\ \forall x.\, (-x)^{-1} &= -x^{-1} \\ \forall x\, y.\, (xy)^{-1} &= x^{-1}y^{-1} \\ \forall x.\, x^{-1} = 0 &\Leftrightarrow x = 0 \\ \forall x.\, x^{-1} > 0 &\Leftrightarrow x > 0 \end{aligned}$$

For the reader who is disturbed by our choice, let us remark that we will discuss the role of partial functions at greater length when we have shown them in action in more complicated mathematical situations. We feel that the treatment of 0^{-1} is unlikely to be significant in practice, because division by zero is normally treated as a special case anyway. This argument, however, might not hold when dealing with every mathematical area. For example in the analysis of poles in complex analysis, the singularities of functions are themselves of direct interest. In other situations, there are specific conventions for accommodating otherwise 'undefined' values, e.g. points at infinity in projective geometry and extended real numbers for infinite measures. Only more experience will decide whether our approach to partiality can deal with such fields in a direct way.

In any case, we think it is important that the reader or user of a formal treatment should be aware of precisely what the situation is. Our decision to set $0^{-1} = 0$ is simple and straightforward, in contrast to some approaches to undefinedness that we consider later. As Arthan (1996) remarks 'all but the most expert readers will be ill-served by formal expositions which make use of devious tricks'. (This is in the context of computer system specification, but probably holds equal weight for pure mathematics.) Note, by the way, that axiomatizing the reals in first order logic gives rise to similar problems, since all function symbols are meant to be interpreted as total functions.[3]

[3] Hodges (1993) points out that for various field-specific notions such as 'subfield' and 'finitely generated' to be instantiations of their model-theoretic generalizations, it's necessary to include the multiplicative inverse in the signature of fields and to take $0^{-1} = 0$.

2.3 Constructing the real numbers

There are well-established methods in classical mathematics for constructing the real numbers out of something simpler (the natural numbers, integers or rationals). If we arrange the number systems in a lattice ($\mathbb{Q}^+$ and $\mathbb{R}^+$ represent the positive rationals and reals respectively), then there are various ways one can attempt to climb from $\mathbb{N}$ up to $\mathbb{R}$, possibly by way of intermediate systems.

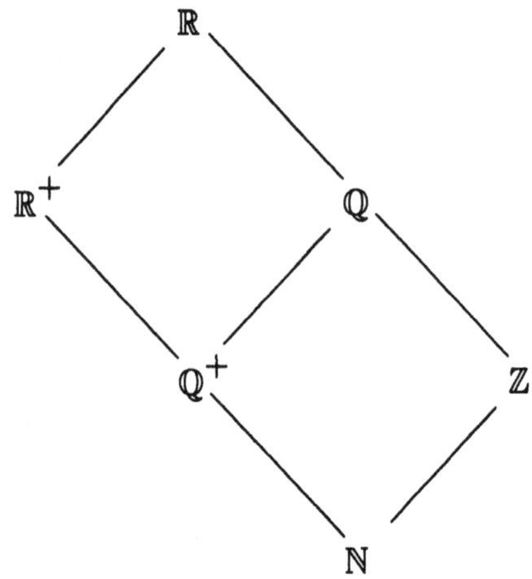

The three best-known are:

- Positional expansions
- Dedekind cuts
- Cauchy sequences

All the methods are conceptually simple but the technical details are substantial, and most general textbooks on analysis, e.g. Rudin (1976), merely sketch the proofs. A pioneering monograph by Landau (1930) was entirely devoted to the details of the construction (using Dedekind cuts), and plenty of similar books have followed, e.g. those by Thurston (1956) (Cauchy sequences), Roberts (1962) (Cauchy sequences), Cohen and Ehrlich (1963) (Cauchy sequences), Lightstone (1965) (positional expansions), Parker (1966) (Dedekind cuts) and Burrill (1967) (positional expansions). Other discussions that survey more than one of these alternatives are Feferman (1964), Artmann (1988) and Ebbinghaus et al. (1990). A very recent collection of papers about the real numbers is Ehrlich (1994).

Before we focus on the choice, we should remark that there are plenty of other methods, e.g. continued fractions, or a technique due to Bolzano based on decreasing nests of intervals. A more radical alternative (though it is in some sense a simple generalization of Dedekind's method), giving a bizarre menagerie of numbers going way beyond the reals, is given by Conway

(1976). As it stands, the construction is hard to formalize, especially in type theory, but Holmes (1998) has formalized a variant sufficing for the reals. Furthermore, there are some interesting methods based on the 'point free topology' construction given by Johnstone (1982). A detailed development using the idea of an intuitionistic formal space (Sambin 1987) is given by Negri and Soravia (1995). This technique is especially interesting to constructivists, since many theorems admit intuitionistic proofs in such a framework, even if their classically equivalent point-set versions are highly nonconstructive. For example, there is a constructive proof by Coquand (1992) of Tychonoff's theorem, which is classically equivalent to the Axiom of Choice.

2.4 Positional expansions

Perhaps the most obvious approach is to model the real numbers by infinite positional (e.g. binary or decimal) sequences. For the sake of simplicity, we will consider binary expansions here, although the base chosen is largely immaterial. It is necessary to take into account the fact that the representation is not unique; for example 0.11111... and 1.00000... both represent the same real number. One can take equivalence classes; this looks like overkill but it is not without advantages, as we shall see. Alternatively one can proscribe either 00000... or 11111....

It is easy to define the orderings, especially if one has taken the approach of proscribing one of the redundant expansions. One simply says that $x < y$ when there is an $n \in \mathbb{N}$ such that $x_n < y_n$ but for all $m < n$ we have $x_m = y_m$. Completeness is rather straightforward.[4] If one proscribes 00000... then it's easier to prove in the least upper bound form; if one proscribes 11111... then the greatest lower bound form is easier. If one uses equivalence classes, both are easy. The idea is to define the least upper bound s of a set of reals S recursively as follows:

$$s_n = max\{x_n \mid x \in S \wedge \forall m < n.\, x_m = s_m\}$$

Addition is harder because it involves carries (in practice the main difficulty is the associative law) and multiplication is harder still, apparently unworkably so. What are the alternatives?

1. It isn't *too* hard to define addition correctly; this is done by Behrend (1956) and de Bruijn (1976). A direct definition of multiplication is probably too difficult. However it is possible to develop the theory of multiplication abstractly via endomorphisms of $\mathbb{R}^+$ — Behrend (1956) gives a particularly elegant treatment, even including logarithms, exponentials

[4] Note, by the way, that in the guise of positional expansions, the Bolzano-Weierstrass theorem (every bounded infinite set has a limit point) is an easy consequence of König's lemma.

and trigonometric functions. The key theorem is that for any $x, y \in \mathbb{R}^+$,[5] there is a unique homomorphism that maps $x \mapsto y$, and this depends only on completeness and a few basic properties of the additive structure.

2. One can relax the imposition that all digits are less than some base, and allow arbitrary integers instead. This approach, taken by Faltin, Metropolis, Ross, and Rota (1975), makes addition and multiplication straightforward, though it makes defining the ordering relation correspondingly more difficult, since one needs to 'normalize' numbers again before a straightforward ordering can be defined. However on balance this is still easier.
3. One can use the supremum property (which as we have already remarked is quite easy to prove) to reduce addition and multiplication to finite expansions only. That is, one can define without too much trouble the addition and multiplication of truncated expansions and take the supremum of all truncations. This approach is used by Burrill (1967) and Abian (1981), while Lightstone (1965) does things similarly using a rather ad hoc limiting process. Since the truncations have 00000... tails, but we want the least upper bound, it works most easily if we've taken equivalence classes of sequences.

2.5 Cantor's method

This method, generally attributed to Cantor but largely anticipated by Meray (1869), identifies a real number with the set of all rational sequences that converge to it. To say that a sequence (s_n) converges to s, written $s_n \to s$ means:

$$\forall \epsilon > 0.\, \exists N.\, \forall n \geq N.\, |s_n - s| < \epsilon$$

This is no good as a definition, because it contains the limit itself, which may not be rational. However, the following similar statement avoids this; it does not matter if we restrict ϵ to rational values, since $\mathbb{Q}$ is dense in $\mathbb{R}$, i.e. between any two distinct reals there is a rational.

$$\forall \epsilon > 0.\, \exists N.\, \forall m \geq N, n \geq N.\, |s_m - s_n| < \epsilon$$

A sequence (s_n) with this property is called a *Cauchy sequence* or *fundamental sequence*. Given the real number axioms, it is quite easy to show that every Cauchy sequence converges. (The converse, that every convergent sequence is a Cauchy sequence, is easy.) Actually, we later sketch how we proved it in our theory. The fact that two series (s_n) and (t_n) converge to the same limit can also be expressed without using the limit itself:

[5] That is, *strictly* positive real numbers.

$$\forall \epsilon > 0.\ \exists N.\ \forall n \geq N.\ |s_n - t_n| < \epsilon$$

It is easy to see that this defines an equivalence relation on Cauchy sequences, and the real numbers can be defined as its equivalence classes. The arithmetic operations can be inherited from those of the rationals in a natural way ($(x + y)_n = x_n + y_n$ etc.) although the supremum presents slightly more difficulty. A complete treatment is given by Cohen and Ehrlich (1963) and Thurston (1956). A similar method, going via the positive rationals to the positive reals, is given by Roberts (1962).

Cantor's method admits of abstraction to more general structures. Given any metric space, that is, a set equipped with a 'distance function' on pairs of points (see later for formal definition), the process can be carried through in essentially the same way. This gives an isometric (distance-preserving) embedding into a complete metric space, i.e. one where every Cauchy sequence has a limit.

Since generality and abstraction are to be striven for in mathematics, it seems desirable to regard the construction of the reals as a special case of this procedure. Taken literally, however, this is circular, since the distance returned by a metric is supposed to be real-valued. On the other hand if we move to the more general structure of a topological space, the procedure seems to have no natural counterpart, since the property of being a Cauchy sequence is not preserved by homeomorphisms. Consider the action of the function from the set of strictly positive reals onto itself that maps $x \mapsto 1/x$. Plainly this is a homeomorphism (under the induced topology given by the usual topology on $\mathbb{R}$) but it maps the sequence of positive integers, which is not a Cauchy sequence, to a Cauchy sequence.

Nevertheless there is a suitable structure lying between a metric and a topological space in generality. This is a uniform space, which while not equipped with an actual notion of distance, has nevertheless a system of *entourages* which (roughly speaking) indicate that certain pairs of points are the *same* distance apart. The completion procedure can be extended in a natural way to show that any uniform space can be embedded in a complete one by a uniformly continuous mapping that has an appropriate universal property. (From a categorical perspective, the 'morphisms' natural to topological, uniform and metric spaces are respectively continuous, uniformly continuous and isometric.)

A topological group is a structure that is both a group and a Hausdorff topological space, such that the group operations are continuous. It is not hard to see that a topological group has enough structure to make it a uniform space, where addition amounts to a 'rigid spatial translation'. Bourbaki (1966) constructs the reals by first giving the rational numbers a topology, regarding this topological group as a uniform space and taking its completion. Although elegant in the context of general work in various mathematical structures, this is too complicated *per se* for us to emulate.

2.6 Dedekind's method

A method due to Dedekind (1872) identifies a real number with the set of all rational numbers less than it. Once again this is not immediately satisfactory as a definition, but it is possible to give a definition not involving the bounding real number that, given the real number axioms, is equivalent. We shall call such a set a *cut*. The four properties required of a set C for it to be a cut are as follows:

1. $\exists x.\ x \in C$
2. $\exists x.\ x \notin C$
3. $\forall x \in C.\ \forall y < x.\ y \in C$
4. $\forall x \in C.\ \exists y > x.\ y \in C$

These state respectively that a cut is not empty, is not $\mathbb{Q}$ in its entirety, is 'downward closed', and has no greatest element. Again the arithmetic operations can be inherited from $\mathbb{Q}$ in a natural way, and the supremum of a set of cuts is simply its union.

- $sup\, S = \bigcup S$
- $X + Y = \{x + y \mid x \in X \wedge y \in Y\}$
- $XY = \{xy \mid x \in X \wedge y \in Y\}$
- $X^{-1} = \{w \mid \exists d < 1. \forall x \in X.\, wx < d\}$

(Note that the more obvious definition $X^{-1} = \{w \mid \forall x \in X.\, wx < 1\}$ fails to give a cut if X is rational, since it has a largest member.) However this definition of multiplication is problematical, because the product of two negative rationals is positive. The two cuts X and Y extend to $-\infty$, so there will exist products of these large and negative numbers that are arbitrarily large and positive. Therefore the set is not a cut. This difficulty is usually noted in sketch proofs given in books, but to carry through in detail the complicated case splits they gloss over would be extremely tedious. Conway (1976) emphasizes the difficulty of constructing $\mathbb{R}$ from $\mathbb{Q}$ by Dedekind cuts:

> Nobody can seriously pretend that he has ever discussed even eight cases in such a theorem — yet I have seen a presentation in which one theorem actually had 64 cases ... Of course an elegant treatment will manage to discuss several cases at once, but one has to work very hard to find such a treatment.

He advocates instead following the path on the lattice diagram through $\mathbb{Q}^+$ and $\mathbb{R}^+$, at least if Dedekind's method is to be used. This avoids the case splits (otherwise it is essentially the same as the signed case presented above), and has other advantages as well. Landau (1930) also follows this route, as does Parker (1966). One apparent drawback of using this path is that we lose the potentially useful intermediate types $\mathbb{Z}$ and $\mathbb{Q}$. However this is not really so, for two reasons: first, it's quite easy to carve these out as subtypes of $\mathbb{R}$ when we're finished; and second, the code used to construct $\mathbb{R}$ from $\mathbb{R}^+$ can be used almost unchanged (and this is where a computer theorem prover scores over a human) to construct $\mathbb{Z}$ and $\mathbb{Q}$ from their positive-only counterparts.

2.7 What choice?

It seems that using positional expansions is a promising and unfairly neglected method. As stressed by Abian (1981) and others, the idea of positional expansions is very familiar, so it can be claimed to be the most intuitive approach. However the formal details of performing arithmetic on these strings is messy; even the case of finite strings, though not really very difficult, is tiresome to formalize.

Cauchy's method is quite elegant, but it does require us to construct the rationals first, and what's more, prove quite a lot of 'analytical' results about them to support the proofs about Cauchy sequences. It is also necessary to verify that all the operations respect the equivalence relation. Thus, when expanded out to full details, it involves quite a lot of work.

The Dedekind method involves a bit of work verifying the cut properties, and again we have to construct the rationals first. On the other hand the proofs are all fairly routine, and it's fairly easy to chug through them in HOL. In fact a previous version of this work (Harrison 1994) was based on Dedekind cuts.

With hindsight, we have decided that an alternative approach is slightly easier. This has been formalized in HOL, and turned out to be a bit better (at least based on size of proof) than the Dedekind construction. As far as we know, it has not been published before. The fundamental idea is simple: we follow Cantor's method, but automatically scale up the terms of the sequences so that everything can be done in the integers or naturals. In fact we use the naturals, since it streamlines the development somewhat; this yields the non-negative reals.[6] Consider Cauchy sequences (x_n) that have $O(1/n)$ convergence, i.e. there is some B such that

$$\forall n.\ |x_n - l| < B/n$$

In terms of the Cauchy sequence alone this means that there is a bound B such that:

$$\forall m, n \in \mathbb{N}.\ |x_m - x_n| < B(1/m + 1/n)$$

and the criterion for x and y to be equal is that there is a B such that:

[6] Note that where we later use $|p-q|$ for naturals p and q, we are really considering an 'absolute difference' function, since the standard 'cutoff' subtraction is always 0 for $p \leq q$. Actually we use the standard definition (see treatises on primitive recursive functions, passim): $\mathtt{diff}(m,n) = (m-n)+(n-m)$.

$$\forall n \in \mathbb{N}.\, |x_n - y_n| < B/n$$

Apart from the multiplicative constant B, this is the bound used by Bishop and Bridges (1985) in their work on constructive analysis. Now suppose we use the natural number sequence (a_n) to represent the rational sequence $x_n = a_n/n$. The above convergence criterion, when multiplied out, becomes:

$$\exists B.\, \forall m, n \in \mathbb{N}.\, |na_m - ma_n| \leq B(m+n)$$

We shall say that a is 'nearly multiplicative'. (Note that we drop from $<$ to $\leq$ to avoid quibbles over the case where $m = 0$ and/or $n = 0$, but this is inconsequential. In some ways the development here works more easily if we exclude 0 from $\mathbb{N}$.) The equivalence relation is:

$$\exists B.\, \forall n \in \mathbb{N}.\, |a_n - b_n| \leq B$$

Before we proceed to define the operations and prove their properties, let us observe that there is a beguilingly simple alternative characterization of the convergence rate, contained in the following theorem.

Theorem 2.7.1. *A natural number sequence (a_n) is 'nearly multiplicative', i.e. obeys:*

$$\exists B \in \mathbb{N}.\, \forall m, n \in \mathbb{N}.\, |na_m - ma_n| \leq B(m+n)$$

iff it is 'nearly additive', that is:

$$\exists B \in \mathbb{N}.\, \forall m, n \in \mathbb{N}.\, |a_{m+n} - (a_m + a_n)| \leq B$$

(the two B's are not necessarily the same!)

Proof. 1. Suppose $\forall m, n \in \mathbb{N}.\, |na_m - ma_n| \leq B(m+n)$. Then in particular for any $m, n \in \mathbb{N}$ we have $|(m+n)a_m - ma_{m+n}| \leq B(2m+n)$ and $|(m+n)a_n - na_{m+n}| \leq B(2n+m)$. Adding these together we get:

$$|((m+n)a_m + (m+n)a_n) - (ma_{m+n} + na_{m+n})| \leq 3B(m+n)$$

hence $\forall m, n \in \mathbb{N}.\, |a_{m+n} - (a_m + a_n)| \leq (3B + a_0)$, where the a_0 covers the trivial case where $m + n = 0$ so $m = n = 0$.

2. Now suppose that (a_n) is nearly additive. Induction on k yields:

$$\forall k, n \in \mathbb{N}.\, k \neq 0 \Rightarrow |a_{kn} - ka_n| \leq Bk$$

and multiplying by n throughout gives:

$$\forall k, n \in \mathbb{N}.\, k \neq 0 \Rightarrow |na_{kn} - (kn)a_n| \leq Bkn \leq B(kn+n)$$

This actually establishes what we want in the special case where m is an exact multiple of n. For the general case, a bit more work is required. First we separate off the following lemma. Suppose $m \neq 0$ and $m \leq n$. Let $q = n \texttt{DIV}\ m$ and $r = n \texttt{MOD}\ m$. Then:

$$n = mq + r$$

so by nearly additivity and the above special case we get:

$$\begin{aligned}
|na_m - ma_n| &= |(mq+r)a_m - ma_{mq+r}| \\
&\leq |(mq+r)a_m - m(a_{mq} + a_r)| + Bm \\
&\leq |(mq)a_m - ma_{mq}| + |ra_m - ma_r| + Bm \\
&\leq Bmq + |ra_m - ma_r| + Bm \\
&\leq B(mq+m) + |ra_m - ma_r| \\
&\leq B(m+n) + |ra_m - ma_r|
\end{aligned}$$

We claim $\forall m, n.\ m \leq n \Rightarrow |na_m - ma_n| \leq (8B + a_0)n$. The proof is by complete induction. If $m = 0$ then the result is trivially true; if not, we may apply the lemma. Now if $r = 0$, the result again follows immediately. Otherwise we may use the above lemma twice so that, setting $s = m \texttt{MOD}\ r$, we get:

$$|na_m - ma_n| \leq B(m+n) + B(r+m) + |sa_r - ra_s|$$

The inductive hypothesis yields $|sa_r - ra_s| \leq (8B + a_0)r$. But note that $2r \leq n$ by elementary properties of modulus, so that

$$\begin{aligned}
2|na_m - ma_n| &\leq 2B(m+n) + 2B(m+r) + (8B + a_0)(2r) \\
&\leq 2B(m+n) + 2B(m+r) + (8B + a_0)n \\
&\leq 4Bn + 4Bn + (8B + a_0)n \\
&\leq 2(8B + a_0)n
\end{aligned}$$

Consequently $|na_m - ma_n| \leq (8B + a_0)n$. Now without regard to which of m and n is larger, we get $|na_m - ma_n| \leq (8B + a_0)(m+n)$ as required. □

This method of constructing the reals was inspired by a posting by Michael Barr on 19th November 1994 to the Usenet group `sci.math.research`, suggesting equivalence classes of the nearly-additive functions as a representation for the reals. The method is originally due to Schanuel, inspired in part by Tate's Lemma,[7] but Schanuel did not regard it as a useful *construction*, since

[7] See for example Lang (1994), p. 598.

commutativity of multiplication is hard to prove, but rather an easy *representation* of the reals, which are considered as already available. Struggling to prove the commutativity of multiplication (see below) we ended up proving the above as a lemma, and hence realizing that this amounts to encoding a certain kind of Cauchy sequence. In fact, the more difficult direction in the above proof is not necessary for the construction; we never use the 'nearly additive' characterization.

2.8 Lemmas about nearly-multiplicative functions

We will use various derived properties of nearly-multiplicative functions in the proofs that follow; for convenience we collect them here.

Lemma 2.8.1. *Every nearly-multiplicative function a has a linear bound, i.e.*

$$\exists A, B.\, \forall n.\, a_n \leq An + B$$

Proof. Instantiating the nearly-multiplicativity property appropriately, we have $\exists B.\, \forall n.\, |na_1 - a_n| \leq B(n+1)$, from which the theorem is immediate. □

Lemma 2.8.2. *For every nearly-multiplicative function a:*

$$\exists B.\, \forall m, n.\, |a_{mn} - ma_n| \leq B(m+1)$$

Proof. We may assume without loss of generality that $n \neq 0$. Instantiating the nearly-multiplicativity property gives $\exists B.\, \forall m, n.\, |na_{mn} - mna_n| \leq B(mn + n)$. Now divide by n. □

Lemma 2.8.3. *Every nearly-multiplicative function a is nearly-additive, i.e.*

$$\exists B \in \mathbb{N}.\, \forall m, n \in \mathbb{N}.\, |a_{m+n} - (a_m + a_n)| \leq B$$

Proof. Given above.

Lemma 2.8.4. *For every nearly-multiplicative function a:*

$$\exists B.\, \forall m, n.\, |a_m - a_n| \leq B|m - n|$$

Proof. We may assume $m = n + k$. There are several straightforward proofs; the easiest is probably to perform induction on k, using the fact that $|a_{k+1} - a_k|$ is bounded; this last fact is immediate from nearly-additivity. □

Lemma 2.8.5. *For all nearly-multiplicative functions a and b:*

$$\exists K, L.\, \forall n.\, |a_n b_n - na_{b_n}| \leq Kn + L$$

Proof. Instantiating the nearly-multiplicative property gives:

$$\exists B.\, \forall n.\, |a_n b_n - n a_{b_n}| \leq B(b_n + n)$$

But now the linear bound property for b yields the result. □

Finally, we will often have occasion to use a few general principles about bounds and linear bounds for functions $\mathbb{N} \to \mathbb{N}$. For example, it is clear by induction that $\forall N.\, (\exists B.\, \forall n \geq N.\, f(n) \leq B) \Leftrightarrow (\exists B.\, \forall n.\, f(n) \leq B)$. The following general principle is used especially often, so we give the proof in detail:

Lemma 2.8.6. *We have* $\exists B.\, \forall n.\, f(n) \leq B$ *iff* $\exists K, L.\, \forall n.\, n f(n) \leq Kn + L$.

Proof. The left-to-right implication is easy; set $K = B$ and $L = 0$. Conversely, suppose $\forall n.\, n f(n) \leq Kn + L$. Then we claim $\forall n.\, f(n) \leq (K + L + f(0))$. For $n = 0$ this is immediate, and otherwise we have

$$n f(n) \leq Kn + L \leq (K + L)n \leq (K + L + f(0))n$$

and since $n \neq 0$ the result follows. □

Note that if we exclude 0 from $\mathbb{N}$, a few of the above results as used in the proof below become rather technically simpler. In particular if we know that $\exists K, L.\, \forall n.\, f(n) \leq Kn + L$, then also $\exists C.\, \forall n.\, f(n) \leq Cn$. It's hard to say without trying it which approach turns out simpler overall. In any case, the standard HOL type of naturals contains 0, which is the main reason why we adopted that alternative.

2.9 Details of the construction

Before we look at the construction in detail, let's list the properties that it suffices to establish.

1. $\forall x, y.\, x + y = y + x$
2. $\forall x\ y\ z.\, x + (y + z) = (x + y) + z$
3. $\forall x.\, 0 + x = x$
4. $\forall x\ y.\, xy = yx$
5. $\forall x\ y\ z.\, x(yz) = (xy)z$
6. $\forall x.\, 1x = x$
7. $\forall x.\, x \neq 0 \Rightarrow x^{-1} x = 1$
8. $\forall x\ y\ z.\, x(y + z) = xy + xz$
9. $\forall x\ y.\, x \leq y \lor y \leq x$
10. $\forall x\ y.\, x \leq y \Leftrightarrow \exists d.\, y = x + d$
11. $\forall x\ y.\, x + y = y \Rightarrow x = 0$
12. $\forall S.\, (\exists x.\, x \in S) \land (\exists M.\, \forall x \in S.\, x \leq M)$
    $\Rightarrow \exists m.\, (\forall x \in S.\, x \leq m) \land \forall m'.\, (\forall x \in S.\, x \leq m') \Rightarrow m \leq m'$

2.9.1 Equality and ordering

As we have already said, we use the following equivalence relation:

$$a \sim b \Leftrightarrow \exists B.\, \forall n \in \mathbb{N}.\, |a_n - b_n| \leq B$$

To show that this is an equivalence relation is trivial. The ordering is defined similarly:

$$a \leq b \Leftrightarrow \exists B.\, \forall n \in \mathbb{N}.\, a_n \leq b_n + B$$

It is easy to see that this respects the equivalence relation, i.e. $x \sim x' \wedge y \sim y' \Rightarrow (x \leq y \Leftrightarrow x' \leq y')$. Welldefinedness, reflexivity, transitivity and antisymmetry are almost immediate from the definitions, though several of these follow anyway from later theorems relating $\leq$ and $+$.

Theorem 2.9.1. *The ordering is total, i.e.* $\forall a, b.\, a \leq b \vee b \leq a$.

Proof. By nearly-multiplicativity, there are A and B such that:

$$\forall m, n.\, |ma_n - na_m| \leq A(m + n)$$

$$\forall m, n.\, |mb_n - nb_m| \leq B(m + n)$$

Now suppose it is *not* the case that $a \leq b \vee b \leq a$. In that case, there are m and n, which we may assume without loss of generality to be nonzero, with:

$$a_n > b_n + (A + B)$$

$$b_m > a_m + (A + B)$$

so

$$ma_n + nb_m > mb_n + na_m + (A + B)(m + n)$$

However this contradicts the fact that:

$$|(ma_n + nb_m) - (mb_n + na_m)| \leq |ma_n + na_m| + |mb_n - nb_m| \leq (A + B)(m + n)$$

so the theorem is true. □

2.9.2 Injecting the naturals

The natural injection ι from N can be defined as follows; evidently it yields a nearly-additive function.

$$\iota(n)_i = ni$$

For brevity, we will denote the injection of n by n^* rather than $\iota(n)$. We use $\iota 0$, $\iota 1$ etc. (which we write 0^*, 1^*) for elements of the positive reals, rather than defining separate constants. We often need the injections anyway, so it seems simpler to have just one way of denoting these elements. Nontriviality of the structure is immediate from the injectivity of ι and the fact that the natural numbers 0 and 1 are distinct.

In explicit HOL quotations, the injection is denoted by '`&`'; the user needs to get accustomed to writing '`&0`', '`&1`', ... This could be avoided by simple interface tricks, but we found it quite acceptable in most situations. HOL's operator overloading does at least allow us to use the same symbols like '+' for natural number and real number addition.

We find that the Archimedean Law holds: $\forall a.\, \exists n \in \mathbb{N}.\, a \leq n^*$. Indeed, when the definition is expanded out, this is precisely the linear bounds lemma. Though the Archimedean property follows at once from completeness, it's useful to have some consequences of the Archimedean law in order to derive completeness.

2.9.3 Addition

Because the scaling factor we are applying to the Cauchy sequences is independent of the sequence, we define addition componentwise as usual. Explicitly, we set:

$$(a + b)_n = a_n + b_n$$

Again, it's easy to see that this respects the equivalence relation. We should also show that when applied to nearly-multiplicative functions it yields another. This is pretty straightforward since

$$|m(a+b)_n - n(a+b)_m| = |m(a_n+b_n) - n(a_m+b_m)| \leq |ma_n - na_m| + |mb_n - nb_m|$$

Furthermore, commutativity and associativity, as well as the facts that 0^* is the unique additive identity and that $\forall a, b.\, a \leq a + b$, are all immediate from the corresponding properties of the natural numbers. The only other fact we need to prove is:

Theorem 2.9.2. $\forall a, b.\, a \leq b \Rightarrow \exists d.\, b \sim a + d$.

Proof. Suppose $a \leq b$. Then by definition there's a B such that

$$\forall n \in \mathbb{N}.\, a_n \leq b_n + B$$

Now define $d_n = (b_n + B) - a_n$. That $b \sim a + d$ and that d is nearly-multiplicative are immediate. □

As already remarked, this gives $a \leq b \Leftrightarrow \exists d.\, b \sim a + d$, and hence allows us to prove a lot of theorems about the ordering more easily. This is a side benefit of dealing with the non-negative reals first.

2.9.4 Multiplication

We could prove completeness now, and then develop the Behrend theory, so avoiding any more explicit definitions. However multiplication is rather easy; the inverse is slightly harder, but not much; and these streamline the later development.[8] The scaling by n seems to get in the way; apparently we need to define $(ab)_n = (a_n b_n / n)$. However, by a previous lemma we have some K and L with:

$$\forall n.\, |a_n b_n - n a_{b_n}| \leq Kn + L$$

This shows that we can very conveniently take *composition of functions* as the definition of multiplication (our sequences are just functions $\mathbb{N} \to \mathbb{N}$ after all). Now the associativity of multiplication is immediate from the associativity of function composition. Most of the other properties are very easy too: obviously the identity function $1_n = n$ is an identity, and distributivity is immediate from nearly-additivity, as is the fact that multiplication respects the equivalence relation and always yields a nearly-multiplicative function. Commutativity is also straightforward, since $|a_n b_n - n a_{b_n}| \leq Kn + L$ and $|b_n a_n - n b_{a_n}| \leq K'n + L'$; hence $n|a_{b_n} - b_{a_n}| \leq (K + K')n + (L + L')$ and the result follows. Now that multiplication is available, we can prove a stronger form of the Archimedean property, which is a useful lemma.

Theorem 2.9.3. $\forall a, k.\, a \not\sim 0^* \Rightarrow \exists n.\, k \leq n^* a$

Proof. By the Archimedean property, it suffices to prove the special case when k is the image of a natural number, i.e. $\forall a, k.\, a \not\sim 0^* \Rightarrow \exists n.\, k^* \leq n^* a$. We know a is nearly-multiplicative; suppose $\forall m, n.\, |m a_n - n a_m| \leq B(m + n)$. Since $a \not\sim 0^*$ we have $\forall C.\, \exists n.\, C \leq a_N$. In particular, if we set $C = B + k$, we have some n so that $B + k \leq a_N$. But then $\forall i.\, (B + k)i \leq i a_N$, and now using nearly-multiplicativity we get $\forall i.\, (B + k)i \leq n a_i + B(n + i)$. This yields $\forall i.\, ki \leq n a_i + Bn$ as required. □

As easy corollaries, if $\forall n.\, n^* a \leq k$ then $a \sim 0^*$, and by subtraction if $\forall n.\, n^* a \leq n^* b + k$ then $a \leq b$.

[8] In fact there are many choices available about which parts to construct and what to develop abstractly; we opt for the extreme of constructing everything.

2.9.5 Completeness

Suppose we have a nonempty set S of our 'reals' that is bounded above. The idea is as follows: for each n, let r_n be the largest r such that there's some $x \in S$ with $x \geq r/n$. Then r_n/n is a Cauchy sequence, and we expect it to give a supremum for S. This works very nicely in our framework, since the scaling by n is already understood.

Theorem 2.9.4. *Given a nonempty set S that is bounded above, then*

$$r_n = max\{r \mid \exists a \in S.\, r^* \leq n^* a\}$$

is a supremum for S.

Proof. Evidently the set mentioned is nonempty (it contains 0). It is also bounded above, because we have some m that is an upper bound for S and by the Archimedean law we have an $N \in \mathbb{N}$ such that $m \leq N^*$ and hence N^* is also an upper bound for S. So for any $a \in S$ and $n \in \mathbb{N}$ we have $n^* a \leq (nN)^*$; hence if $\exists a \in S.\, r^* \leq n^* a$, we must have $r^* \leq (nN)^*$, that is $r \leq nN$. Thus the posited maximum element always exists, and we have:

$$\forall n.\, \exists a \in S.\, r_n^* \leq n^* a$$

but by maximality of r_n (since we know $\leq$ is a total order):

$$\forall n.\, \forall a \in S.\, n^* a \leq (r_n + 1)^*$$

The first of these shows that for any $n \in \mathbb{N}$ there's an a with $\forall i.\, i^* r_n^* \leq i^* n^* a$, and by the second $i^* a \leq (r_i + 1)^*$, so:

$$\forall n, i \in \mathbb{N}.\, i r_n \leq n r_i + n$$

From this and the equivalent

$$\forall n, i \in \mathbb{N}.\, n r_i \leq i r_n + i$$

it is immediate that r is nearly-multiplicative. Furthermore:

$$\forall n \in \mathbb{N}.\, \forall i \geq n.\, i r_n \leq n r_i + i$$

so

$$\forall n \in \mathbb{N}.\, \exists B.\, \forall i.\, i r_n \leq n r_i + i + B$$

But expanded with the definition, this says precisely that:

$$\forall n \in \mathbb{N}.\, r_n^* \leq n^* r + 1^*$$

We also know $\forall a \in S.\, \forall n.\, n^* a \leq (r_n + 1)^*$. Consequently

$$\forall a \in S. \forall n. n^* a \leq n^* r + 2^*$$

But by the Archimedean Lemma, this means $\forall a \in S. a \leq r$; in other words r is an upper bound for S.

To see that it is a *least* upper bound is similar; in fact slightly easier. Suppose z is an upper bound for S, i.e. $\forall a \in S. a \leq z$. Then $\forall a \in S. \forall n. n^* a \leq n^* z$. But we know that $\forall n. \exists a \in S. r^*_n \leq n^* a$; therefore $\forall n. r^*_n \leq n^* z$.

We noted above that $\forall n, i \in \mathbb{N}. nr_i \leq ir_n + i$. This immediately yields $\forall n \in \mathbb{N}. n^* r \leq r^*_n + 1^*$. Combining this with $\forall n. r^*_n \leq n^* z$, we find:

$$\forall n. n^* r \leq n^* z + 1^*$$

Again appealing to the Archimedean Lemma, we get $r \leq z$ as required. □

2.9.6 Multiplicative inverse

We could derive the multiplicative inverse abstractly via:

$$a^{-1} = sup\{x \mid ax \leq 1\}$$

but this would at least require us to prove the *denseness* of the ordering (the naturals obey all the other axioms after all). We elect to follow an explicit construction. The scaling becomes a little messy, and we need to perform division explicitly. We define a^{-1} to be 0^* in the case where $a \sim 0^*$. This is not so much because of our decision to set $0^{-1} = 0$ in the reals (here we are only dealing with the nonnegative reals, so that could be incorporated later) as to avoid the condition $a \not\sim 0^*$ in the closure and welldefinedness theorems (see below); that would complicate the automatic lifting to equivalence classes. Otherwise we set:

$$a^{-1}_n = n^2 \texttt{DIV}\ a_n$$

Theorem 2.9.5. *For any a, the corresponding a^{-1} is nearly-multiplicative.*

Proof. If $a \sim 0^*$, the result is immediate. Otherwise, a bit more work is needed. Note first that if $a \not\sim 0^*$, then by the Archimedean lemma we can find an A such that for all sufficiently large n (say $n \geq N$) we have $n \leq Aa_n$; and in particular $a_n \neq 0$ (we can assume without loss of generality that $N > 0$). So for $n \geq N$ we have:

$$|a_n a^{-1}_n - n^2| \leq a_n$$

and therefore for any m:

$$|m a_m a_n a^{-1}_n - m n^2 a_m| \leq m a_m a_n$$

Using this twice, assuming both $n \geq N$ and $m \geq N$, we find that

$$a_m a_n |m a_n^{-1} - n a_m^{-1}| \leq (m+n) a_m a_n + mn |m a_n - n a_m|$$

But we know a_n is linearly bounded in n, and by nearly-multiplicativity we also have $|ma_n - na_m| \leq K(m+n)$ for some K. Combining this with the lower bound for a_n noted above, we find that for sufficiently large m and n we have $|ma_n^{-1} - na_m^{-1}| \leq B(m+n)$ for some B, as required.

It remains only to deal with the cases where either $m < N$ or $n < N$. By symmetry, it suffices to consider the former. Now for each particular m, we claim $|ma_n^{-1} - na_m^{-1}|$ is linearly bounded in n; therefore by induction there is a uniform linear bound for all $m < N$ as required. To justify our claim, we only need to show that a_n^{-1} is linearly bounded in n. But we know that $n \leq Aa_n$ for any $n \geq N$, so $n \leq Aa_n$ and thus $na_n^{-1} \leq Aa_n a_n^{-1} \leq An^2$; since we may assume $n \neq 0$, the result follows. □

Theorem 2.9.6. *For $a \not\sim 0$ we have $a^{-1}a \sim 1^*$.*

Proof. By elementary properties of division we have for sufficiently large n that $a_n \neq 0$ and so $|a_n^{-1} a_n - n^2| \leq a_n$; and a_n has a linear bound, say $An + B$. Moreover, by an earlier lemma, since we now know a^{-1} is nearly-multiplicative, we have some K and L with $\forall n.\ |a_n^{-1} a_n - n a_{a_n}^{-1}| \leq Kn + L$. Consequently $\forall n.\ |n(a^{-1}a)_n - n^2|$ is linearly bounded in n, and the result follows. □

Once we have the above, the fact that inverse respects the equivalence relation follows at once, since if $a \sim b$ we have either that $a \sim b \sim 0^*$, in which case the result is immediate, or that $a \not\sim 0^*$ and $b \not\sim 0^*$, in which case we have:

$$b^{-1} \sim b^{-1}1 \sim b^{-1}(a^{-1}a) \sim b^{-1}(a^{-1}b) \sim (b^{-1}b)a^{-1} \sim 1a^{-1} \sim a^{-1}$$

2.10 Adding negative numbers

It was convenient to define the nonnegative reals above; had we started with integer sequences, function composition would have been a bit messy to use. In any case, it's not significantly harder to extend $\mathbb{R}^+$ to $\mathbb{R}$ than it is to extend $\mathbb{N}$ to $\mathbb{Z}$. Which method should we use? The most obvious approach is to add a boolean 'sign bit', representing $+n$ by $(true, n)$ and $-n$ by $(false, n)$. One needs to do something about the double representation of zero as $(true, 0)$ and $(false, 0)$; either take equivalence classes or disallow one of them. In any case, proving the theorems is an astonishingly messy procedure because of all the case splits. For example, the associative and distributive laws give rise to lots of trivially different subgoals.

With his customary prescience, Conway (1976) anticipates this problem and proposes instead the other well-known alternative: represent a signed number as the difference $x - y$ of two unsigned ones using the pair (x, y). Apart from quibbles about zero denominators, this is the precise analog, with addition taking the place of multiplication, of the construction of the (positive) rationals as pairs of (naturals or) integers. It is necessary to take equivalence classes, since each real has infinitely many representatives. But we needed equivalence classes for the previous stage anyway, and as we shall show below, it's easy to handle them generically. We define the equivalence relation as:

$$(x, x') \sim (y, y') \Leftrightarrow x + y' = x' + y$$

the ordering as

$$(x, x') \leq (y, y') \Leftrightarrow x + y' \leq x' + y$$

and the basic constants and operations as follows:

$$0 = (0, 0)$$

$$1 = (1, 0)$$

$$-(x, x') = (x', x)$$

$$(x, x') + (y, y') = (x + y, x' + y')$$

$$(x, x')(y, y') = (xy + x'y', xy' + x'y)$$

It seems a bit awkward to define the multiplicative inverse directly, so we do it casewise: if $x = x'$ we say $(x, x')^{-1} = (0, 0)$ (this is our $0^{-1} = 0$ choice); if $x' < x$ then we say $((x - x')^{-1}, 0)$, and conversely if $x < x'$ we say $(0, (x' - x)^{-1})$. (Of course we have 'half subtraction' available in the positive reals since $x \leq y \Rightarrow \exists d.\ y = x + d$.) Transforming the supremum property is a bit tedious. We have:

> Every nonempty set of positive reals that is bounded above has a supremum.

The first step is to transfer this result to the type of reals. Although not vacuous (formally, the positive reals are a completely different type), this is straightforward because the type bijections define an isomorphism between the *type* of positive reals and the positive elements of the type of reals. The theorem now becomes

> Every nonempty set of real numbers that is bounded above, and all of whose elements are positive, has a supremum.

We generalize this in two stages. First it is simple to prove the following strengthening:

> Every nonempty set of real numbers that is bounded above, and that contains at least one positive element, has a supremum.

(The property 'nonempty' is actually superfluous here, but we keep it in for regularity.) This follows because l is a supremum of the whole set if and only if it is a supremum of the positive elements of it, since any positive number is greater than any negative number.

Finally we prove the lemma that for any d, positive or negative, l is a supremum of S if and only if $l + d$ is of $\{x + d \mid x \in S\}$. Now this can be used to reduce the case of any nonempty bounded set to the above, by choosing a d to 'translate' it such that it has at least one positive element. We now have the full result:

> Every nonempty set of real numbers that is bounded above has a supremum.

2.11 Handling equivalence classes

Most of the above is rendered in HOL in quite a straightforward way, and does not deserve detailed consideration. However we would like to look at the new tool we developed for defining new types of equivalence classes of a given type — the steps from $\mathbb{N}$ to $\mathbb{R}^+$ and from $\mathbb{R}^+$ to $\mathbb{R}$ both require the use of equivalence classes, and the procedure is tedious to do by hand, so an automated tool is useful.

2.11.1 Defining a quotient type

Suppose we have a representing type ρ, on which a binary relation $R : \rho \to \rho \to bool$ is defined (we'll write R infix when used in a binary context). It's pretty straightforward to automate the definition of the new type. We just need to select the appropriate subsets of ρ, namely those that are R-equivalence classes. Since $R\,x = \lambda y.\, R\,x\,y$, this is simply:

$$\{R\,x \mid x : \rho\}$$

or more formally (we'll use sets and predicates interchangeably)

$$\lambda r.\, \exists x : \rho.\, r = R\,x$$

Trivially this predicate is inhabited, so we can define a new type α in bijection with it. The theorems returned by the type definition function are as follows, where mk and $dest$ are the abstraction and representation functions respectively:

$$\forall a : \alpha.\, mk(dest(a)) = a$$

$$\forall r : \rho \to bool.\, (\exists x : \rho.\, r = R\, x) \Leftrightarrow (dest(mk(r)) = r)$$

2.11.2 Lifting operations

All the above just takes a few lines to automate (we don't even need to know that R is an equivalence relation). However the more interesting task is to automate the 'lifting' of operators and predicates on ρ up to α. Our package is essentially limited to 'first order' operators. It works as follows.

We distinguish two cases, a function f that returns something of type ρ that we want to lift to α, and a function P that returns something we don't want to lift (we use P because this other type is usually Boolean, and so P is a predicate, but this is not necessarily the case). We assume that they take a mixture of arguments: $x_1, \ldots, x_n$ that are of type ρ and we want to lift to α, and $y_1, \ldots, y_m$ that we don't. Note that some of these y_i might still be of type ρ, but are not to be lifted (this has not happened in our use of the package, but is perfectly conceivable). It may help the reader to keep in mind concrete examples like $+ : \rho \to \rho \to \rho$ and $\leq: \rho \to \rho \to bool$.

The function that automates this lifting takes a welldefinedness theorem, showing that the function respects the equivalence class:

$$\begin{array}{l}(x_1\, R\, x_1') \land \cdots \land (x_n\, R\, x_n') \land (y_1 = y_1') \land \cdots \land (y_m = y_m') \\ \Rightarrow (f\; x_1\; \ldots\; x_n\; y_1\; \ldots\; y_m)\; R\; (f\; x_1'\; \ldots\; x_n'\; y_1'\; \ldots\; y_m')\end{array}$$

or

$$\begin{array}{l}(x_1\, R\, x_1') \land \cdots \land (x_n\, R\, x_n') \land (y_1 = y_1') \land \cdots \land (y_m = y_m') \\ \Rightarrow (P\; x_1\; \ldots\; x_n\; y_1\; \ldots\; y_m = P\; x_1'\; \ldots\; x_n'\; y_1'\; \ldots\; y_m')\end{array}$$

Note that, even if some of the y_i are of type ρ, we can distinguish those that are supposed to be lifted from those that aren't by whether R or equality is used in the welldefinedness theorem. The package allows the x_i and y_j to be intermixed arbitrarily; it does however insist that all the operators to be lifted are curried.[9] The definitions of lifted operations f^* and P^* that the package makes are quite natural:

$$\begin{array}{l}f^*\; X_1\; \ldots\; X_n\; y_1\; \ldots\; y_m = \\ mk(\lambda u.\, \exists z_1\; \ldots\; z_n.\; (f\; z_1\; \ldots\; z_n\; y_1\; \ldots\; y_m)\; R\; u\; \land \\ \qquad\qquad\qquad\qquad dest(X_1) z_1 \land \cdots dest(X_n) z_n)\end{array}$$

and

[9] In other words, they are higher order functions $\sigma_1 \to \cdots \to \sigma_n \to \tau$ rather than functions on Cartesian products $\sigma_1 \times \cdots \times \sigma_n \to \tau$.

$$\begin{aligned}&P^* \, X_1 \, \ldots \, X_n \, y_1 \, \ldots \, y_m = \\ &\varepsilon u. \exists z_1 \, \ldots \, z_n. \, (P \, z_1 \, \ldots \, z_n \, y_1 \, \ldots \, y_m = u) \land \\ &\qquad\qquad\qquad dest(X_1) z_1 \land \cdots dest(X_n) z_n\end{aligned}$$

Forgetting about the type bijections for a moment, these are just what one would expect, for example $X_1 +^* X_2 = \{u \mid \exists z_1 \, z_2. \, z_1 + z_2 \; R \; u \land z_1 \in X_1 \land z_2 \in X_2\}$. However, these definitions are rather inconvenient to work with. As well as the definition, the package derives a theorem of the form:

$$\begin{aligned}&mk(R(f \, x_1 \, \ldots \, x_n \, y_1 \, \ldots \, y_m)) = \\ &f^* \, (mk(R \, x_1)) \, \ldots \, (mk(R \, x_n)) \, y_1 \, \ldots \, y_m\end{aligned}$$

or

$$\begin{aligned}&P \, x_1 \, \ldots \, x_n \, y_1 \, \ldots \, y_m = \\ &P^* \, (mk(R \, x_1)) \, \ldots \, (mk(R \, x_n)) \, y_1 \, \ldots \, y_m\end{aligned}$$

These are very useful, since they can be mechanically applied as rewrite rules to 'bubble' the $mk \circ R$ up or down in a term (see below). The derivations that need to be automated are fairly straightforward. First, the definition is instantiated appropriately, then the simplification $dest(mk(R \; x)) = R \; x$ (easily derived from the type bijection theorems) is applied to each of the n instances. Then a bit of trivial logic using the welldefinedness theorem gives the result. In the 'P' case we perform an eta-conversion to eliminate u at the end. Note by the way that nothing in the above derivation uses the fact that R is symmetric; any preorder would do.[10] We are not aware of any use for this observation, though.

A word about deriving welldefinedness theorems in particular instances. Often they are trivial, but sometimes it can create baffling complications if a direct proof is attempted. However by exploiting the transitivity of the equivalence relation, one can establish welldefinedness for one argument at a time. What's more, one can often exploit symmetry of the operator concerned. For example, we often prove first $\forall x \; x' \; y. \, x \sim x' \Rightarrow x + y \sim x' + y$; then using symmetry we get at once $\forall x \; y \; y'. \, y \sim y' \Rightarrow x + y \sim x + y'$. Now these can be plugged together by transitivity to give the full welldefinedness theorem.

2.11.3 Lifting theorems

The final tool in the suite lifts whole theorems. These must be essentially first order, i.e. any quantifiers involving type ρ must be *exactly* ρ. The first stage is to use the following theorem; for efficiency, this is proved schematically

[10] We noticed this because the 'symmetry theorem' argument to the proof tool had its type generalized by the ML compiler, indicating that it wasn't used anywhere. Perhaps this is the first time a mathematical generalization has been suggested in this way!

for a generic pair of type bijections then instantiated with each call (similar remarks apply to other general theorems that we use).

$$\forall P. (\forall x : \rho. P(mk(R\, x))) \Leftrightarrow (\forall a : \alpha. P(a))$$

The proof is rather straightforward, since precisely everything in α is an isomorphic image of an R-equivalence class. We also prove the same thing for the existential quantifier. Now, simply higher order rewriting with the derived theorems from the function-lifting stage together with these quantifier theorems gives the required result. The derived theorems will introduce $mk(R\, x)$ in place of x at the predicate level and bubble it down to the variable level; then the quantifier theorems will eliminate it. We assume all variables in the original theorem are bound by quantifiers; if not, it's trivial to generalize any free ones. We should add that as well as the theorems for each relation like $\leq$, we derive another for equality, which takes the place of the equivalence relation itself in the lifted theorem:

$$\forall x\, y. x\, R\, y \Leftrightarrow (mk(R\, x) = mk(R\, y))$$

We have explained that the tool is limited to first order quantifiers. Unfortunately the completeness theorem for the positive reals is higher order:

```
|- !P. (?x. P x) /\ (?M. !x. P x ==> x nadd_le M)
       ==> (?M. (!x. P x ==> x nadd_le M) /\
                (!M'. (!x. P x ==> x nadd_le M')
                      ==> M nadd_le M'))
```

However this special case is easily dealt with by making P itself locally just another predicate to lift, with Q its corresponding lifted form. That is, we throw in the following trivial theorem with the other theorems returned by the operation lifter:

```
(\x. Q (mk_hreal ((nadd_eq) x))) = P
|- Q (mk_hreal ((nadd_eq) x)) = P x
```

Then we call the theorem lifter, and get:

```
(\x. Q (mk_hreal ((nadd_eq) x))) = P
|- (?x. Q x) /\ (?M. !x. Q x ==> x hreal_le M)
   ==> (?M. (!x. Q x ==> x hreal_le M) /\
            (!M'. (!x. Q x ==> x hreal_le M')
                  ==> m hreal_le M'))
```

following which we instantiate P to make the hypothesis reflexive, and so discharge it. After a generalization step and an alpha conversion from Q to P, we get exactly what we would want by analogy with the lifting of first order theorems:

```
|- !P. (?x. P x) /\ (?M. !x. P x ==> x hreal_le M)
       ==> (?M. (!x. P x ==> x hreal_le M) /\
                (!M'. (!x. P x ==> x hreal_le M')
                      ==> M hreal_le M'))
```

Generalizing the package to more general higher order quantifiers is an interesting problem. It seems quite difficult in the case of existentials, since predicates in the unlifted type need to respect the equivalence relation, for the corresponding lifted form to be derivable in some situations. For example, sets proved to exist must contain x iff they contain all x' with $x\ R\ x'$. It seems the smooth and regular automation of this is not trivial.

2.12 Summary and related work

The reals construction described here includes 146 saved theorems, which are developed in 1973 lines of ML, including comments and blank lines. The tool for defining quotient types is an additional 189 lines. There was already an old library for defining quotient types in HOL, due to Ton Kalker. However that was much less powerful, being unable to handle the automatic lifting of first order theorems.

The first construction of the reals in a computer theorem prover was by Jutting (1977), who in a pioneering effort translated the famous 'Grundlagen der Analysis' by Landau (1930) into Automath. His effort took much longer than ours, which though a long time in the planning, took only a few days to translate into HOL. Even an early version of the work (Harrison 1994) done when the author was still a relative novice, took only 2 weeks. The comparison is rather unfair in that Jutting did much on Automath itself during his work, and advances in computer technology must have made things easier. However, a lot of the difference must be due to the superiority of the HOL theorem proving facilities, giving some indication of how the state of the art has moved forward in the last decade or so. A construction in the very different Metamath system (Megill 1996) has just been completed at time of writing.[11]

The reals can also be developed in a way that is 'constructive' in the Bishop style, as expounded by Bishop and Bridges (1985). The usual construction is an elaboration of Cauchy's method where the rate of convergence of a Cauchy sequence is bounded explicitly. The resulting objects do not enjoy all the properties of their classical counterparts; for example $\forall x, y.\ x \leq y \vee y < x$ is not provable. The definition of the constructive reals has been done in NuPRL by Chirimar and Howe (1992), with a proof of their completeness, i.e. that every Cauchy sequence converges. Much of the construction, as well as some work on completing a general metric space, has

[11] Personal communication.

been done by Jones (1991) in the LEGO prover (which is also based on a constructive logic).

Mizar (Trybulec 1978), IMPS (Farmer, Guttman, and Thayer 1990) and PVS (Owre, Rushby, and Shankar 1992), among other systems, assume axioms for the real numbers in their initial theory. This is clearly a reasonable policy if the objective is to get quickly to some more interesting high-level mathematics. However our approach has the merit of being more systematic and keeps the primitive basis of the system small and uncluttered. In fact, the reals have been constructed in Mizar more than once, but because the primitive basis involves the real numbers it is difficult to retrofit these constructions into the theory development; certainly at time of writing this has not been done.

3. Formalized Analysis

To support practical requirements, e.g. elementary properties of the transcendental functions, a significant amount of real analysis is required. We survey how this was formalized in HOL, focusing on the parts that bring out interesting general issues about theorem proving and the formalization of mathematics. The development we describe covers topology, limits, sequences and series, Taylor expansion, differentiation and integration.

3.1 The rigorization and formalization of analysis

For some time after the development of calculus, Newton, Leibniz and their followers seemed unable to give a completely satisfactory account of their use of 'infinitesimals', quantities that they divided by one minute and assumed zero the next. Indeed, perhaps it was foundational worries, rather than pedagogical considerations, which persuaded Newton to rewrite all the proofs in his *Principia* in geometric language. Attempts were made to place the use of infinitesimals on a firmer footing: Newton came quite close to stating the modern limit concept, and Lagrange made an attempt to found everything on infinite series. However some like Euler continued to rely on intuition, amply justifying it by their astonishing facility in manipulating infinite series and getting correct interesting results such as $\Sigma_{i=1}^{\infty} 1/i^2 = \pi^2/6$.

One of the triumphs of mathematics in the nineteenth century was the rigorization of analysis. People like Cauchy, Bolzano and Weierstrass gave precise 'ϵ-δ' definitions of notions such as limits, continuity, differentiation and integration. For example a function $f : \mathbb{R} \to \mathbb{R}$ is said to be continuous (on $\mathbb{R}$) precisely when:

$$\forall x \in \mathbb{R}.\ \forall \epsilon > 0.\ \exists \delta > 0.\ \forall x'.\ |x - x'| < \delta \Rightarrow |f(x) - f(x')| < \epsilon$$

Now in a rigorous treatment, this is actually a *definition*. However it is important, if our theories of continuous functions are to have their psychological or practical significance, that this correspond to our intuitive notion of what a continuous function is. That is, even if unobvious at first sight, it must be seen in retrospect to be the 'right' definition. Is this the case here?

Perhaps the most intuitive feature of continuous functions is that they attain intermediate values:

$$\forall x, x', z \in \mathbb{R}.\ x < x' \wedge (f(x) < z < f(x') \vee f(x') < z < f(x)) \\ \Rightarrow \exists w.\ x < w < x' \wedge f(w) = z$$

This property is called 'Darboux continuity'. Why not take that as the definition of continuity instead? In general, where there are several apparently equally attractive choices to be made, which one should be selected? Such worries can be allayed when the various plausible-looking definitions are all provably equivalent. For example, the alternative definitions of computability in terms of Turing machines, Markov algorithms, general recursive functions, untyped λ-calculus, production systems and so forth all turned out so. But here this is not the case: continuity implies Darboux continuity but not conversely (we shall see an example later). The usual definition of continuity has probably won out because it is intuitively the most satisfying, leads to the tidiest theory or admits the most attractive generalization to other metric and topological structures. But note that it also led to the counterintuitive pathologies of real analysis such as Bolzano's and Weierstrass's examples of everywhere continuous nowhere differentiable functions. This shows how the rigorous version of a concept can take on an unexpected life of its own.

Our HOL formalization of analysis follows the techniques that have now become standard in mathematics. It does not require such difficult analyses of informal concepts, since modern analysis is already quite rigorous. The most difficult decision we had to take was the precise theory of integration to develop (more on this later). But sometimes the demands of complete formalization and the exigencies of computer implementation can throw new light on informal, even though rigorous, concepts. After all, the development of mathematical logic around the turn of the century was itself spurred by foundational worries, this time over Cantorian set theory and its relatives. It merely takes to an extreme foundational and reductionist tendencies that were already there.

3.2 Some general theories

Our initial approach to formalizing real analysis was utilitarian: the aim was to produce a theory that would be useful in verification applications. This means, above all, having a large number of algebraic theorems, and also a large suite of theorems about the transcendental functions (*sin*, *log* etc.) However, the transcendental functions in particular are most easily dealt with in the context of a reasonable theory of analysis. Moreover, the application to computer algebra systems demands at least elementary theories about differentiation and integration. This motivated some development of pure analysis, most of the effort involved in which has been amply repaid.

Modern analysis has been abstracted away from its concrete roots in theorems about sequences in ℝ, analytic functions on ℂ and so on. Many of these now arise as special cases of rather general theorems dealing with topological spaces, filters, Riemann surfaces etc. This generalization has been motivated by several factors. First, it can lead to economy (at least in written presentation), since several theorems that look different can be seen as instances of the same general one. Second, it can be useful in making only *necessary* assumptions explicit, so leading to generalization even of the concrete instances. Finally, the general concepts themselves become interesting and suggest new and fruitful connections. All these are often subsumed under a broad feeling that the general, abstract forms are more elegant, but this feeling is a complicated mixture of aesthetic and pragmatic considerations.

In our computer approach, the pragmatic angle comes to the fore. Generalization is a genuinely useful tool for avoiding duplication of work. Textbooks can (and do) get away with saying 'the theorems about arithmetic on limits of real functions are directly analogous to those for real sequences' and leave it at that, but a computer needs much more explicit guidance even than a poor student. There has been some work in systems such as Nuprl on transformation tactics (IMPS also has a similar but less formal idea in 'proof by emacs'), which attempt to formalize these techniques of proving by analogy. But by far the most straightforward way is to follow the traditional mathematical line of generalization where it clearly offers economies. Our intention was to use abstract concepts only insofar as they seemed likely to be useful. This usually means that we actually want several distinct instances of the abstract concept. However it's possible that even if only one instance is required, abstraction can be worthwhile, because the process can actually make proofs easier, or at least less cluttered. For example, many slightly messy proofs in real analysis have rather elegant topological versions. The choice of a level of abstraction that is most useful in practice is therefore, in general, difficult. (It may even happen that one ends up using a less general instance as a lemma. For example, Gauss' proof that if a ring R is a unique factorization domain then so is its polynomial ring $R[x]$, uses as a lemma the fact that the ring of polynomials over a field is a UFD.) We shall describe the development of two more abstract theories in HOL and contrast their relative usefulness.

3.2.1 Metric spaces and topologies

The HOL implementation of metric spaces and topologies is a fairly direct transcription of typical textbook definitions. For example:

```
|- ismet (m:A#A->real) = (!x y. (m(x,y) = &0) = (x = y)) /\
                         (!x y z. m(y,z) <= m(x,y) + m(x,z))
```

However we do use one little trick to make proofs easier in the HOL framework: we define new types of topologies and metric spaces. More precisely we define type operators: given any type α there are corresponding types (α)*topology* and (α)*metric*. HOL types are required to be nonempty, but that is guaranteed here since on any set S one can define the trivial discrete metric:

$$\rho(x, y) = \text{if } x = y \text{ then } 0 \text{ else } 1$$

and the corresponding discrete topology which is simply the set of *all* subsets of S; trivially this obeys all the closure properties required. The idea is to avoid a proliferation of hypotheses of the form '...is a topology' or '...is a metric space' by encoding such information in the terms. The price is the appearance of explicit type bijections, but the bijection $(\alpha)topology \to ((\alpha \to bool) \to bool)$ is called simply 'open', allowing the natural reading of `open(top) A` as 'A is open in the topology *top*'. It is now simply a theorem without hypotheses that, for example, $open(top)A \wedge open(top)B \Rightarrow open(top)(A \cap B)$. The introduction of the additional function *open* serves to *make manifest* some of the properties of the topology. This can be compared to the technique, already quite common in HOL, of using $\vdash P(\texttt{SUC}\ n)$ rather than $\vdash n \neq 0 \Rightarrow P(n)$ for theorems about the natural numbers. Though perhaps just a trick, forced on us by HOL's limited facilities for dealing with conditional equations and the like, it can be turned to good account in some situations.

It should be admitted that the HOL theories of topologies and metric spaces have not so far been useful. In all our work, we just use the standard topology and metric on the real line; it's not clear that proving a few results in an abstract framework makes them significantly easier. In fact, we prove many theorems in a concrete way even when they have an attractive topological generalization — this is explicitly noted in a few places below. On the other hand, if we came to develop multivariate or complex analysis, these theories might come into their own. They are a little limited in that metrics and topologies are only defined on whole types, rather than on arbitrary subsets. Since HOL does not have a mechanism for defining subtypes in a completely transparent way (they must be accompanied by explicit coercions), this is too inflexible to form the basis for a serious development of topology. Moreover, the HOL type system is too restrictive for a number of classical results. For example, Tychonoff's theorem contemplates an infinite Cartesian product of topological spaces, which needn't all be of the same 'type' in the HOL sense.

Nevertheless, the HOL theory of topology was once applied, surprisingly smoothly, to produce a proof of A. H. Stone's theorem that every metrizable space is paracompact (every open cover has a locally finite refinement). This was suggested on the QED mailing list[1] by Andrzej Trybulec as an interesting case study in the relative power and flexibility of theorem proving systems. In response, a proof given by Engelking (1989) was translated directly into HOL

[1] On 17th June 1994; available on the Web as `ftp://ftp.mcs.anl.gov/pub/qed/archive/56`.

by the present author. The textbook proof occupies about a page, whereas the HOL proof is 700 lines long and took almost 10 hours to construct. However this compares quite favourably with other present-day systems. As far as we know, the only other system to have been used to prove this theorem is Mizar, and the process took at least as long. However this excursion into general topology has not been followed up with more substantial work, at least not by us.

3.2.2 Convergence nets

Several notions of 'limit' arise in real analysis; those that are especially useful to us are:

1. A function $f : \mathbb{R} \to \mathbb{R}$ is said to have limit y_0 as $x \to x_0$ iff $\forall \epsilon > 0.\, \exists \delta > 0.\, \forall x.\, 0 < |x - x_0| < \delta \Rightarrow |f(x) - y_0| < \epsilon$. So a function f is continuous at x_0 iff $f(x) \to f(x_0)$ as $x \to x_0$.
2. A sequence of natural numbers (s_n) is said to have limit l (as $n \to \infty$) iff $\forall \epsilon > 0.\, \exists N \in \mathbb{N}.\, \forall n \in \mathbb{N}.\, n \geq N \Rightarrow |s_n - l| < \epsilon$.
3. A function $f : \mathbb{R} \to \mathbb{R}$ is said to have limit y_0 as $x \to \infty$ iff $\forall \epsilon > 0.\, \exists K.\, \forall x.\, |x| \geq K \Rightarrow |f(x) - y_0| < \epsilon$.

(And one could easily think of more, e.g. in the first case distinguish between left-sided and right-sided limits, and in the third distinguish between $+\infty$ and $-\infty$.) These are obviously rather close similarities between them. (Indeed the first and the third can be considered the same if ∞ is not just used as a figure of speech, as here, but added to the real line or complex plane — the '1-point compactification' — with the appropriate properties. However it's not very convenient for us to do that.) Moreover, we want to prove the same theorems about all of them, including:

1. The limit is unique, i.e. a function or sequence cannot converge to two different limits (this holds in an arbitrary Hausdorff topological space in fact).
2. The limit of a negation is the negation of the limit; the limit of an absolute value is the absolute value of the limit. Provided the limit is nonzero, the same holds for multiplicative inverse.
3. The limit of a constant is that constant.
4. The limit of a sum, difference or product is respectively the sum, difference or product of the limits; the same holds for division provided the second limit is nonzero.
5. If one function or sequence is $\leq$ another everywhere, then the limits are in the same relation (this doesn't sharpen to $<$, e.g. consider $1/n$ and $1/n^2$).
6. If $f - g \to 0$ and either f or g has a limit, then f and g have the same limit; in particular if $f(x) = g(x)$ sufficiently close to the limit.

7. If the limit is nonzero, then close enough to the limit, the value of the function or sequence is nonzero.

There are admittedly a few that are special to certain cases. For example the useful fact that if a sequence has a limit then it is bounded does not generalize to the other types of limit. Nevertheless the overwhelming bulk of the interesting facts are common to all three cases. So much so that rather than prove them all individually we used a generalization: the theory of nets.[2] This is a good example of how the requirements of a formal presentation can drive the invention of new simplifying concepts. To give a similar example, the equating of real sequences with functions $\mathbb{N} \to \mathbb{R}$ which we tacitly assume (the subscripting s_n being simply the application of s to argument n) appears to have been made first by Peano as part of his project of formalization. Our use of nets is quite prosaic; we do not prove deeper properties, such as the fact that classic theorems equating sequential and pointwise convergence generalize to arbitrary topological spaces if sequences are replaced by nets. (For example the Bolzano-Weierstrass theorem is as follows: a set is compact iff every net has an accumulation point.[3])

Nets are simply functions out of a set X with a directed partial order, i.e. a partial order $\sqsubseteq$ such that $\forall x, y \in X. \exists z \in X. x \sqsubseteq z \land y \sqsubseteq z$. Actually in the HOL theory, we never use any partial order properties, so simply specify $\forall x, y \in X. \exists z \in X. \forall w \in X. z \sqsubseteq w \Rightarrow x \sqsubseteq w \land y \sqsubseteq w$. For the three kinds of limit, we specialize X and $\sqsubseteq$ as follows:

1. For limits of functions $f : \mathbb{R} \to \mathbb{R}$ at $x_0 \in \mathbb{R}$, X is $\mathbb{R} - \{x_0\}$ and we define the order by $x \sqsubseteq x' \Leftrightarrow 0 < |x' - x_0| \leq |x - x_0|$. Note that limits at different points give rise to different nets. (This kind of net is in fact generalized to reverse inclusion of neighbourhoods in a topological space and the above derived by specialization.)
2. For sequences, X is $\mathbb{N}$ and the order is the usual ordering $\leq$ on $\mathbb{N}$.
3. For limits of real functions at infinity, X is $\mathbb{R}$ and the ordering is $x \sqsubseteq x' \Leftrightarrow |x| \leq |x'|$.

Intuitively, being larger according to the ordering $\sqsubseteq$ means being closer to the limit point. Accordingly, we say that a net $f : X \to \mathbb{R}$ has a limit y_0 iff:

$$\forall \epsilon > 0. \exists x \in X. \forall x'. x \sqsubseteq x' \Rightarrow |f(x') - y_0| < \epsilon$$

Notice that the special case of limits of the first kind actually differs somewhat from the way it was stated above, being:

[2] Essentially we arrived at a similar notion ourselves; they are almost forced on one when attempting to generalize all the above-mentioned limit concepts.

[3] Note by the way that this theorem cannot be stated in precisely that form in the HOL logic without a notion of type quantification as proposed by Melham (1992), since it involves quantifying over all nets with arbitrary index set.

$$\forall \epsilon > 0.\, \exists z.\, 0 < |z - x| \wedge \forall x.\, 0 < |x - x_0| \leq |z - x| \Rightarrow |f(x) - y_0| < \epsilon$$

rather than

$$\forall \epsilon > 0.\, \exists \delta > 0.\, \forall x.\, 0 < |x - x_0| < \delta \Rightarrow |f(x) - y_0| < \epsilon$$

In the case of the reals they are easily seen to be equivalent, but for a general metric space this is no longer true unless x_0 is known to be a limit point (i.e. there are distinct points arbitrarily close to it). Since we do actually define pointwise limits for an arbitrary metric space, in fact for an arbitrary topological space, this is significant. The '$\leq$' version does turn out to be more convenient for the general net theorems. If one looks at the definitions of limit in a metric space given in analysis texts, they usually give a conditional definition: 'if x_0 is a limit point then ...'. Most formal logical systems only sanction unconditional definitions, though it may be that the expansion of the definition is subject to definedness conditions. In the HOL logic a definitional expansion is always valid, even if without further information it is impossible to derive much of interest from it.

It turned out to be perfectly straightforward to prove in HOL all the desired properties under the more general limit notion given by nets. Then they can be trivially specialized to the three cases at hand. We only deal with the first and second kinds of limit in the present book. More details of the theory of nets and their now more popular relatives filters (these are well-known in model theory as well as analysis) are given in the classic book by Kelley (1975) and many more modern books on general topology such as Bourbaki (1966).

3.3 Sequences and series

A basic theory of sequences is now derived by specializing the net theorems. Before we consider how the theory is further developed and applied to infinite series, let us reflect on the relationship between formal and informal notation for the limits of sequences.

We have already remarked on how from a formal point of view, a sequence can be regarded, à la Peano, as a function, meaning that s_n is, formally speaking, the application of the function $s : \mathbb{N} \to \mathbb{R}$ to the argument $n : \mathbb{N}$. So while it is common to talk about 'the sequence (s_n)' (we've done so ourselves), it would be simpler to talk about 'the sequence s', since s_n is merely its value at a particular point; in fact the formal version of (s_n) is perhaps the η-equivalent $\lambda n.\, s_n$. One of the merits of formalization in lambda-calculus (or equivalent), is that it makes the free/bound variable distinction and the functional dependency status completely explicit. Here is an example of the specialization of one of the net theorems (the infix '-->' denotes 'tends to').

```
|- !x x0 y y0. x --> x0 /\ y --> y0
            ==> (\n. x(n) * y(n)) --> (x0 * y0)
```

We define a (higher order) constant *lim* so that the informal statement $lim_{n \to \infty} s_n$ is rendered simply as *lim s*. Indeed, it is clear that n is not actually meant to be a free variable in the informal version; rather, '$lim_{n \to \infty} \ldots$' or '... as $n \to \infty$' is viewed as a binding operation. The HOL formalization looks quite different, but if we perform an η-expansion on s, we get $s = \lambda n. s_n$, so *lim s* can equally well be written $lim(\lambda n.\ s_n)$. Now, there are already a number of so-called 'binders' defined in HOL. From a logical point of view, these are just ordinary higher order functions. However during parsing and printing, the notation $Bx.\ t[x]$ (where B is the binder) is regarded as shorthand for $B(\lambda x.\ t[x])$. The quantifiers, for example, are implemented in this way; what is parsed and printed in standard logical notation $\forall x. P[x]$ is really expanded to $\forall(\lambda x. P[x])$.[4] We do exactly the same with sequential limits, and with lots of other operations we define later. This means that something very like the informal notation can be used, (with a more sophisticated interface, exactly the same), e.g. $lim\ n.\ (n-1)/(n-2)$. This is far more than just a trick: it explicates all variable binding operations just in terms of lambda binding, which is both economical and clarifying.

There is a respect, however, in which the HOL formalization does not work out so well, and this is also illustrated by the *lim* operation. We define:

```
|- lim f = @l. f --> l
```

Now consider this variant of the above theorem on the product of limits:

```
?- !x x0 y y0. (lim x = x0) /\ (lim y = y0)
            ==> (lim (\n. x(n) * y(n)) = x0 * y0)
```

This theorem cannot be proved! The reason is connected with the issue of partial and total functions which we have already mentioned briefly. We already have a theorem asserting that limits are unique, i.e. if $f \to l$ and $f \to l'$ then $l = l'$. From that and the defining property of the ε operator, it is certainly possible to deduce $lim\ f = l$ from $f \to l$. However the reverse is not true. The *lim* operation is a HOL function, and HOL functions are all total. So even if f does not have a limit, there is some l with $lim\ f = l$. This explains why we should not expect to prove the above theorem. (On the contrary, if $x_n = n$ and $y_n = \frac{1}{n}$, it must be false, since otherwise it would imply $0 = 1$.) The 'functional' form $lim\ f = l$ contains ***essentially less information*** than the relational form $f \to l$. Therefore, in our subsequent development, we almost always employ the relational form, and the functional form is seldom useful.

[4] This elegant device originated with Church (1940); subsequently Landin (1966) was one of the first to emphasize how many other notational devices, e.g. `let`-expressions, could be regarded as syntactic sugar on top of λ-calculus. Landin, by the way, is credited with inventing the term 'syntactic sugar'.

If one looks at analysis texts they usually say something like 'if $s_n \to l$ as $n \to \infty$, then we write $lim_{n \to \infty} s_n = l$'. So taken literally, reading 'if' as 'iff' as one conventionally does for definitions, the whole construct is some kind of *contextual definition* which is really to be regarded as a shorthand for the relational statement. Contextual definitions are those that do not necessarily refer directly to well-defined entities in the object logic, but are to be regarded as shorthands for possibly quite structurally different statements there. The use of proper classes in ZF set theory is a good example, and one can even look at cardinal arithmetic this way, that is, $|A| = |B|$ is really an abbreviation for 'there exists a bijection between the sets A and B', and so on.

From one point of view then, our sticking to a purely relational formalization is defensible, in that it could be said to constitute an *analysis* of what the informal statement means. One could even say that it is through the metalanguage ML that the functional versions should be interpreted, not in the object logic. However, the fact remains that the relational form can be very inconvenient to work with. The inconvenience comes to the fore when such constructs are nested, the prime example being the nested differentiation operations in differential equations. Here, differential equations as written in textbooks need to be accompanied by a long string of differentiability assumptions which in informal usage are understood implicitly. Therefore one might ask: is there a better formalism in which such statements can be formalized in a way that keeps them close to informal convention?

One simple possibility is to use an untyped system like standard set theory. Here, the lack of types gives more freedom to adopt special values in the case of undefinedness. For example, many functions that we want to be undefined in certain places have a natural 'type' $X \to Y$. (The inverse function $\mathbb{R} \to \mathbb{R}$, and the limit operation $(\mathbb{N} \to \mathbb{R}) \to \mathbb{R}$ are just two we have discussed here.) One might adopt the convention of extending their ranges to $Y \cup \{Y\}$ and giving the function the value Y in the case of undefinedness.[5] This would seem to give many of the benefits of a first-class notion of definedness without complicating the foundational system.

A more radical approach is to adopt a logic in which certain terms can be 'undefined'. Then, on the understanding that $s = t$ means 's and t are defined and equal', the statement $lim\ s = l$ would, assuming that l is defined, incorporate the information that s does actually converge. Such a logic is implemented by the IMPS system (Farmer, Guttman, and Thayer 1990), which was expressly designed for the formalization of mathematics, and otherwise has a type theory not dissimilar to HOL's. However some dislike the idea of complicating the underlying logic, either because of a desire for simplicity, or because of concern that proofs are likely to become cluttered with definability assumptions. The original LCF systems described by Gordon, Milner,

[5] We are assuming here that $Y \notin Y$, but one could surely find counterparts to our convention in set theories where this is not guaranteed (Holmes 1998). Even there, $Y \notin Y$ is still guaranteed for 'small' sets, which includes pretty well all concrete sets used in mathematics.

and Wadsworth (1979) and Paulson (1987) implemented a similar logic (a special 'bottom' element denoted undefinedness), as did the first version of the LAMBDA hardware verification tool, and in both cases, the clutter was considerable.

An alternative approach, long used by the Nuprl system and more recently by PVS, is to make all functions total, but exploit a facility for transparent subtypes. In such a scheme, lim would have not type $(\mathbb{N} \to \mathbb{R}) \to \mathbb{R}$ but rather $\{s \mid \exists l.\ s \to l\} \to \mathbb{R}$. Now the logic is still almost as simple (and subtypes are desirable for other reasons too, as we have already noted). Now if an assertion $lim\ s = l$ is well-typed, then s must converge. However there is still an additional load of proof obligations involved in typechecking, which is no longer decidable as in HOL. Moreover, it means that the underlying types can become extremely complicated and counterintuitive. Finally, it is less flexible than the IMPS approach, which, as it actually features a definedness operator, can employ its own bespoke notions of equality. For example in many informal contexts it seems that the equality $s = t$ is interpreted as 'quasi-equality' (using IMPS terminology), i.e. 'either s and t are both undefined, or they are both defined and equal'. On such a reading, for example, the equation $\frac{d}{dx}(1/x) = -1/x^2$ is strictly valid. Actually Freyd and Scedrov (1990) use a special asymmetric 'Venturi tube' equality meaning 'if the left hand side is defined then so is the right and they are equal'. For other contrasts between the approaches to undefinedness, consider the following:

$$\forall x \in \mathbb{R}.\ tan(x) = 0 \Rightarrow \exists n \in \mathbb{Z}.\ x = n\pi$$

Assuming that $tan(x)$ is defined as $sin(x)/cos(x)$, this formula distinguishes all the major approaches to undefinedness:

- In our formalization with $0^{-1} = 0$ it is false, since $tan(x) = sin(x)/cos(x)$ is also 0 at the values where $tan(x)$ is conventionally regarded as 'undefined', i.e. when $x = \pm\frac{2n+1}{2}\pi$.
- Had we just used an arbitrary value for 0^{-1} (say $\varepsilon x.\ \bot$) then the formula would be neither provable nor refutable, since that would require settling whether the arbitrary value is in fact 0.
- In the IMPS approach, the theorem is true, since $tan(x) = 0$ implies that $tan(x)$ is defined. (It makes no difference whether equality is interpreted as strict or quasi-equality, since 0 is certainly defined.)
- For approaches relying on total functions out of subtypes, the truth of this formula depends on how typechecking and logic interact. However in the usual scheme, as used for example by PVS, the above formula is a typing error without a restriction on the quantified variable. In typechecking $P[x] \Rightarrow Q[x]$, the formula $P[x]$ is assumed when typechecking $Q[x]$, but an assertion that $P[x]$ is well-typed is not.

3.3.1 Sequences

Now let us survey the actual development of the theory of sequences. The most important theorems to us are those concerning Cauchy sequences; (s_n) is said to be a Cauchy, or fundamental, sequence, if:

$$\forall \epsilon > 0.\ \exists N.\ \forall m, n \geq N.\ |s_n - s_m| < \epsilon$$

This looks rather similar to the fact that the sequence is convergent to some limit l:

$$\exists l.\ \forall \epsilon > 0.\ \exists N.\ \forall n \geq N.\ |s_n - l| < \epsilon$$

In fact, these turn out to be provably equivalent, i.e. the reals are (Cauchy) complete. The Cauchy criterion for convergence is useful in practice because it allows us to prove that a sequence converges without needing to postulate the limit; as we shall see, this is especially convenient when dealing with infinite series.

The proof that a sequence is Cauchy iff it is convergent was taken from Burkill and Burkill (1970), a standard textbook on analysis, and formalized directly in HOL. One way is rather easy. Suppose (s_n) is convergent. Then, given any $\epsilon > 0$, let us specialize the definition of convergence to $\epsilon/2$. We have some N such that $\forall n \geq N.\ |s_n - l| < \epsilon/2$. Therefore if $m \geq N$ and $n \geq N$ then, using the triangle law:

$$|s_n - s_m| \leq |s_n - l| + |s_m - l| < \epsilon/2 + \epsilon/2 = \epsilon$$

The above was straightforward, but it illustrates an interesting feature of typical 'ϵ-δ' proofs in analysis. Very often one sets out to establish some overall bound on ϵ, say, and to get this, one instantiates other ϵ-δ properties (either other ϵ's or sometimes N's in the case of sequences and series) and uses the triangle law and similar reasoning to get the result. The required instantiations, for example $\epsilon/2$ in our example, generally follow not just from the fact to be proved, but from the structure of the intended proof. Taking the finished proof for granted, the reasoning is not deep, but it's often difficult to guess the right instantiations until the proof structure has been developed. From the point of view of HOL, this means that it's desirable to have the proof and the instantiations (as found in a textbook for example) fixed in one's mind before touching the keyboard. However the Isabelle system (Paulson 1994) allows the use of 'logic variables' whose instantiations can be delayed, and sometimes automatically inferred by higher order unification (Huet 1975). It would be a very interesting exercise to try some ϵ-δ proofs in Isabelle — they may be much more natural to write.

Now let us return to Burkill and Burkill's proof of the other direction and examine its HOL formalization. It uses the auxiliary notion of a 'subsequence'. Intuitively, a subsequence of a sequence s is another that picks out some, but not necessarily all, elements of s, in order. Though this is a very informal description, arriving at a formal counterpart is not difficult. The most direct formalization, which we used in the HOL proof, is as follows. Define a 'reindexing' function $k : \mathbb{N} \to \mathbb{N}$ to be one that is strictly increasing (by an easy induction, this is equivalent to $\forall n.\ k(n) < k(\mathtt{SUC}\ n)$, which is actually the definition we use). We now say that t is a subsequence of s iff there is a reindexing function k such that $t = s \circ k$.

Now we prove the following attractive theorem: *every* sequence s has a monotonic subsequence t, i.e. one where either $\forall m, n. m \leq n \Rightarrow t_m \leq t_n$ or else $\forall m, n. m \leq n \Rightarrow t_m \geq t_n$.[6] Call n a *terrace point* if we have $\forall m > n.\ s_m \leq s_n$. If there are infinitely many such terrace points, we can just form a decreasing sequence by successively picking them (formally, we define the reindexing function by primitive recursion over the naturals). If on the other hand there are only finitely many terrace points, then suppose N is the last one (or $N = 0$ if there are none). Now for *any* $n > N$, there is an m with $s_m > s_n$ (otherwise n would be a terrace point); to avoid invoking AC, suppose m is the least such number. Hence we can choose a (strictly) increasing subsequence by repeatedly making such choices; this again translates easily into a primitive recursive definition. Hence the theorem is proved.

We just need two additional lemmas to get the main result:

- A bounded and monotonic sequence converges. Suppose the sequence is increasing, the other case being analogous. Consider the set $\{s_n \mid n \in \mathbb{N}\}$. This must have a supremum l such that for any $\epsilon > 0$, there exists an N with $|s_N - l| < \epsilon$. But because the sequence is increasing, this means that $\forall n \geq N.\ l - \epsilon < s_n \leq l$, so the sequence in fact converges to l.
- Every Cauchy sequence is bounded. For any $\epsilon > 0$, say $\epsilon = 1$, we can find an N such that $\forall m, n \geq N.\ |s_m - s_n| < \epsilon$, so

$$max(s_0, \ldots, s_{N-1}, s_N + \epsilon)$$

(which can be proved to exist by induction) is an upper bound.

Putting all these together, we get the result. Suppose s is a Cauchy sequence; let t be a monotonic subsequence. Since s is bounded, so is t, and the latter therefore converges to a limit l. But now by the Cauchy property, s must also converge to l.

We then derive various other standard properties of sequences. Notably we prove the useful fact that if $|c| < 1$ then $c^n \to 0$ as $n \to \infty$. This is used later to prove the convergence of some important series.

---

[6] Nothing depends on deeper properties of the reals; it holds for any total order. It is nonconstructive, though Erdös and Szekeres (1935) prove the following elegant finite version: every sequence of n^2+1 reals must have a monotonic subsequence of length $n+1$. Some such finite form follows from Ramsey's theorem, but this bound is much sharper than a Ramsey number, and is in fact the best possible.

3.3.2 Series

The sum of an infinite series $\Sigma_{i=k}^{\infty} s_i$ is by definition the limit as $n \to \infty$ of $\Sigma_{i=k}^{n} s_i$. Therefore the first stage in the development of a theory of infinite series is to define the notion of (finite) summation. Once again the summation and 'sums to' operators are higher order functions, but may be used as binders giving something close to conventional notation. However the finite summation is not perhaps defined in the most natural way. We use:

```
|- (Sum(m,0) f = &0) /\
   (Sum(m,SUC n) f = Sum(m,n) f + f(n + m))
```

This means that `Sum(m,n) f` actually represents $\Sigma_{i=m}^{m+n-1} f(i)$. This rather counterintuitive definition was chosen because it simplifies the development of the theory somewhat; in particular many theorems about `Sum(m,n) f` can be proved very directly using induction on n. The disparity with the usual notation was not considered important, since it is usually hidden inside the theory of infinite series rather than used explicitly. In retrospect, we rather regret the decision. But let us at least look at some of the theorems we derived.

```
|- !f n p. Sum(0,n) f + Sum(n,p) f = Sum(0,n + p) f

|- !f m n. Sum(m,n) f = Sum(0,m + n) f - Sum(0,m) f

|- !f m n. abs(Sum(m,n) f) <= Sum(m,n)(\i. abs(f i))

|- !f g m n. (!r. m <= r /\ r < (n + m) ==> (f r = g r))
             ==> (Sum(m,n) f = Sum(m,n) g)

|- !f g m n. Sum(m,n)(\i. f i + g i) = Sum(m,n) f + Sum(m,n) g

|- !f c m n. Sum(m,n)(\i. c * f i) = c * Sum(m,n) f

|- !n f c. Sum(0,n) f - &n * c = Sum(0,n)(\p. (f p) - c)

|- !f K m n. (!p. m <= p /\ p < m + n ==> (f p) <= K)
             ==> Sum(m,n) f <= &n * K

|- !n k f. Sum(0,n)(\m. Sum(m * k,k) f) = Sum(0,n * k) f

|- !f n k. Sum(0,n)(\m. f(m + k)) = Sum(0,n + k) f - Sum(0,k) f

|- !f m k n. Sum(m + k,n) f = Sum(m,n)(\r. f(r + k))
```

The above are all easy to prove. We also have a slightly more difficult theorem about permuting a sum, the proof being taken from the early pages of Lang (1994).

```
|- !n p. (!y. y < n ==> (?!x. x < n /\ (p x = y)))
         ==> (!f. Sum(0,n) (\i. f(p i)) = Sum(0,n) f)
```

Moving on to infinite series, we have as usual a higher order relation, called '`sums`', to indicate that a series converges to the stated limit. There is also a constant '`summable`' meaning that some limit exists. The properties of infinite series that we use are mostly elementary consequences of theorems about finite summations and theorems about limits. For example we have another set of theorems justifying performing arithmetic operations term-by-term on convergent series, e.g.

```
|- !x x0 y y0. x sums x0 /\ y sums y0
               ==> (\n. x(n) + y(n)) sums (x0 + y0)
```

For the sake of making a nice theory, there are also a few classic results relating 'absolute convergence' (where the absolute values of the terms form a convergent series) and bare convergence. But true to our pragmatic orientation, we are mainly interested in providing tools for proving later that *particular* infinite series converge. An important lemma in deriving such results is a Cauchy-type criterion for summability, which follows easily from the corresponding theorem for sequences:

```
|- !f. summable f =
       !e. &0 < e ==> ?N. !m n. m >= N ==> abs(Sum(m,n) f) < e
```

The two main 'convergence test' theorems we prove are the comparison test, i.e. that if the absolute values of the terms of a series are bounded, for sufficiently large n, by those of a convergent series, then it is itself convergent (there is another version which asserts that f is absolutely convergent, an easy consequence of this one):

```
|- !f g. (?N. !n. n >= N ==> abs(f(n)) <= g(n)) /\ summable g
         ==> summable f
```

and the classic 'ratio test':

```
|- !f c N. c < &1 /\
           (!n. n >= N ==> abs(f(SUC n)) <= c * abs(f(n)))
           ==> summable f
```

This latter result follows quite easily from the fact that the geometric series $\Sigma_i c^i$ converges to $1/(1-c)$ if $|c| < 1$, and the Cauchy criterion.

3.4 Limits, continuity and differentiation

Once again we specialize the net theorems to give various theorems for pointwise limits. Here the infix notation `f --> l` (f tends to l) takes an additional argument which indicates the limit point concerned.[7] Next we define the notion of continuity. A function f is continuous at a point x when $f(z) \to f(x)$ as $z \to x$. It is easy, given the arithmetic theorems on limits, to prove this equivalent to the fact that $f(x+h) \to f(x)$ as $h \to 0$. We actually take this as our definition, since it simplifies the relationship with differentiation, which has a similar definition. We say that f has derivative l at a point x if $(f(x+h) - f(x))/h \to l$ as $h \to 0$. Here are the actual HOL definitions; '`f contl x`' should be read 'f is continuous at x', '`(f diffl l)(x)`' as 'f is differentiable with derivative l at the point x', and '`f differentiable x`' as 'f is differentiable at the point x'.[8]

```
|- f contl x = ((\h. f(x + h)) --> f(x))(&0)

|- (f diffl l)(x) = ((\h. (f(x+h) - f(x)) / h) --> l)(&0)

|- f differentiable x = ?l. (f diffl l)(x)
```

One of the first theorems we prove is the equivalent form of continuity:

```
|- !f x. f contl x = (f --> f(x))(x)
```

Yet another suite of theorems about arithmetic combinations, this time of continuous functions, are then proved. Once again they are simple consequences of the theorems for pointwise limits, which in turn are just instances of the general net theorems. For example, if two functions are continuous, so is their sum, product etc. The cases of multiplicative inverse and division include a condition that the function divided by has a nonzero value at the point concerned:

```
|- !x. contl f x /\ contl g x /\ ~(g x = &0)
       ==> contl (\x. f(x) / g(x)) x
```

There is one special property of continuous functions that is not directly derived from limit theorems, though the proof is easy and is rendered in HOL without difficulty. This is that the composition of continuous functions is continuous. We remark on it now because it plays a significant role in the theory of differentiation that follows.

---

7 The arrow symbol is actually a front end translation for an underlying constant `tends_real_real` in this case. The HOL interface map feature is employed so that the same arrow can be used in different places for different kinds of limits.

8 The 'definition' of continuity is actually a theorem derived from the underlying definition in terms of topological neighbourhoods. However we do not discuss the more general form in detail, since the topology theory was heavily elided above.

```
|- !f g x. f contl x /\ g contl (f x) ==> (g o f) contl x
```

We do also define a functional form of the derivative, which can be used as a binder, but again because of its totality, it is less useful than the relational form.

```
|- deriv f x = @l. (f diffl l)(x)
```

The derivative, whether written in a relational or functional style, illustrates especially well how reduction to lambda-calculus gives a simple and clear analysis of bound variables. The everyday Leibniz notation, as in:

$$\frac{d}{dx}(x^2) = 2x$$

actually conceals a rather subtle point. The variable x obviously occurs free in the right-hand side of the above equation and bound in the left. But it isn't *just* a bound variable on the left, because changing the variable name changes the right hand side too! If we write the above out formally using our definitions, we get *deriv* $(\lambda x.\, x^2)\ x = 2x$. Now the situation on the left hand side becomes clear. There are really two separate instances of x, one bound, one free, which the Leibniz notation conflates. A precisely similar situation can occur in integration, but here the standard notation separates the two instances:

$$\int_0^x 2x\ dx = x^2$$

Indeed, careful authors usually abandon the Leibniz derivative notation in more advanced work, or indicate with a subscript the point at which the resulting derivative is to be calculated. The formalized view we have taken of the derivative as simply a higher order function is reflected in much of present-day functional analysis, and the HOL notion of binder acts as a nice link between this and more familiar notations. Another derivative notation that seems clear is the use of the prime, $f'(x)$. However the author has witnessed a heated debate on `sci.math` among good mathematicians over whether $f'(g(x))$ denotes the derivative of f evaluated at $g(x)$ (this view seems most popular) or the derivative of $f \circ g$ evaluated at x ('the prime notation (f') is a shorthand notation for derivative of a univariate function with respect to the free variable.')

3.4.1 Proof by bisection

A useful tool for some of the proofs that follow is proof by bisection. This is a classic technique, going back to Bolzano, for proving some property $P(a, b)$ of the endpoints holds for a closed interval $[a, b]$.[9] One just needs to prove that (1) if the property holds for each half of an interval, it holds for the whole interval; and (2) for any point of the interval, it holds for any sufficiently small subinterval containing that point. The reasoning is by contradiction as follows. Suppose $P(a, b)$ is false. Then by (1) it must fail in one half of the interval, say the left (we can avoid AC by always picking the left interval if it fails in both halves). So $P(a, c)$ is false, where $c = (a + b)/2$. Now bisect $[a, c]$ and so on. In this way a decreasing nest of intervals is derived for which P fails. It is an easy consequence of the completeness of the reals that there is a point x common to all these intervals, but since the intervals get arbitrarily small, (2) yields a contradiction. Here is the formal HOL statement of the principle:

```
|- !P. (!a b c. a <= b /\ b <= c /\ P(a,b) /\ P(b,c)
                ==> P(a,c)) /\
      (!x. ?d. &0 < d /\
                !a b. a <= x /\ x <= b /\ b - a < d ==> P(a,b))
      ==> !a b. a <= b ==> P(a,b)
```

This is a good example of how recurrent proof themes can be embedded in theorems; it would not be hard to write a special 'bisection tactic' to apply it automatically. The above is used several times in the following development, as noted explicitly. The principle has the look of a sort of induction theorem. Actually, if we step up to the more general framework of a topological space, it can be seen as a form of induction over an open covering of a compact set, which by the Heine-Borel theorem may be assumed finite.[10]

3.4.2 Some elementary analysis

We proceed to prove some of the classic theorems of elementary real analysis:

- A function continuous on a closed interval is bounded. This can be proved by bisection, since boundedness has the required composition property, and the boundedness for sufficiently small regions follows immediately from continuity.

---

[9] We use in our discussion the standard analysis notations $[a, b] = \{x \mid a \leq x \leq b\}$ and sometimes $(a, b) = \{x \mid a < x < b\}$; though in fact neither is used in the HOL development. We hope context will distinguish the latter from an ordered pair. An explicit assumption $a \leq b$ often appears in the HOL formalizations of theorems where it is assumed without comment in analysis texts; though some of these theorems also turn out to hold for an empty interval.

[10] The Heine-Borel theorem for $\mathbb{R}$ states that if a (finite) interval of the reals of the form $[a, b]$ is covered by (i.e. contained in the union of) a family of open sets, then there is a finite subcover of that covering. We don't actually prove this in HOL, since there were no applications that could not be done equally well by direct bisection. However the Heine-Borel theorem is itself often proved by bisection.

- A function continuous on a closed interval attains its supremum and infimum. The following slick proof is taken from Burkill (1962). Suppose f does not attain its supremum M. Then the function defined by $\lambda x.(M - f(x))^{-1}$ is continuous on the interval (a previous theorem about continuity assures us of this because the denominator is never zero), and therefore *it* is bounded, by K say, which must be strictly positive. But this means that we have $M - f(x) \geq K^{-1}$, which is a contradiction because M is a *least* upper bound.
- Rolle's theorem: if f is continuous for $a \leq x \leq b$ and differentiable for $a < x < b$, and in addition $f(a) = f(b)$, then there is some $a < x < b$ with $f'(x) = 0$. We know that f attains its bounds, and in fact its derivative must be zero there, otherwise it would exceed its bounds on one side or the other. Abian (1979) uses an ingenious variant of bisection to give a very elegant proof of this result.
- The Mean Value Theorem states that if f is continuous for $a \leq x \leq b$ and differentiable for $a < x < b$, then there is some $a < x < b$ with $f(b) - f(a) = (b - a)f'(x)$. A proof is easy by applying Rolle's theorem to the function:

$$\lambda x.\ f(x) - \frac{f(b) - f(a)}{b - a} x$$

- A function whose derivative is zero on an interval is constant on that interval. This is an immediate corollary of the Mean Value Theorem. As pointed out by Richmond (1985), this can also be proved directly by bisection, using the property:

$$P(x, y) \equiv f(y) - f(x) \leq C(y - x)$$

  for any positive C.
- The Intermediate Value Theorem. This states that all continuous functions f are Darboux continuous, i.e. if for any interval $[a, b]$, y lies between $f(a)$ and $f(b)$, then there is an x between a and b such that $f(x) = y$. Intuitively it says that if a continuous function starts below a horizontal line and ends above it, then it must cross the line. This, or to be precise its contrapositive, is also proved by bisection. Suppose f is continuous on $[a, b]$ but never attains the value y. Then it is easy to see by bisection that y cannot lie between $f(a)$ and $f(b)$.
- Taylor's theorem, in its Maclaurin form, i.e. centred on zero. This is derived, following Burkill (1962), by iterating the Mean Value Theorem. It is not used directly in the developments detailed in the present chapter, where functions are *defined* directly by their power series. However it is useful for obtaining specific numerical results, since it gives precise error bounds on finite truncations of the series. The HOL form of it is as follows:

```
|- !f diff h n.
        &0 < h /\
        0 < n /\
        (diff(0) = f) /\
        (!m t. m < n /\ &0 <= t /\ t <= h
               ==> (diff(m) diffl diff(SUC m)(t))(t))
        ==> ?t. &0 < t /\ t < h /\
                (f(h) = Sum(0,n)
                   (\m. (diff(m)(&0) / &(FACT m)) * (h pow m)) +
                        ((diff(n)(t) / &(FACT n)) * (h pow n)))
```

This perhaps looks a little overwhelming! Read informally it says that if $f^{(n)}$ (written `diff(n)` in HOL) represents the nth derivative of f in the interval $[0, h]$ (where we assume $h > 0$), i.e. $f^{(n)}(x)$ gives the value of the nth derivative at x, then

$$f(h) = \Sigma_{m=0}^{n-1} \frac{f^{(m)}(0)h^m}{m!} + R$$

with the remainder R expressible as $\frac{f^{(n)}(t)h^n}{n!}$ for some t with $0 < t < h$. Note that when $n = 1$ this is simply the Mean Value Theorem, as expected from the proof.

3.4.3 The Carathéodory derivative

For practical use, we want to be able to prove theorems about the derivatives of specific functions. The various combining theorems (derivatives of sum and product etc.) are mostly straightforward. The easiest way to prove the rules for inverses and quotients is to prove first that $\lambda x.\, x^{-1}$ has derivative $-1/x^2$ at all points x other than 0, and then use the chain rule. First however we need to prove the chain rule, and that does turn out to be trickier than expected. In Leibnizian notation the theorem is very suggestive:

$$\frac{dy}{dx} = \frac{dy}{du}\frac{du}{dx}$$

It would seem that to prove it we need simply observe that the above is true for finite differences Δx, and consider the limit. However this does not work easily, because we have to consider the possibility that Δu may be zero even when Δx is not. Crudely speaking, the problem is that limits are not compositional: if $f(x) \to y_0$ as $x \to x_0$ and $g(y) \to z_0$ as $y \to y_0$, it may not be the case that $(g \circ f) \to z_0$ as $x \to x_0$. The reason is that the definition of limit:

$$\forall \epsilon > 0.\, \exists \delta > 0.\, \forall y.\, 0 < |y - y_0| < \delta \Rightarrow |g(y) - z_0| < \epsilon$$

includes the extra property that $0 < |y - y_0|$, i.e. $y \neq y_0$. This is necessary since in many situations (e.g. the derivative) the function whose limit is being considered might be undefined or nonsensical at $y = y_0$.

The usual proofs of the chain rule therefore split into two separate cases, which makes the result rather messy. There are rumours that a large proportion of American calculus texts get the proof wrong. Certainly, the author has seen one that explicitly noted that the chain rule's proof is too complicated to be given. There is a way out, however, Continuity *is* compositional as we have already noted, and the chain rule follows quite easily from the following alternative characterization of differentiability, due to Carathéodory. A function f is differentiable at x with derivative $f'(x)$ iff there is a function g_x, continuous at x and with value $f'(x)$ there, such that for all x':

$$f(x') - f(x) = g_x(x')(x' - x)$$

The equivalence with the usual definition is easy to establish. The theorem about the differentiation of inverse functions is also eased by using the Carathéodory characterization, as pointed out by Kuhn (1991). Here are the HOL versions of the chain rule and theorems about the continuity and differentiability of (left) inverse functions.

```
|- !f g x.
      (f diffl l)(g x) /\ (g diffl m)(x)
      ==> ((f o g) diffl (l * m))(x)

|- !f g x d.
      &0 < d /\
      (!z. abs(z - x) < d ==> (g(f(z)) = z)) /\
      (!z. abs(z - x) < d ==> f contl z)
      ==> g contl (f x)

|- !f g l x d.
      &0 < d /\
      (!z. abs(z - x) < d ==> (g(f(z)) = z)) /\
      (!z. abs(z - x) < d ==> f contl z) /\
      (f diffl l)(x) /\
      ~(l = &0)
      ==> (g diffl (inv l))(f x)
```

Automated support, in the shape of a function DIFF_CONV, is provided for proving results about derivatives of specific functions. This is treated at more length in a later chapter. Let us just note that the ability to automate things like this is a benefit of the programmability of LCF-style systems.

3.5 Power series and the transcendental functions

At last we have reached the stage of having the analytical tools to deal with the transcendental functions. First we bring together the theories of infinite series and differentiability, proving a few results about power series, in particular that they are characterized by a 'circle of (absolute) convergence':

```
|- !f x z. summable (\n. f(n) * (x pow n)) /\ abs(z) < abs(x)
            ==> summable (\n. abs(f(n)) * (z pow n))
```

within which they can be differentiated term-by-term:

```
|- !c K. summable(\n. c(n) * (K pow n)) /\
         summable(\n. (diffs c)(n) * (K pow n)) /\
         summable(\n. (diffs(diffs c))(n) * (K pow n)) /\
         abs(x) < abs(K)
         ==> ((\x. suminf (\n. c(n) * (x pow n))) diffl
                (suminf (\n. (diffs c)(n) * (x pow n))))(x)
```

Here the function `diffs` represents the coefficients in the 'formal' derivative series, i.e.

```
|- diffs c = (\n. &(SUC n) * c(SUC n))
```

The above result about term-by-term differentiation was in fact perhaps the most difficult single proof in the whole development of analysis described in this chapter. Had we been developing analysis for its own sake, we would have proved some general results about uniform convergence. As it is, we prove the result by direct manipulation of the definition of derivative, following the proof of Theorem 10.2 given by Burkill and Burkill (1970). The theorem as we proved it requires both the first and second formal derivative series to converge within the radius of convergence. This does in fact follow in general, but we did not bother to prove it in HOL because the power series that we are concerned with differentiate 'to each other', so we already have convergence theorems.

The functions *exp*, *sin* and *cos* are defined by their power series expansions (as already remarked, we do not need Taylor's theorem to do this):

$$\begin{aligned} exp(x) &= 1 + x + \frac{x^2}{2!} + \frac{x^3}{3!} + \dots \\ sin(x) &= x - \frac{x^3}{3!} + \frac{x^5}{5!} - \frac{x^7}{7!} + \dots \\ cos(x) &= 1 - \frac{x^2}{2!} + \frac{x^4}{4!} - \frac{x^6}{6!} + \dots \end{aligned}$$

For example, the actual HOL definition of *sin* is:

```
|- sin(x) = suminf(\n. (sin_ser) n * (x pow n))
```

where `sin_ser` is defined to be:

```
\n. if EVEN n then &0
    else ((--(&1)) pow ((n - 1) DIV 2)) / &(FACT n)
```

We show using the ratio test that the series for *exp* converges, and hence by the comparison test that the other two do. Now by our theorem about differentiating infinite series term by term, we can show that the derivative of *sin* at x is $cos(x)$, and so on. Furthermore, a few properties like $cos(0) = 1$ are more or less immediate from the series. The effort in proving the theorem about differentiation term-by-term is now repaid, since these facts alone are enough to derive quite easily all the manipulative theorems we want. The technique we use to prove an identity $\forall x.\ f(x) = g(x)$ is essentially to show that (1) this is true for some particularly convenient value of x, usually 0, and (2) that the derivative of $f(x) - g(x)$ or $f(x)/g(x)$ or some similar function, is zero, so the function must be constant, meaning $f(x) = g(x)$ everywhere. This method was our own invention, inspired by the way Bishop and Bridges (1985) prove such identities by comparing *every term* of the respective Taylor expansions of f and g. It does not seem to be widely used; despite quite an extensive search, we have only found a similar technique in one analysis text: Haggarty (1989), though he does not use the method systematically, proves (in Appendix A) the addition formula for *sin* by proving that the following has a derivative of zero w.r.t. x:

$$sin(a + x)cos(b - x) + cos(a + x)sin(b - x)$$

As an example, to show that $exp(x+y) = exp(x)exp(y)$, consider the function:

$$\lambda x.\ exp(x + y)exp(-x)$$

Our automatic conversion, with a little manual simplification, shows that this has a derivative that is 0 everywhere. Consequently, by a previous theorem, it is constant. But at $x = 0$ it is just $exp(y)$, so the result follows; this also shows that $exp(x)$ is nonzero everywhere, given that it is nonzero for $x = 0$.

Likewise we can prove $\forall x.\ sin(x)^2 + cos(x)^2 = 1$ by observing that the left hand side has zero derivative w.r.t. x. The addition formulas for *sin* and *cos* can also be proved in a similar way. Rather than use Haggarty's method, we prove them together by differentiating:

$$\begin{aligned}\lambda x.\ &(sin(x + y) - (sin(x)cos(y) + cos(x)sin(y)))^2 + \\ &(cos(x + y) - (cos(x)cos(y) - sin(x)sin(y)))^2\end{aligned}$$

(Of course, this would itself be very tedious to do by hand, but using `DIFF_CONV` it is essentially automatic.) Periodicity of the trigonometric functions follows from the addition formulas and the fact that there is a least $x > 0$

with $cos(x) = 0$. This latter fact is proved by observing that $cos(0) > 0$ and $cos(2) < 0$. The Intermediate Value Theorem tells us that there must therefore be a zero in this range, and since $sin(x)$ is positive for $0 < x < 2$, cos is strictly decreasing there, so the zero is unique. (These proofs involve some fiddly manipulations of the first few terms of the series for sin and cos, but most of the actual calculation can be automated, as described in the next chapter.) The zero is in fact $\pi/2$, and this serves as our definition of π. We define $tan(x) = sin(x)/cos(x)$ and derive its basic properties without great difficulty.

The functions ln, asn, acs and atn are defined as the inverses of their respective counterparts exp, sin, cos and tan. Their continuity and differentiability (in suitable ranges) follow from the general theorems about inverse functions, with a bit of algebraic simplification. For example we have that $\frac{d}{dx}(cos^{-1}(x)) = -1/\sqrt{1-x^2}$ for $-1 < x < 1$, or in HOL:

```
|- !x. --(&1) < x /\ x < &1
       ==> (acs diffl --(inv(sqrt(&1 - x pow 2))))(x)
```

A few basic theorems about n^{th} roots are also included. The definition of roots does not actually use logarithms directly, but simply asserts them as inverses to the operations of raising to the nth power (choosing the positive root where there is a choice):

```
|- root(n) x = @u. (&0 < x ==> &0 < u) /\ (u pow n = x)
```

However when we come to deriving theorems about roots, by far the easiest way is to use the relationship with logarithms.

3.6 Integration

A consequence of the definitional approach is that we must be particularly careful about the way we define mathematical notions. In some cases, the appropriate definitions are uncontroversial. However many areas of mathematics offer a range of subtly different approaches. Integration is a particularly difficult case; its history is traced by Dalen and Monna (1972) and Pesin (1970). For a long time it was considered as the problem of quadrature (finding areas). However, once Newton and Leibniz had discovered that it is (broadly speaking) a converse operation to differentiation, many people began to think of it that way instead. Undergraduate mathematics courses usually present the Riemann integral. At a more advanced level, Lebesgue theory or some more abstract descendant seems dominant; consider the following quote from Burkill (1965)

> It has long been clear that anyone who uses the integral calculus in the course of his work, whether it be in pure or applied mathematics, should normally interpret integration in the Lebesgue sense. A

few simple principles then govern the manipulation of expressions containing integrals.

We shall consider these notions in turn and explain our selection of the Kurzweil-Henstock gauge integral. For our later application to computer algebra, it is particularly important to get clear the relationship between differentiation and integration. Ideally we would like the Fundamental Theorem of Calculus

$$\int_a^b f'(x)dx = f(b) - f(a)$$

to be true whenever f is differentiable with derivative $f'(x)$ at all points x of the interval $[a, b]$.

3.6.1 The Newton integral

Newton actually *defined* integration as the reverse of differentiation. Integrating f means finding a function that when differentiated, gives f (called an *antiderivative* or *primitive*). Therefore the Fundamental Theorem is true by definition for the Newton Integral.

Newton's approach however has certain defects as a formalization of the notion of the area under a curve. It is not too hard to prove that all derivatives are Darboux continuous, i.e. attain all intermediate values. Consequently, a simple step function:

$$f(x) = \begin{cases} 0 \text{ if } x < 1 \\ 1 \text{ if } x \geq 1 \end{cases}$$

which intuitively has a perfectly well-defined area, does not have a Newton integral. Of course, this would not have troubled Newton or Leibniz, since it is only quite recently that step functions, and others not defined by simple expressions involving algebraic and transcendental functions, have been accepted as functions at all. But they appear quite naturally in some parts of contemporary physics and engineering.

3.6.2 The Riemann integral

The Riemann integral defines the area under a curve in terms of the areas of strips bounded by the curve, as the width of the strips tends to zero. It handles the step function but has other defects. Integrals over infinite intervals have to be written as limiting cases of other integrals in various ad hoc ways. The integral does not have convenient convergence properties: limits of sequences of integrable functions can fail to be integrable. And, particularly relevant to the present work, the Fundamental Theorem of Calculus fails to hold (the example given below for the Lebesgue integral also serves for the Riemann).

3.6.3 The Lebesgue integral

The Lebesgue integral is superior to the Riemann integral in a number of important respects. It accommodates infinite limits without any ad hoc devices, and obeys some useful convergence theorems. Any (directly) Riemann integrable function is also Lebesgue integrable, and some functions that have no Riemann integral nonetheless have a Lebesgue integral, the classic example being the indicator function of the rationals:

$$f(x) = \begin{cases} 1 \text{ if } x \in \mathbb{Q} \\ 0 \text{ if } x \notin \mathbb{Q} \end{cases}$$

One feature that the Lebesgue integral shares with the Riemann integral is that the Fundamental Theorem of Calculus is *still* not generally true. The following counterexample was given in Lebesgue's thesis:

$$f(x) = \begin{cases} 0 & \text{if } x = 0 \\ x^2 sin(1/x^2) & \text{if } x \neq 0 \end{cases}$$

This is an inevitable consequence of the fact that the Lebesgue integral, in common with the Riemann integral, is *absolute*, meaning that whenever f is integrable, so is $|f|$.

3.6.4 Other integrals

Various integrals have been proposed that extend the Lebesgue integral and for which the Fundamental Theorem is true. The first was due to Denjoy (1912) who, starting with the Lebesgue integral, constructed a sequence of integrals by a process of transfinite recursion called 'totalisation'. A very simple characterization of the Denjoy integral was given by Perron (1914), but it is not constructive and the development of the theory uses theorems about the Lebesgue integral.

3.6.5 The Kurzweil-Henstock gauge integral

Surprisingly recently it was observed that a simple modification of the Riemann limit process could give an integral equivalent to the Denjoy and Perron integrals. This seems to have first been made explicit by Kurzweil (1958), but its later development, in particular the proof of Lebesgue-type convergence theorems, was mainly due to Henstock (1968), who discovered the integral independently at much the same time. It is known as the 'generalized Riemann Integral', the 'Kurzweil-Henstock gauge integral' or simply 'gauge integral'. In the following, we give a sketch of the definition of this integral following the terminology given by McShane (1973). A fuller introduction may be found in the undergraduate textbook by DePree and Swartz (1988) or in the definitive treatise by Henstock (1991).

The limiting process involved in the gauge integral seems rather obscure at first sight, but the intuition can be seen quite clearly if we consider integrating a derivative. Suppose f is differentiable for all x lying between a and b. Then given any such x and any $\epsilon > 0$, we know that there exists a $\delta > 0$ such that whenever $0 < |y - x| < \delta$

$$\left|\frac{f(y) - f(x)}{y - x} - f'(x)\right| < \epsilon$$

For some fixed ϵ, this δ can be considered as a function of x that always returns a strictly positive real number, i.e. a *gauge*.

Consider now splitting the interval $[a, b]$ into a ***tagged division***, i.e. a finite sequence of non-overlapping intervals, each interval $[x_i, x_{i+1}]$ containing some nominated point t_i called its *tag*. We shall say that a division is δ-fine (or fine with respect to a gauge δ) if for each interval in the division:

$$[x_i, x_{i+1}] \subseteq (t_i - \delta(t_i), t_i + \delta(t_i))$$

As we shall see later, a δ-fine division exists for any gauge δ. For any such division, the usual Riemann-type sum

$$\sum_{i=0}^{n} f'(t_i)(x_{i+1} - x_i)$$

is within $(b - a)\epsilon$ of $f(b) - f(a)$, because:

$$\begin{aligned}
&\left|\sum_{i=0}^{n} f'(t_i)(x_{i+1} - x_i) - (f(b) - f(a))\right| \\
&= \left|\sum_{i=0}^{n} f'(t_i)(x_{i+1} - x_i) - \sum_{i=0}^{n}(f(x_{i+1}) - f(x_i))\right| \\
&= \left|\sum_{i=0}^{n}[(f(x_{i+1}) - f(x_i)) - f'(t_i)(x_{i+1} - x_i)]\right| \\
&\leq \sum_{i=0}^{n} |(f(x_{i+1}) - f(x_i)) - f'(t_i)(x_{i+1} - x_i)| \\
&< \sum_{i=0}^{n}(x_{i+1} - x_i)\epsilon \\
&= (b - a)\epsilon
\end{aligned}$$

In general, for any function f, not just a derivative, we say that it has ***gauge integral*** I on the interval $[a, b]$ if for any $\epsilon > 0$, there is a gauge δ such that for any δ-fine division, the usual Riemann-type sum approaches I closer than ϵ:

$$\left| \sum_{i=0}^{n} f(t_i)(x_{i+1} - x_i) - I \right| < \epsilon$$

So the above reasoning shows that a derivative f' always has gauge integral $f(b) - f(a)$ over the interval $[a, b]$, i.e. that the Fundamental Theorem of Calculus holds.

As hinted earlier, the gauge integral is nonabsolute, but it has all the attractive convergence properties of the Lebesgue integral. There is quite a simple relationship between the two integrals: f has a Lebesgue integral precisely when both f and $|f|$ have a gauge integral. A more surprising connection is that dropping the requirement that each tag is a member of the corresponding interval gives exactly the Lebesgue integral, but without requiring any of the usual measure-theoretic machinery. On the other hand, if we restrict the gauge to be constant, rather than permit it to vary with x, we get one of the several equivalent formulations of the Riemann integral. The smallness of the perturbation to the Riemann definition is striking.

Another interesting feature of the gauge integral was pointed out by Thompson (1989). By iterating the Fundamental Theorem one can arrive at a version of Taylor's theorem with an integral form of remainder that requires significantly weaker hypotheses about the nth derivative than are needed for the ('Cauchy') form of the remainder which we derived above. The proof generalizes quite directly to the complex and vector-valued cases, whereas the proof we have used based on the Mean Value Theorem is inherently one-dimensional.

3.6.6 Formalization in HOL

All the concepts involved in the gauge integral admit a fairly straightforward HOL formalization. First we define the notion of a division and of a tagged division. These are based on functions x and t that pick out the points of division and the tags respectively; we always have $x_i \leq t_i \leq x_{i+1}$. The divisions are all finite, but we find it more convenient to use functions rather than lists. These functions are arranged so that when they reach the right hand limit $x_n = b$ of the interval $[a, b]$, they repeat indefinitely, i.e. $x_m = b$ for $m \geq n$. The number of elements can be recovered as the least n with $x_n = x_{n+1}$. (This means we cannot have empty intervals in the division unless $a = b$, but nothing seems to be lost by that.) Predicates for testing whether a function represents a division (`division`) or a tagged division (`tdiv`) are defined, together with a function `dsize` for extracting the size of a division, as follows:

```
|- division(a,b) D =
        (D 0 = a) /\
        (?N. (!n. n < N ==> D n < D(SUC n)) /\
             (!n. n >= N ==> (D n = b)))

|- tdiv(a,b) (D,p) =
   division(a,b) D /\ (!n. D n <= p n /\ p n <= D(SUC n))

|- dsize D =
     @N. (!n. n < N ==> D n < D(SUC n)) /\
         (!n. n >= N ==> (D n = D N))
```

Next come the definitions of the notion of g being a gauge over the set (in practice always an interval) E, and the fact that a tagged division is δ-fine w.r.t. a gauge δ:

```
|- gauge E g = (!x. E x ==> &0 < (g x))

|- fine g(D,p) = !n. n < dsize D ==> (D(SUC n) - D n) < g(p n)
```

Next comes the Riemann sum over a tagged division:

```
|- rsum(D,p) f = Sum(0,dsize D) (\n. f(p n) * (D(SUC n) - D n))
```

Finally, we can now define a constant `Dint`, where `Dint(a,b) f k` means 'the definite integral of f over the interval $[a, b]$ is k'. As usual we employ a relational form, though the reader may prefer to think of it as $\int_a^b f(x)dx = k$.

```
|- Dint(a,b) f k =
     !e. &0 < e ==>
         ?g. gauge (\x. a <= x /\ x <= b) g /\
             !D p. tdiv(a,b)(D,p) /\ fine g (D,p)
                   ==> abs(rsum(D,p) f - k) < e
```

We then develop a little basic theory. There are few results that are very deep. A serious theory would include the Monotone and Dominated convergence theorems for integrals of limits. One important lemma we do prove is that for any gauge δ there is a δ-fine division. Yet again, the proof is easy using bisection. This yields the fact that the integral is uniquely defined. Finally, we carry through in HOL the proof of the Fundamental Theorem of Calculus, which was given informally above.

```
|- !f f' a b.
        a <= b /\ (!x. a <= x /\ x <= b ==> (f diffl (f' x))(x)
        ==> Dint(a,b) f' (f b - f a)
```

Since this is one of the most important mathematical theorems of all time, standing at the root of much of modern science and mathematics, it seems a fitting point on which to end this chapter.

3.7 Summary and related work

The theories described in this chapter include 368 theorems that are saved at the top level. Some of these are 'big name' results, others minor lemmas. The total ML source is 7634 lines long, including comments and blank lines. As well as these analytical results we have discussed, there are a further 266 basic algebraic theorems that are derived from the real 'axioms'. Many of these are established using an automated tool which we discuss later.

A number of theorem provers have been used to formalize significant parts of analysis. Many Mizar articles in the *Journal of Formalized Mathematics* are devoted to such topics.[11] The IMPS system (Farmer, Guttman, and Thayer 1990) was designed with a view to doing analysis at a fairly abstract level, and several examples are described by Farmer and Thayer (1991). Very recently some work similar to that described here has been done by Dutertre (1996) in PVS, and his method, relying heavily on advanced features of the PVS type system, provides an interesting contrast with the present approach. Forester (1993) has done some work which, while modest in scope compared to these other efforts, is all done constructively. For example, he formalizes a constructive proof of the Intermediate Value theorem that allows arbitrary approximation of the relevant point.

Our work is probably unique in its combination of scope and focus. Rather than a piecemeal development of interesting theory, we systematically build up analytical infrastructure for real applications. Moreover, our work is distinguished from these others by the fact that it uses a definitional foundation of the reals rather than an axiomatization.

There are many attractive avenues for future research. It would be well worth experimenting to find the right type system to support this and other branches of mathematics in a clean way. Moreover, it would be interesting to explore further the potential for automatic theorem proving in analysis. This might turn out to be more effective using some version of Nonstandard Analysis, since the proofs there very often have a cleaner, more 'algebraic' flavour.[12]

---

[11] This journal is available on the Web from `http://math.uw.bialystok.pl/ Form.Math/`.

[12] Such an idea has already been investigated by Ballantyne and Bledsoe (1977), for example.

4. Explicit Calculations

For some applications, and even in the course of quite high-level mathematical proofs, it is necessary to perform calculations with numbers of various kinds. Here we describe how this can be done in HOL; we implement fairly standard algorithms, but with the unusual twist of working completely by inference. The two main contributions are a new scheme for using numerals in HOL, and an inference-performing version of the 'function closure' approach to exact real arithmetic.

4.1 The need for calculation

It is not really our intention to use the HOL theory of reals like a pocket calculator to evaluate specific numerical expressions. Apart from anything else, it will be orders of magnitude slower. On the other hand it will arguably give a higher level of assurance that its answer is correct, so there may be a few niche applications in the generation of tables of constants with guaranteed accuracy. After all, this is what Babbage designed his computers for! In any case, there are rather a lot of situations in our work where explicit numerical calculation is necessary. We will later describe decision procedures where cancellation between equations and inequalities requires some simple arithmetic on rational constants which form the coefficients. Later we shall even have applications for real number calculation, to verify some precomputed constants in a floating point algorithm that we analyze. Rather than discuss all of these separately on demand, we collect them all in the present chapter. Note however that they are actually implemented at different points in the HOL theory development.

4.2 Calculation with natural numbers

The fundamental requirement is for calculation with numeral constants; for example, we want to be able to pass from the term '$3 + 5$' to the theorem $\vdash 3+5 = 8$. This simple requirement has in fact been problematical in HOL for many years. The `HOL88` and `hol90` systems implement numerals as an infinite constant family, with defining equations of the form $\vdash n =$ `SUC` m (e.g. $\vdash 8 =$ `SUC 7`) returned on demand by a function called `num_CONV`. By programming in the usual LCF manner, it's possible to implement conversions that will repeatedly use the definitions of the numerals and the arithmetic operators to give the answer. Actually, the first such system was programmed by the present author relatively recently (Harrison 1991) as the so-called `reduce` library. For example given '3+5' it might use the primitive recursive definition of addition:

```
|- (!n. 0 + n = n) /\
   (!m n. SUC m + n = SUC (m + n))
```

to evaluate it as follows (in fact it uses a slightly more efficient variant):

```
3 + 5
SUC 2 + 5
SUC (2 + 5)
SUC (SUC 1 + 5)
SUC (SUC (1 + 5))
SUC (SUC (SUC 0 + 5)))
SUC (SUC (SUC (0 + 5)))
SUC (SUC (SUC 5))
SUC (SUC 6)
SUC 7
8
```

Such an approach requires time proportional to 10^n for n-digit numbers. It is therefore completely impractical for large numbers. There is another criticism to be made too: the infinite family of constants is hacked crudely on top of what is otherwise a strictly foundational theorem prover. The correctness of the result depends on the accuracy of the ML compiler's bignums package (including conversion between numbers and strings) which is used to produce the axiom instances. Actually, the `hol90` system doesn't even use bignums at all; it relies on machine arithmetic. This means that to ensure consistency it must fail if the numbers wrap, giving a strict limit on the range of numbers that are practical.

For some time it has been proposed to use a positional representation of numerals in the HOL logic.[1] For example, one can use lists of booleans to represent binary numbers, tagged by an appropriate constant defined to map such a list to the corresponding natural number. Assuming the head is the least significant bit, the term `NUMERAL [T; F; T; F; F; T]` represents binary 100101, or decimal 37; the number can always be parsed and printed in that form (the potential for error reappears here in translation, but it is less pernicious since it does not threaten logical consistency). The earliest

[1] See for example the messages from Phil Windley and Paul Loewenstein to the info-hol mailing list on 26 May 1989.

HOL implementation effort appears to have been due to Phil Windley; subsequently Leonard (1993) released an extensive library containing a complete suite of functions for arithmetic on positional representations using arbitrary radix, given some small fixed family of constants for the digits.

These positional representations inside the logic tackle both the problems of efficiency and reliability. Against that, since numerals are no longer constants, the sizes of terms and the time spent by rewriting conversions etc. traversing them are both increased. However this does not seem to be a significant disadvantage. The biggest problem is that it requires the theory of lists or something similar, and that relies on a certain amount of natural number arithmetic, all using numerals! This means that in order to take the revised definition of numeral as standard, it would be necessary to retrofit it to all the previous arithmetic theorems. Accordingly, for the present work, we use a similar but more direct method.

When defining the type of numbers, we use '_0' to play the role of zero. As soon as the type is established, a constant `NUMERAL` is declared, which is equal to the identity on the type `:num`. What is parsed and printed as '`0`' actually expands to '`NUMERAL _0`'. As soon as addition is defined (using `0` in its definition), we define two further constants:

```
|- BIT0 n = n + n

|- BIT1 n = SUC(n + n)
```

The rather artificial definition of the second is because multiplication (which uses numeral 1 in its definition) has not yet been defined. Now these constants are sufficient to express any number in binary. For example, we implement 37 as:

```
NUMERAL (BIT1 (BIT0 (BIT1 (BIT0 (BIT0 (BIT1 _0))))))
```

The reader may wonder why we use the constant `NUMERAL` at all, instead of just using `BIT0`, `BIT1` and `0`. The reason is that in that case one number becomes a subterm of another (e.g. 1 is a subterm of 2), which can lead to some surprising accidental rewrites. Besides, the `NUMERAL` constant is a useful tag for the prettyprinter.

The parser and printer transformations established, the theory of natural numbers can now be developed as usual. But when we want to perform arithmetic, the situation is now much better. Most of the arithmetic operations are defined by primitive recursion, indicating a simple evaluation strategy for unary notation (look at the evaluation of $3 + 5$ above for an example). But many of them have an almost equally direct strategy in terms of our binary notation.[2] For example the following theorems, easily proved, can be used directly as rewrite rules to perform arithmetic evaluation.

[2] Another nice example, though we don't actually implement it, is the GCD function. Knuth (1969) gives a simple algorithm based on $gcd(2m, 2n) = 2gcd(m, n)$,

```
|- (!n. SUC (NUMERAL n) = NUMERAL (SUC n)) /\
   (SUC _0 = BIT1 _0) /\
   (!n. SUC (BIT0 n) = BIT1 n) /\
   (!n. SUC (BIT1 n) = BIT0 (SUC n))
```

or

```
|- (!m n. (NUMERAL m = NUMERAL n) = (m = n)) /\
   ((_0 = _0) = T) /\
   (!n. (BIT0 n = _0) = (n = _0)) /\
   (!n. (BIT1 n = _0) = F) /\
   (!n. (_0 = BIT0 n) = (_0 = n)) /\
   (!n. (_0 = BIT1 n) = F) /\
   (!m n. (BIT0 m = BIT0 n) = (m = n)) /\
   (!m n. (BIT0 m = BIT1 n) = F) /\
   (!m n. (BIT1 m = BIT0 n) = F) /\
   (!m n. (BIT1 m = BIT1 n) = (m = n))
```

or

```
|- (!m n. NUMERAL m + NUMERAL n = NUMERAL (m + n)) /\
   (_0 + _0 = _0) /\
   (!n. _0 + BIT0 n = BIT0 n) /\
   (!n. _0 + BIT1 n = BIT1 n) /\
   (!n. BIT0 n + _0 = BIT0 n) /\
   (!n. BIT1 n + _0 = BIT1 n) /\
   (!m n. BIT0 m + BIT0 n = BIT0 (m + n)) /\
   (!m n. BIT0 m + BIT1 n = BIT1 (m + n)) /\
   (!m n. BIT1 m + BIT0 n = BIT1 (m + n)) /\
   (!m n. BIT1 m + BIT1 n = BIT0 (SUC (m + n)))
```

Therefore, as well as greater efficiency and greater reliability, there is the convenience of just being able to use HOL's workhorse rewriting mechanism, since our numbers can be, and are, stored in 'fully expanded' form rather than wrapped in separate constants symbols which need to be unfolded explicitly. However there are a few functions (e.g. division and factorial) where a rewrite rule seems either hard to make efficient or not even possible. There are a few other tricky matters, e.g. the multiplication rewrite rule can leave denormalized numbers with a tail 'BIT0 _0' (i.e. a leading zero) unless the special case `1 * n = n` is always done in preference, so it's generally necessary to throw in another rewrite to eliminate these zeros. Anyway, many operations can be implemented much better by directing the application of the rewrite rules precisely. In particular, expressing one of the standard division algorithms as

$gcd(2m+1, 2n) = gcd(2m+1, n)$ and $gcd(2m+1, 2n+1) = gcd(m-n, 2n+1)$. This outperforms Euclid's method on machines where bitwise operations are relatively efficient; our in-logic implementation would surely exhibit the same characteristics even if our 'bits' are rather large!

a set of rewrite rules is tedious, whereas it's easy to implement a derived rule by reducing it to other operations based on the theorem:

$$m = nq + r \land r < n \Rightarrow m \texttt{ DIV } n = q \land m\texttt{MOD } n = r$$

with the appropriate values of q and r discovered externally in ML and converted back into HOL terms. Accordingly, we add a whole suite of conversions along the lines of the old **reduce** library, which can be used where efficiency matters. For example, they implement m^{2n+1} by evaluating m^n once then multiplying it by itself and by m, whereas the obvious rewrite would duplicate the evaluation of m^n. One optimization we have not made at time of writing is to use the well-known $O(n^{log_2(3)})$ multiplication algorithm (Knuth 1969). However it is probably worthwhile to do so; we previously added it to Leonard's numeral library, and found that it was more efficient on examples over about 20 (decimal) digits. Here are a few timings for the current version:[3]

`2 + 2`	0.02
`1 EXP 1000`	0.07
`12 * 13`	0.12
`100 MOD 3`	0.15
`2 EXP (4 + 5) * 2`	0.15
`(1 EXP 3) + (12 EXP 3)`	0.18
`(9 EXP 3) + (10 EXP 3)`	0.43
`12345 * 12345`	0.72
`(2 EXP 32) DIV ((3 EXP 6) DIV 2)`	1.70
`2 EXP 1000`	6.80
`3 EXP 100`	31.21

Of course, compared with direct computer implementations of multiprecision arithmetic, these are risibly slow. However they aren't bad considering that everything is happening by primitive inference. We shall see that they are fast enough for many of the intended applications.

4.3 Calculation with integers

The next stage is to perform calculation with integers, that is, with real numbers of the form '`&n`' or '`--(&n)`', rather than on members of the integer type itself. We do not treat '`--(&0)`' as a valid integer constant, and none of our procedures will produce such a number. However, regarded as a composite expression, the procedure for negation will reduce it to '`&0`'. All these procedures are conceptually easy to write, albeit tedious to make efficient. They

[3] A reminder that these are in CPU seconds under interpreted CAML Light on a Sparc 10.

work by storing a proforma theorem justifying the result in terms of natural number arithmetic for various combinations of signs. For example we have:

```
|- (&m <= &n = m <= n) /\
   (--(&m) <= &n = T) /\
   (&m <= --(&n) = (m = 0) /\ (n = 0)) /\
   (--(&m) <= --(&n) = n <= m)
```

Functions are provided for all the comparisons ($\leq$, $<$, $\geq$, $>$ and $=$), unary negation and absolute value, addition, subtraction and multiplication. From these are derived functions for powers and finite summations.

4.4 Calculation with rationals

For the decision procedures to be described in the next chapter, it's convenient to be able to perform rational arithmetic. It will also prove useful for performing algebraic simplification in the computer algebra chapter. A previous version of that work, described by Harrison and Théry (1993), was handicapped by the extreme slowness of rational arithmetic (inherited from slow natural number arithmetic).

Rational numbers are assumed to be of the form m/n with m and n integer constants and $n > 0$. We do not require the fraction to be cancelled (though some results will only be cancelled if the arguments are). Moreover, for the sake of readability, we also allow integer constants to be treated directly as rationals. To avoid a multiplicity of special cases in the body of the algorithm, some algorithms are preceded by a preprocessing pass that transforms every integer argument n into $n/1$; moreover any results of the form $n/1$ are converted to n. The relational operations are all straightforward. Via pre-stored theorems such as:

```
|- &0 < y1 ==> &0 < y2 ==>
       (x1 / y1 <= x2 / y2 = x1 * y2 <= x2 * y1)
```

they are reduced to integer relational operations together with proof obligations concerning the positivity of the denominators, also handled automatically by the integer arithmetic routines. The unary operations of negation, absolute value and multiplicative inverse are also easy. Subtraction is implemented by addition and negation; division by multiplication and inverse. These two basic binary operations of addition and multiplication again use a proforma theorem to reduce the problem to integer arithmetic; the appropriate result, cancelled down, is found outside the logic then proved by means of this theorem. For example, the theorem justifying multiplication is:

```
|- &0 < y1 ==> &0 < y2 ==> &0 < y3
   ==> (x1 * x2 * y3 = y1 * y2 * x3)
   ==> (x1 / y1 * x2 / y2 = x3 / y3)
```

Powers are calculated by raising numerator and denominator separately to the appropriate power. Note that if the result is already cancelled, no further cancellation will be necessary, since $gcd(x^n, y^n) = gcd(x, y)^n = 1^n = 1$. Here are a few timings.

`&1 / &2 + &1 / &2`	0.30
`(&3 / &4) pow 5`	0.40
`(&2 / &3) pow 10`	0.81
`&355 / &113 - &22 / &7`	0.83
`(&1 / &2) / (&7 / &8) pow 3 - &11 + &12 * (&5 / &8)`	1.05
`(&22 / &7) pow 3 - (&355 / &113) pow 3`	9.87

4.5 Calculation with reals

Computers seldom provide facilities for exact calculation with real numbers; instead, floating-point approximations are normally used. The main reason for this is probably efficiency, and this is crucial given the enormous number of calculations involved in typical applications like weather forecasting and other physical simulations. However, it is well-known that floating point arithmetic is difficult to analyze mathematically, and in the hands of an unskilled or careless practitioner, can lead to serious errors.

Actually, later in this book we will prove a few formal results about the accuracy of some floating point arithmetic functions. But for the purpose of using real number calculation as support in formal mathematical proofs, we need to retain definite error bounds at all stages. For example, we cannot conclude that $x \leq y$ simply because their floating point approximations x' and y' are in that relation. However if we know $|x - x'| < 2^{-(n+1)}$, $|y - y'| < 2^{-(n+1)}$ and $x' \leq y' - 2^{-n}$, *then* we can safely draw the conclusion $x \leq y$.

The method we describe here is like the above methods for integer and rational arithmetic, except that instead of returning *equational* theorems at each stage, the conversions yield theorems asserting inequalities on the error bound. These are all in the following canonical form: given a real expression x and a desired accuracy of n bits, a theorem of the following form giving an integer approximation k is returned:

$$\vdash |k - 2^n x| < 1$$

Note that in order to use integer arithmetic, which is more efficient than rational, everything is scaled up by 2^n. The above says, equivalently, that $k/2^n$ is within $1/2^n$ of x.

Now suppose we want to approximate $x + y$, given approximations to x and y. Clearly $|k - 2^n x| < 1$ and $|l - 2^n y| < 1$ is sufficient to ensure $|(k+l) - 2^n(x+y)| < 2$, but not that it is < 1. Instead, we need to approximate

x and y to a *higher* level of accuracy than n bits. This phenomenon occurs with most arithmetic operations, and means that it's impossible to fix a single accuracy at the outset and do all calculations to that precision. Instead, we make all the arithmetic conversions, given a desired accuracy for the result, evaluate the subexpressions to the required higher accuracy. That is, the accuracy n as well as the expression itself becomes a parameter which varies (usually increases) as recursive calls stack up.

Such schemes for exact real arithmetic work very naturally in a higher order functional programming language. A real number can actually be represented by the function that given n, returns the n-bit approximation k_n. The arithmetic operators simply combine such functions, and then the result can be evaluated to arbitrary precision by applying it to the appropriate argument; the subexpressions will then automatically be approximated to the right accuracy. The first implementation along these lines was due to Boehm, Cartwright, O'Donnel, and Riggle (1986). More recently a high-performance implementation in CAML Light has been written by Ménissier-Morain (1994), whose thesis contains detailed proofs of correctness for all the algorithms for elementary transcendental functions. We have drawn heavily on her work in what follows. Our work differs from that of Bohm and Ménissier-Morain in that we produce a *theorem* at each stage asserting that the accuracy is as required.

Actually, we maintain two functions in parallel, one that simply returns an answer, and one that produces a theorem. The point is that sometimes intermediate exploration of expressions to different levels of precision is necessary, e.g. to find a lower bound for inversion or an upper bound for multiplication. Because proving these theorems in the logic is highly inefficient, we arrange the routines so all this exploration is done without inference.

In a standard technique, both functions retain a cache of the highest precision already evaluated. Then when lower precision is required, it can be calculated cheaply from the cached value (requiring inference in one case, but it's not too expensive). However it may happen that this causes different approximations to be given for the same precision at different times. We will always have $|x_n - 2^n x| < 1$ and $|x'_n - 2^n x| < 1$, but this does not necessitate $x_n = x'_n$, merely that they differ by no more than 1 (recall that both are integers so $|x_n - x'_n| < 2$ is equivalent to $|x_n - x'_n| \leq 1$). And since the no-inference version is used more, there is the possibility that the same query will yield different answers with and without inference. We attempt to implement the algorithms so that the inference version for a given expression is invoked just for one accuracy. But we have to be careful that discrepancies between the inference and non-inference versions do not cause failure to meet the bounds necessary for the proforma theorems. We shall see below a few instances of this.

Let us now see how the operations are defined. For the sake of clarity, we will consistently confuse the real number x with the approximating function, so x_n represents the n-bit approximation. Let us just isolate one general point. Most of the operations, as we have noted, require the evaluation of subexpressions to greater accuracy, say another m bits. In order to rescale the resulting integer k, it is necessary to divide it by 2^m. However since we are dealing with integer arithmetic, we cannot in general represent $k/2^m$ exactly. If we merely use truncating division, the error here may be almost 1 (e.g. consider $63/2^6$). We must therefore round it to the nearest number to keep the error down to $\frac{1}{2}$. We explain the algorithms by means of a function NDIV such that for any integer x and nonzero natural number p, the following holds:

$$|x \texttt{ NDIV } p - \frac{x}{p}| \leq \frac{1}{2}$$

This function can be expressed in terms of standard truncating division on the integers, DIV: we have $x \texttt{ NDIV } p = (x + p \texttt{ DIV } 2) \texttt{ DIV } p$. Indeed, we have $x + p \texttt{ DIV } 2 = p((x + p \texttt{ DIV } 2) \texttt{ DIV } p) + e$ where $0 \leq e < p$, and the result follows by subtracting $p \texttt{ DIV } 2$ from both sides. In fact, the function is not defined in HOL: we simply state a relational equivalent involving multiplication. That is, rather than say $x \texttt{ NDIV } y = z$ we say $2|yz - x| \leq |y|$. Actually, this is a weaker condition since there may be two values of z that satisfy this. However that is inconsequential for any of the theorems we use.

4.5.1 Integers

If $r \in \mathbb{Z}$ we represent it by r_n where:

$$r_n = 2^n r$$

The fact that $|r_n - 2^n r| < 1$ is immediate; in fact the error is zero.

4.5.2 Negation

$$(-x)_n = -x_n$$

We have $|(-x)_n - 2^n(-x)| = |-x_n + 2^n x| = |x_n - 2^n x| < 1$ as required.

4.5.3 Absolute value

$$|x|_n = |x_n|$$

Observing that $||x| - |y|| \leq |x - y|$ we have $||x|_n - 2^n|x|| = ||x_n| - |2^n x|| \leq |x_n - 2^n x| < 1$.

4.5.4 Addition

$$(x+y)_n = (x_{n+2} + y_{n+2}) \text{ NDIV } 4$$

We have the following correctness proof:

$$\begin{aligned}
|(x+y)_n - 2^n(x+y)| &= |((x_{n+2}+y_{n+2}) \text{ NDIV } 4) - 2^n(x+y)| \\
&\le \frac{1}{2} + |(x_{n+2}+y_{n+2})/4 - 2^n(x+y)| \\
&= \frac{1}{2} + \frac{1}{4}|(x_{n+2}+y_{n+2}) - 2^{n+2}(x+y)| \\
&\le \frac{1}{2} + \frac{1}{4}|x_{n+2} - 2^{n+2}x| + \frac{1}{4}|y_{n+2} - 2^{n+2}y| \\
&< \frac{1}{2} + \frac{1}{4}1 + \frac{1}{4}1 \\
&= 1
\end{aligned}$$

Note that many authors take a base of 4 instead of 2; one reason is that in all bases B above 4 the algorithm $(x+y)_n = (x_{n+1}+y_{n+1})$ NDIV B works. By contrast, we need an extra 2 bits of evaluation. However, from a practical point of view, evaluation to two extra binary digits is no worse than one extra quaternary one.

4.5.5 Subtraction

$$(x-y)_n = (x_{n+2} - y_{n+2}) \text{ NDIV } 4$$

Correctness follows from combining the addition and negation theorems.

4.5.6 Multiplication by an integer

$$(mx)_n = (mx_{n+p+1}) \text{ NDIV } 2^{p+1}$$

where $2^p \ge |m|$. For correctness, we have:

$$\begin{aligned}
|(mx)_n - 2^n(mx)| &\le \frac{1}{2} + |\frac{mx_{n+p+1}}{2^{p+1}} - 2^n(mx)| \\
&= \frac{1}{2} + \frac{|m|}{2^{p+1}}|x_{n+p+1} - 2^{n+p+1}x| \\
&< \frac{1}{2} + \frac{|m|}{2^{p+1}} \\
&\le \frac{1}{2} + \frac{1}{2}\frac{|m|}{2^p} \\
&\le \frac{1}{2} + \frac{1}{2} = 1
\end{aligned}$$

4.5.7 Division by an integer

$$(x/m)_n = x_n \text{ NDIV } m$$

For correctness, we can ignore the trivial cases when $m = 0$, which should never be used, and when $m = \pm 1$, since then the result is exact. Otherwise, we assume $|x_n - 2^n x| < 1$, so $|x_n/m - 2^n x/m| < \frac{1}{|m|} \leq \frac{1}{2}$, which, together with the fact that $|x_n \text{ NDIV } m - x_n/m| \leq \frac{1}{2}$, yields the result.

4.5.8 Finite summations

We define arbitrary finite summations directly rather than implement them by iterating binary addition, since the error bound is kept tighter by this implementation. Note that the correctness theorems for (binary) addition and multiplication by a natural number can be seen as special cases of this theorem.

$$(\Sigma_{i=0}^{m-1} x^{(i)})_n = (\Sigma_{i=0}^{m-1} x_{n+p+1}^{(i)}) \text{ NDIV } 2^{p+1}$$

where p is chosen so that $2^p \geq m$. For each i we have $|x_{n+p+1}^{(i)} - 2^{n+p+1} x^{(i)}| < 1$, so unless $m = 0$, when the result holds trivially, we can reason as follows:

$$\left|(\Sigma_{i=0}^{m-1} x_{n+p+1}^{(i)}) - 2^{n+p+1} \Sigma_{i=0}^{m-1} x^{(i)}\right| < m \leq 2^p$$

Dividing this throughout by 2^{p+1} and combining with the basic property of NDIV, we find:

$$\begin{aligned}
&\left|(\Sigma_{i=0}^{m-1} x_{n+p+1}^{(i)}) \text{ NDIV } 2^{p+1} - 2^n \Sigma_{i=0}^{m-1} x^{(i)}\right| \\
\leq &\left|(\Sigma_{i=0}^{m-1} x_{n+p+1}^{(i)}) \text{ NDIV } 2^{p+1} - (\Sigma_{i=0}^{m-1} x_{n+p+1}^{(i)})/2^{p+1}\right| \\
&+ \left|(\Sigma_{i=0}^{m-1} x_{n+p+1}^{(i)}) - 2^{n+p+1} \Sigma_{i=0}^{m-1} x^{(i)}\right| /2^{p+1} \\
\leq &\ \frac{1}{2} + \left|(\Sigma_{i=0}^{m-1} x_{n+p+1}^{(i)}) - 2^{n+p+1} \Sigma_{i=0}^{m-1} x^{(i)}\right| /2^{p+1} \\
< &\ \frac{1}{2} + \frac{2^p}{2^{p+1}} = \frac{1}{2} + \frac{1}{2} = 1
\end{aligned}$$

4.5.9 Multiplicative inverse

We will use the following result.

Lemma 4.5.1. *If $2e \geq n + k + 1$, $|x_k| \geq 2^e$ and $|x_k - 2^k x| < 1$, where x_k is an integer and e, n and k are natural numbers, then if we define*

$$y_n = 2^{n+k} \text{ NDIV } x_k$$

we have $|y_n - 2^n x^{-1}| < 1$, i.e. the required bound.

Proof. The proof is rather tedious and will not be given in full. We just sketch the necessary case splits. If $|x_k| > 2^e$ then a straightforward analysis gives the result; the rounding in NDIV gives an error of at most $\frac{1}{2}$, and the remaining error is $< \frac{1}{2}$. If $|x_k| = 2^e$ but $n + k \geq e$, then although the second component of the error may now be twice as much, i.e. < 1, there is no rounding error because $x_k = \pm 2^e$ divides into 2^{n+k} exactly. (We use here the fact that $2^e - 1 \leq 2^{e-1}$, because since $2e \geq n + k + 1$, e cannot be zero.) Finally, if $|x_k| = 2^e$ and $n + k < e$, we have $|y_n - 2^n \frac{1}{x}| < 1$ because both $|y_n| \leq 1$ and $0 < |2^n \frac{1}{x}| < 1$, and both these numbers have the same sign. □

The HOL version of this theorem is as follows. Note that we need to make explicit, in the first two conjuncts, that m has an integral value:

```
|- (?m. (b = &m) \/ (b = --(&m))) /\
   (?m. (a = &m) \/ (a = --(&m))) /\
   SUC(n + k) <= 2 * e /\
   &2 pow e <= abs(a) /\
   abs(a - &2 pow k * x) < &1 /\
   &2 * abs(a * b - &2 pow (n + k)) <= abs(a)
   ==> abs(b - &2 pow n * inv(x)) < &1
```

Now suppose we wish to find the inverse of x. First we evaluate x_0. There are two cases to distinguish:

1. If $|x_0| > 2^r$ for some natural number r, then choose the least natural number k (which may well be zero) such that $2r + k \geq n + 1$, and set $e = r + k$. It is easy to see that the conditions of the lemma are satisfied. Since $|x_0| \geq 2^r + 1$ we have $|x| > 2^r$, and so $|2^k x| > 2^{r+k}$. This means $|x_k| > 2^{r+k} - 1$, and as x_k is an integer, $|x_k| \geq 2^{r+k} = 2^e$ as required. The condition that $2e \geq n = k + 1$ is easy to check. Note that if $r \geq n$ we can immediately deduce that $y_n = 0$ is a valid approximation, but this may not follow from the theorem version of x_k. The above still works in that case, though it is not quite as efficient.
2. If $|x_0| \leq 1$, then we call the function '`msd`' that returns the least p such that $|x_p| > 1$. Note that this may in general fail to terminate if $x = 0$. Now we set $e = n + p + 1$ and $k = e + p$. Once again the conditions for the lemma are satisfied. Since $|x_p| \geq 2$, we have $|2^p x| > 1$, i.e. $|x| > \frac{1}{2^p}$. Hence $|2^k x| > 2^{k-p} = 2^e$, and so $|x_k| > 2^e - 1$, i.e. $|x_k| \geq 2^e$.

4.5.10 Multiplication of real numbers

First we choose r and s so that $|r - s| \leq 1$ and $r + s = n + 2$. That is, both r and s are slightly more than half the required precision. We now evaluate x_r and y_s, and select natural numbers p and q that are the corresponding 'binary logarithms', i.e. $|x_r| \leq 2^p$ and $|y_s| \leq 2^q$. Generally we pick p and q as small as possible to make this true, except that we will later require $p+q \neq 0$, so if necessary we bump one of them up by 1. (Note that in this case $y_n = 0$ is a valid approximation, but again this may not follow from the theorem version.) Now set:

$$\begin{aligned} k &= n + q - s + 3 = q + r + 1 \\ l &= n + p - r + 3 = p + s + 1 \\ m &= (k + l) - n = p + q + 4 \end{aligned}$$

We claim that $z_n = (x_k y_l)$ NDIV 2^m has the right error behaviour, i.e. $|z_n - 2^n(xy)| < 1$. If we write:

$$\begin{aligned} 2^k x &= x_k + \delta \\ 2^l y &= y_l + \epsilon \end{aligned}$$

with $|\delta| < 1$ and $|\epsilon| < 1$, we have:

$$\begin{aligned} |z_n - 2^n(xy)| &\leq \frac{1}{2} + |\frac{x_k y_l}{2^m} - 2^n(xy)| \\ &= \frac{1}{2} + 2^{-m}|x_k y_l - 2^{k+l}xy| \\ &= \frac{1}{2} + 2^{-m}|x_k y_l - (x_k + \delta)(y_l + \epsilon)| \\ &= \frac{1}{2} + 2^{-m}|\delta y_l + \epsilon x_k + \delta\epsilon| \\ &\leq \frac{1}{2} + 2^{-m}(|\delta y_l| + |\epsilon x_k| + |\delta\epsilon|) \\ &\leq \frac{1}{2} + 2^{-m}(|y_l| + |x_k| + |\delta\epsilon|) \\ &< \frac{1}{2} + 2^{-m}(|y_l| + |x_k| + 1) \end{aligned}$$

Now we have $|x_r| \leq 2^p$, so $|2^r x| < 2^p + 1$. Thus $|2^k x| < 2^{q+1}(2^p + 1)$, so $|x_k| < 2^{q+1}(2^p + 1) + 1$, i.e. $|x_k| \leq 2^{q+1}(2^p + 1)$. Similarly $|y_l| \leq 2^{p+1}(2^q + 1)$. Consequently:

$$\begin{aligned} |y_l| + |x_k| + 1 &\leq 2^{p+1}(2^q + 1) + 2^{q+1}(2^p + 1) + 1 \\ &= 2^{p+q+1} + 2^{p+1} + 2^{p+q+1} + 2^{q+1} + 1 \\ &= 2^{p+q+2} + 2^{p+1} + 2^{q+1} + 1 \end{aligned}$$

Now for our error bound we require $|y_l| + |x_k| + 1 \leq 2^{m-1}$, or dividing by 2 and using the discreteness of the integers:

$$2^{p+q+1} + 2^p + 2^q < 2^{p+q+2}$$

We can write this as $(2^{p+q} + 2^p) + (2^{p+q} + 2^q) < 2^{p+q+1} + 2^{p+q+1}$, which is true because we have either $p > 0$ or $q > 0$.

4.5.11 Transcendental functions

All the transcendental functions we implement (namely *exp*, *ln*, *sin* and *cos*) are evaluated via their Taylor expansions. We do not claim this is the most efficient method possible, but it is simple and adequate for our purposes. In work at very high levels of precision, the fastest known algorithms, e.g. those described by Brent (1976), use a quadratically convergent iteration based on the Gauss-Legendre arithmetic-geometric mean (AGM). However, these need to be supported by asymptotically fast multiplication, preferably the sophisticated algorithms with complexity $O(n\ log(n)\ loglog(n))$, for them to be superior to Taylor series; even then the crossover only happens at very high precision. Other interesting possibilities are to use Chebyshev polynomials, or some variant of the CORDIC algorithm. (Later we verify a floating point CORDIC algorithm; in fact precomputing its constant table is the main requirement for the present work!)

The definition of the transcendental functions like *exp* as limits of their power series expansion does not directly yield an error bound on truncations of the series. However we can get such an error bound from Taylor's theorem and (by now) pre-proved facts about the transcendental functions. (In any case, the series expansion for $ln(1+x)$ is arrived at using Taylor's theorem, rather than from the definition as an inverse function.) Since, to be sure of reasonably fast convergence, we only consider the functions in a limited range such as $[-1, 1]$, on which the functions are all monotonic, Taylor's theorem gives a simple expression for the error in truncation in terms of the next term in the series with the upper bound substituted for the variable. For example, for the exponential function we have:

```
|- abs x <= &1
   ==> abs(exp x - Sum(0,m) (\i. x pow i / &(FACT i)))
       < &3 * inv(&(FACT m))
```

Actually, results of this kind can be derived by much more elementary reasoning where the series concerned is decreasing and alternating, i.e. successive terms are of opposite signs. This is the case for $sin(x)$ and $cos(x)$, but not for $exp(x)$ for positive x nor $ln(1+x)$ for negative x.

Calculating the truncated power series by direct use of addition and multiplication would lead to grossly pessimistic error bounds, and hence calculation to excessive accuracy. We use two refinements to avoid this. First, we use summations directly, rather than iterated addition. But moreover, it generally happens that because of division by $n!$ in the Taylor series, the overall error does not build up badly. We saw above that x_n suffices to calculate $(x/m)_n$ to the same accuracy. But if we refine this proof, we find that even a larger error in x_n may be eliminated by the process of division. If $|x_n - 2^n x| < K$ then we have $|x_n \texttt{ NDIV } m - 2^n(x/m)| < K/m + \frac{1}{2}$. When m is large enough, this is still < 1, so the division is enough to compensate for the error in successive multiplications. Taking the exponential function as an example, we have some m so that:

$$e^x \approx \Sigma_{i=0}^{m-1} x^i/i!$$

Now suppose $|x| \leq 1$, and let us denote the guaranteed error bound for the the ith term by k_i, i.e.

$$|t_n^{(i)} - 2^n x^i/i!| \leq k_i$$

If we simply calculate the next term as follows:

$$t_n^{i+1} = (x_n t_n^{(i)}) \texttt{ NDIV } (2^n(i+1))$$

then we can see by following through the error analysis for multiplication (we will not give details here) that:

$$k_{i+1} = \frac{2k_i}{i+1} + \frac{1}{(i+1)!} + \frac{1}{2}$$

We can assume $k_0 = 0$, since the constant 1 is represented exactly by 2^n. Then using the above formula we find that the errors build up then decay as follows (in the HOL proofs, the rational arithmetic routines are of the utmost use here): $k_1 = \frac{3}{2}$, $k_2 = \frac{5}{2}$, $k_3 = \frac{7}{3}$, $k_4 = \frac{41}{24}$. Thereafter, it is an easy induction that $k_n \leq 2$, and by considering the cases, we see that the *total* error in the summation of m terms is always $\leq 2m$.

Putting all this together, we can arrive at a routine for calculating $exp(x)$ to n-bit accuracy, assuming $|x| \leq 1$. First, we find m such that $|e^x - \Sigma_{i=0}^{m-1} x^i/i!| < \frac{1}{2^{n+2}}$ and hence $|2^n e^x - 2^n \Sigma_{i=0}^{m-1} x^i/i!| < \frac{1}{4}$; by the above Taylor theorem it suffices that $3 \times 2^{n+2} \leq m!$. Now the error in the summation will be bounded by $2m$, so if we evaluate x to $p = n + e + 2$ bits where $2m \leq 2^e$, the error in the summation, after rescaling by 2^{e+2}, will be $\leq \frac{1}{4}$. Finally, we have an additional error $\leq \frac{1}{2}$ from the rounding in division by $2^n(i+1)$, and the overall error is < 1 as required. This reasoning is all embedded in the following HOL theorem:

```
|- abs x <= &1
   ==> abs(s - &2 pow p * x) < &1
   ==> (n + e + 2 = p) /\ &3 * &2 pow (n + 2) <= &(FACT m) /\
       &2 * &m <= &2 pow e /\ (t 0 = &2 pow p) /\
       (!k. SUC k < m
            ==> &2 * abs(t (SUC k) * &2 pow p * &(SUC k)
                         - s * t k) <= &2 pow p * &(SUC k)) /\
       abs(u * &2 pow (e + 2) - Sum(0,m) t) <= &2 pow (e + 1)
   ==> abs(u - &2 pow n * exp x) < &1
```

To apply this theorem, given a desired n, the numbers m, e and p are calculated as above, and then x evaluated recursively to p bits giving an approximation s. For example, if we wish to evaluate $exp(\frac{1}{2})$ to 10 bits, then we require the evaluation of $m = 8$ terms, and we moreover have $e = 4$ and so $p = 16$. Now the subevaluation of $\frac{1}{2}$ yields the theorem:

```
|- abs(&32768 - &2 pow 16 * inv(&2)) < &1
```

and so the value $s = 32768$. The appropriate sequence of values t_i is then calculated outside the logic: $t_0 = 65536$, $t_1 = 32768$, $t_2 = 8192$, $t_3 = 1365$, $t_4 = 171$, $t_5 = 17$, $t_6 = 1$ and $t_7 = 0$. A hypothesis asserting these equivalences is made. The final numerical value is calculated: $u = (t_0 + \cdots + t_7)$ NDIV $2^{e+2} = 1688$. Now the proforma theorem above is instantiated:

```
|- abs(inv(&2)) <= &1
   ==> abs(&32768 - &2 pow 16 * inv(&2)) < &1
   ==> (10 + 4 + 2 = 16) /\
       &3 * &2 pow (10 + 2) <= &(FACT 8) /\
       &2 * &8 <= &2 pow 4 /\
       (t 0 = &2 pow 16) /\
       (!k. SUC k < 8
            ==> &2 *
                abs(t(SUC k) * &2 pow 16 * &(SUC k)
                    - &32768 * t k) <= &2 pow 16 * &(SUC k)) /\
       abs(&1688 * &2 pow (4 + 2) - Sum(0,8) t) <=
       &2 pow (4 + 1)
   ==> abs(&1688 - &2 pow 10 * exp(inv(&2))) < &1
```

After modus ponens with the theorem about x and s, the body of the restricted quantifier is expanded automatically and is rewritten with the assumptions about the t_i as well as the theorem $\vdash 2^{16} = 65536$ which need only be proved once. The entire antecedent of this theorem can be reduced to $\top$ automatically by the natural number and integer arithmetic routines already discussed (the process takes around 10 seconds). Moreover the hypothesis about the t_i is easily removed using CHOOSE and a simple automatic proof procedure to justify the existence of such a t, since this variable no longer appears in the conclusion. The result is:

```
abs(inv(&2)) <= &1
|- abs(&1688 - &2 pow 10 * exp(inv(&2))) < &1
```

The final assumption of a bound on the argument can be dealt with automatically provided x is sufficiently less than 1 for the system to be able to prove it (see the next section). For larger arguments, systematic use is made of $e^{2x} = (e^x)^2$ until the argument is provably in range. Similar approaches work for other functions; notably to calculate $ln(x)$ we find k and x' such that $x = 2^k(1+x')$ and $-\frac{1}{4} \leq x' < \frac{1}{2}$, then evaluate $ln(x) = ln(1+x') + k\ (ln(1+\frac{1}{2}) - ln(1-\frac{1}{4}))$. This allows us to assume $-\frac{1}{4} \leq x \leq \frac{1}{2}$ in the core function to evaluate the Taylor series:

$$ln(1+x) = x - \frac{x^2}{2} + \frac{x^3}{3} - \frac{x^4}{4} + \cdots$$

Such a strong bound is necessary anyway for an acceptable convergence rate, since compared with the series for *exp*, *sin* and *cos*, the ith term has a denominator $i+1$ rather than $i!$ or $(2i)!$. Even so, the series converges more slowly, so evaluating logarithms tends to be somewhat slower than evaluating the other functions. Therefore, an alternative that might be more efficient would be to calculate the logarithm outside the logic and justify its accuracy by evaluating its exponential. We do not explore this possibility in detail here, but note that is has something in common with a 'finding vs checking' theme discussed later. Here are some times for the present implementation calculating constants used in a later floating point algorithm: the evaluation of $ln(1+2^{-i})$ for various i and various accuracies n:

Evaluation	10 bits	20 bits	30 bits	40 bits	50 bits
$ln(1+\frac{1}{2})$	19.33	62.05	156.73	276.30	478.73
$ln(1+\frac{1}{4})$	15.72	43.07	104.90	182.08	302.68
$ln(1+\frac{1}{8})$	14.25	40.10	77.35	140.77	232.63
$ln(1+\frac{1}{16})$	13.38	30.98	68.75	116.50	198.45
$ln(1+\frac{1}{32})$	10.52	34.28	60.43	104.62	181.65

4.5.12 Comparisons

Note that comparison is, in general, uncomputable; if $x = y$ there is in principle no way of proving or refuting *any* comparison between x and y. If $x \neq y$ they are all provable, but can take an arbitrarily large amount of computation if x and y are very close together. To decide the ordering relation of x and y it suffices to find an n such that $|x_n - y_n| \geq 2$. For example, if $x_n \geq y_n + 2$ we have

$$2^n x > x_n - 1 \geq y_n + 1 > 2^n y$$

and so $x > y$. Actually, the search for the required n is conducted without inference. This means that the same n might not suffice for the theorem-producing version. Accordingly, we search instead for an n with $|x_n - y_n| \geq 4$; it is clear that this suffices.

4.6 Summary and related work

Our work here makes no claims to significant originality in the basic algorithmic details, which are largely taken from the literature already cited. The main contribution is a demonstration that it is feasible to do this kind of thing using just logic. We're clearly close to the limit of what can realistically be done by inference. But we have showed that it's possible to integrate the kinds of modest explicit calculations we find in proofs via inference, maintaining logical purity without hacks. Though slow, it is still faster than a human! Finally, it does have external applications when one wants a very high level of assurance. We have showed how to use the system for generating constant tables for floating point operations.

Our rewrite system for natural number arithmetic is in fact similar to the system DA discussed by Walters and Zantema (1995) and said to be 'perfect for natural number arithmetic'. Some time ago, Paulson implemented in Isabelle a representation of integers using 2s complement notation, which still allows one to give simple rewrite rules for many arithmetic operations, while avoiding the separate sign and magnitude in our representation. As far as we know, no theorem prover other than HOL has support for exact real arithmetic.

5. A Decision Procedure for Real Algebra

We describe a HOL implementation of a quantifier elimination procedure for the first order theory of reals, including multiplication. Quite a few interesting and nontrivial mathematical problems can be expressed in this subset. While the complexity of deciding this theory restricts practical applications, our work is a good example of how a sophisticated decision procedure may be coded in the LCF style. In particular, it illustrates the power of encoding patterns of inference in proforma theorems, theorems that we use some mathematical analysis to establish. For practical use, we establish more efficient procedures for the linear case.

5.1 History and theory

The elementary (first order) theory of reals with which we are concerned permits atomic formulas involving the equality (=) and ordering ($<$, $\leq$, $>$ and $\geq$) relations, based on terms constructed using the operations of addition, subtraction, negation and multiplication from first order variables and rational constants. Arbitrary first order terms may be constructed from these atoms, involving all propositional connectives and *first order* quantifiers (i.e. quantification over real numbers). In practice, we can also eliminate division and multiplicative inverse by appropriate combinations of case splits and multiplications. Moreover, various extra terms such as x^n (for a fixed numeral n) and $|x|$ can similarly be eliminated.

The completeness and decidability of this theory was first proved by Tarski (1951), who did it by exhibiting a quantifier elimination procedure. However the situation is quite delicate: several similar-looking theories are undecidable. For example, as proved by Gabbay (1973), Tarski's decision procedure no longer works intuitionistically. And an analogous theory of rationals is undecidable; this follows from a clever construction due to Julia Robinson (1949), which shows that the integers are arithmetically definable in the first order theory of rationals, given which the undecidability follows from well-known results such as Gödel's incompleteness theorem. It is still an open problem whether the theory of reals including exponentiation is decidable, though it has been shown recently by Wilkie (1996) that this theory and several related ones are *model complete* (Robinson 1963). For the complex numbers the corresponding theory is certainly not decidable, as pointed out in Tarski's original paper, since elementary number theory is included (essentially because e^{ix} is periodic).

For a recursively enumerable theory, completeness implies decidability, simply because a set $S \subseteq \mathbb{N}$ with both S and $\mathbb{N} - S$ recursively enumerable is recursive. In general, Tarski was probably more interested in completeness; perhaps the initial publication of his monograph by the RAND Corporation led him to emphasize the more 'practical' question of decidability. Quantifier elimination gives a concrete procedure for systematically transforming an arbitrary formula ψ into a new formula ψ', containing no free variables that were not already free in ψ, such that $A \models \psi \Leftrightarrow \psi'$ where A are the axioms for a real closed field which we give below. A well-known example of such an equivalence is the criterion for solvability of a quadratic equation:

$$A \models (\exists x.\, ax^2 + bx + c = 0) \Leftrightarrow a \neq 0 \wedge b^2 \geq 4ac \vee a = 0 \wedge (b \neq 0 \vee c = 0)$$

And this suffices for completeness and decidability, since if ψ is a closed formula, the equivalent ψ' involves no variables at all, and any ground formulas like $0 < 1 + 1 \wedge 0 = 0$ are either true or false in all models of the axioms. This is not true for arbitrary axiomatic theories, e.g. in the theory of algebraically closed fields, formulas of the form $1 + \ldots + 1 = 0$ etc. are neither provable nor refutable without additional axioms specifying the characteristic of the field.[1] Quantifier elimination does however always imply *model completeness*, which together with the so-called 'prime model property' implies completeness. The notion of model completeness, and its use to prove the completeness of elementary real algebra, was all worked out by Robinson (1956). Compared with Tarski's work, Robinson's proof is more elegantly 'algebraic' and less technically intricate. And it too implies decidability, as we have noted. But quantifier elimination is a more appealing foundation for a decision procedure, since it directly gives rise to an algorithm, rather than merely assuring us that exhaustive search will always terminate. We therefore implement a quantifier elimination procedure in HOL, working by inference.

Tarski's original method was a generalization of a classical technique due to Sturm for finding the number of real roots of a polynomial.[2] Sturm's theorem cannot be applied directly; although one can replace $0 \leq x$ by $\exists d.\, x = d^2$ and $0 < x$ by $\exists d.\, d^2x = 1$, the elimination of the first quantifier by Sturm's method reintroduces inequalities, so the procedure is circular. Tarski's procedure is rather complicated and inefficient (its complexity is 'nonelementary',

---

[1] The characteristic is the least p — necessarily prime — such that $\overbrace{1 + \ldots + 1}^{p \text{ times}} = 0$, or 0 if, as in the case of $\mathbb{C}$, there is no such p.

[2] Since the original thesis was written, we needed to prove this theorem in HOL for other reasons — see Appendix B.

i.e. not bounded by any finite tower of exponentials in its input size); better quantifier elimination procedures were developed by Seidenberg (1954) and Cohen (1969) among others. Seidenberg's proof has even found its way into the undergraduate algebra textbook by Jacobson (1989), which also has an excellent presentation of Sturm's algorithm. Collins (1976) proposed a method of Cylindrical Algebraic Decomposition (CAD),[3] which is usually more efficient and has led to renewed interest, especially in the computer algebra community. At about the same time L. Monk, working with Solovay, proposed another relatively efficient technique.[4] Even these algorithms tend to be doubly exponential in the number of quantifiers to be eliminated, i.e. of the form:

$$\sim 2^{2^{kn}}$$

where n is the number of quantifiers and k is some constant. Recent work by Vorobjov (1990) has improved this to 'only' being doubly exponential in the number of *alternations* of quantifiers. These sophisticated algorithms would be rather hard to implement as HOL derived rules, since they depend on some quite highbrow mathematics for their justification. However there is a relatively simple algorithm given by Kreisel and Krivine (1971), which we chose to take as our starting point. A more leisurely explanation of the Kreisel and Krivine algorithm, complete with pictures, is given by Engeler (1993). We modify Kreisel and Krivine's algorithm slightly for reasons of efficiency. No criticism of their work is implied by this (though we point out a few minor inaccuracies in their presentation); they were merely presenting quantifier elimination as a theoretical possibility, whereas we are aiming actually to run the procedure.

5.2 Real closed fields

We should note that quantifier elimination does not require the full might of the real number axioms. The 'axioms' characterizing the reals that we have derived from the definitional construction are all first order, except for the completeness property, which is second order. The usual technique in such situations for arriving at a reasonable first order version is to replace the second order axiom with an infinite axiom schema. However in this case it turns out that an ostensibly weaker set of axioms suffices for quantifier elimination. This being so, all instances of the proposed completeness schema are derivable from these axioms (their negations cannot be, since they hold

[3] A related technique was earlier proposed by Łojasiewicz (1964).

[4] Leonard Monk kindly sent the present author a manuscript describing the method. This appears in his UC Berkeley PhD thesis, but as far as we know, the most substantial *published* reference is a fairly sketchy summary given by Rabin (1991).

in the standard model). First we demand that every nonnegative number has a square root:

$$\forall x.\, x \geq 0 \Rightarrow \exists y.\, x = y^2$$

and second that all polynomials of odd degree have a root, i.e. we have an infinite set of axioms, one like the following for each *odd* n.

$$\forall a_0, \ldots, a_n.\, a_n \neq 0 \Rightarrow \exists x.\, a_n x^n + a_{n-1} x^{n-1} + \cdots + a_1 x + a_0 = 0$$

These axioms characterize so-called ***real closed fields***. The real numbers are one example, but there are plenty of others, e.g. the (countable) field of computable real numbers.[5] Real closed fields also have a straightforward algebraic characterization. A field is said to be ***formally real*** if whenever a sum of squares is zero, all the elements in the sum are zero (equivalently, -1 is not expressible as a sum of squares). A field is real closed iff it is formally real but has no formally real proper algebraic extension (an algebraic extension results from adjoining to the field the roots of polynomial equations).

Our quantifier elimination procedure uses certain facts that are derived directly in our HOL theory of reals. Notably we make use of the intermediate value theorem for polynomials. We know all these facts can be derived from the axioms for a real closed field, but we do not make the effort of doing so, since we cannot envisage any interesting applications except to the reals. Nevertheless, if one were prepared to go to the effort of proving the facts in full generality (the proofs in algebra texts generally rely on the extension to the complex field) it could be fitted into the algorithm fairly easily.

5.3 Abstract description of the algorithm

First we will describe the algorithm in general terms, noting how it differs from that given by Kreisel and Krivine. In order to eliminate all quantifiers from an arbitrary formula, it is sufficient to be able to eliminate a single existential quantifier with a quantifier-free body. Then this procedure can be iterated starting with the innermost quantifier, transforming $\forall x.\, P[x]$ into $\neg\exists x.\, \neg P[x]$ first if necessary. Accordingly, we will now focus on that special case.

---

[5] Though we do not discuss the computable reals explicitly, our procedures in the previous chapter effectively give proofs that certain real functions are computable. We shall touch on this again when discussing theoretical aspects of floating point arithmetic.

5.3.1 Preliminary simplification

We place the quantifier-free body in negation normal form, i.e. push all negations down to the level of atomic formulas. Then literals are transformed as follows:

$$\begin{aligned}
&x < y \longrightarrow y > x \\
&x \leq y \longrightarrow y > x \lor x = y \\
&x \geq y \longrightarrow x > y \lor x = y \\
&x \not< y \longrightarrow x > y \lor x = y \\
&x \not\leq y \longrightarrow x > y \\
&x \not\geq y \longrightarrow y > x
\end{aligned}$$

This leaves only unnegated literals of the form $x = y$, $x > y$ and $x \neq y$. Further, we can assume the right-hand arguments are always zero by transforming $x = y$ to $x - y = 0$, $x > y$ to $x - y > 0$ and $x \neq y$ to $x - y \neq 0$. The body is now placed in disjunctive normal form, and the existential quantifier distributed over the disjuncts, i.e.

$$(\exists x.\ P[x] \lor Q[x]) \longrightarrow (\exists x.\ P[x]) \lor (\exists x.\ Q[x])$$

Now we eliminate the existential quantifier from each disjunct separately. By construction, each formula we have to consider is of the form:

$$\exists x.\ \bigwedge_k p_k(x) = 0 \land \bigwedge_l q_l(x) > 0 \land \bigwedge_m r_m(x) \neq 0$$

where each $p_k(x)$, $q_l(x)$ and $r_m(x)$is a polynomial in x; it involves other variables too, but while eliminating x these are treated as constant. Of course some of them may be bound by an outer quantifier, and so will be treated as variables later.

5.3.2 Reduction in context

It is convenient for a formal description — and this is reflected in the HOL implementation of the algorithm — to retain, while the algorithm runs, a set of assumptions that certain coefficients are zero, or nonzero, or have a certain sign. These arise from case splits and may be 'discharged' after the algorithm is finished with a subformula. For example, if we deduce $a = 0 \vdash (\exists x.\ P[x]) \Leftrightarrow Q_0$ and $a \neq 0 \vdash (\exists x.\ P[x]) \Leftrightarrow Q_1$, then we can derive:

$$\vdash (\exists x.\ P[x]) \Leftrightarrow a = 0 \land Q_0 \lor a \neq 0 \land Q_1$$

This means that we tackle each formula not just in isolation, but in a context of assumptions. At the outer level, however, the context is empty.

5.3.3 Degree reduction

We distinguish carefully between the formal degree of a polynomial, and the actual degree. The formal degree of $p(x)$ is simply the highest power of x occurring in some monomial in $p(x)$. For example in x^3+3xy^2+8, the variables x, y and z have formal degrees 3, 2 and 0 respectively. However this does not exclude the possibility that the coefficient of the relevant monomial might be zero for some or all values of the other variables. The actual degree in a given context is the highest power occurring whose coefficient a is associated with an assumption $a \neq 0$ in the context.

We need to deal with formulas of the following form:

$$\exists x. \bigwedge_k p_k(x) = 0 \wedge \bigwedge_l q_l(x) > 0 \wedge \bigwedge_m r_m(x) \neq 0$$

It is a crucial observation that we can reduce such a problem to a finite set of other problems involving similar existential terms, but each one having the following properties:

- There is at most one equation.
- For all equations, inequalities and inequations, the formal and actual degrees of the relevant polynomials are equal, i.e. there is a context containing an assumption that each of their leading coefficients is nonzero.
- The degree of x in the equation, if any, is no more than the lowest formal degree of x in any of the original equations.
- If there is an equation, then the degree of x in all the inequalities and inequations is strictly lower than its degree in the equation.

The basic method for doing this is to use the equation with the lowest actual degree to perform elimination with the other equations and inequalities, interjecting case splits where necessary. (Obviously if a polynomial does not involve x, then it can be pulled outside the quantifier and need no longer figure in our algorithm.) This can be separated into three phases.

Degree reduction of other equations. If there are any equations, pick the one, say $p_1(x) = 0$ where $p_1(x)$ has the lowest nonzero formal degree, say $p_1(x) = ax^n + P(x)$. If there is no assumption in context that $a \neq 0$ then case-split over $a = 0$, reducing the equation to $P(x) = 0$ in the true branch, then call recursively on both parts (there may now be a *different* equation with lowest formal degree in the true branch if $n = 1$ and so the original equation is now pulled outside the quantifier). If there are no equations left, then we are finished.

In the remaining case, we use $ax^n + P(x) = 0$ and the assumption $a \neq 0$ to reduce the degree of the other equations. Suppose $p_2(x) = 0$ is another equation, of the form $bx^m + P'(x)$ where, since $p_1(x)$ was chosen to be of least degree, $m \geq n$. The following, since $a \neq 0$, is easily seen to be a logical equivalence.

$$\vdash (p_1(x) = 0) \wedge (p_2(x) = 0) = (p_1(x) = 0) \wedge (bx^{m-n}p_1(x) - ap_2(x) = 0)$$

But now we have reduced the formal degree of the latter equation. The whole procedure is now repeated. Eventually we have at most one equation with x free.

Degree reduction of inequalities. If we have one equation $p_1(x) = 0$ with $p_1(x)$ of the form $ax^n + P(x)$ left, we may again suppose that $a \neq 0$. It's now useful to know the sign of a, so we case-split again over $a < 0 \vee 0 < a$ unless it is already known. Consider the case where $0 < a$, the other being similar. Now if the polynomial on the left of an inequality, $q_1(x)$ say, is of the form $bx^m + Q(x)$ with $m \geq n$, we can reduce its degree using the following:

$$\vdash (p_1(x) = 0) \wedge q_1(x) > 0 \Leftrightarrow (p_1(x) = 0) \wedge (aq_1(x) + (-1)bx^{m-n}p_1(x) > 0)$$

which is again easily seen to be true. After repeating this on all inequalities as much as possible, we finish by case-splitting over the leading coefficients in the inequalities, so we may thereafter assume them to be nonzero.

Degree reduction of inequations. This part is similar to the previous stage, except that since we do not need to keep the sign fixed in an inequality; we only need the information that $a \neq 0$. Given an equation $ax^n + P(x)$ with $a \neq 0$, and an inequation $bx^m + R(x) \neq 0$ with $m \geq n$, we reduce the degree of the latter using the following:

$$\vdash (p_1(x) = 0) \wedge r_1(x) \neq 0 \Leftrightarrow (p_1(x) = 0) \wedge (ar_1(x) + (-1)bx^{m-n}p_1(x) \neq 0)$$

Again, this is followed by case splits.

5.3.4 The main part of the algorithm

We now need to consider formulas $\exists x.\ \bigwedge_l q_l(x) > 0 \wedge \bigwedge_m r_m(x) \neq 0$ and $\exists x.\ p(x) = 0 \wedge \bigwedge_l q_l(x) > 0 \wedge \bigwedge_m r_m(x) \neq 0$, in a context where all the polynomials involved have equal formal and actual degrees, and the degrees of the inequalities and inequations is lower than that of the equation. The idea of the algorithm, in a nutshell, is to transform each such formula into an equivalent where at least one of the polynomials $q_l(x)$ or $r_m(x)$ occurs in an *equation* like $q_i(x) = 0$. It can then be used as above to reduce the degrees of the other polynomials. The transformation is achieved by a clever use of the intermediate value property.

To make the termination argument completely explicit, we will, following Kreisel and Krivine, define the degree of a formula (with respect to x) as follows:

- The degree of x in $p(x) = 0$ is the degree of x in $p(x)$
- The degree of x in $q(x) > 0$ or $r(x) \neq 0$ is *one greater than* the degree of x in $q(x)$ or $r(x)$, respectively.
- The degree of x in a non-atomic formula is the highest degree of x in any of its atoms.

This is based on the idea that, as suggested by the sketch of the method above, a polynomial is 'more valuable' when it occurs in an equation, so transferring the same polynomial from an inequation or inequality to an equation represents progress, reflected in a reduction in degree.

It is clear that if the body of a quantifier has zero degree in the quantified variable, the elimination of the quantifier is trivial, the following being the case:

$$\vdash (\exists x.\, A) = A$$

Actually we can stop at degree 1. Then there can only be a single equation, all inequations and inequalities having been rendered trivial by elimination using that equation. And the quantifier can now be eliminated very easily because:

$$\vdash (\exists x.\, ax + b = 0) = a \neq 0 \lor b = 0$$

Moreover, because of a previous case-split, we always know, per construction, that $a \neq 0$ in context, so this can be reduced to $\top$. Therefore we will have a terminating algorithm for quantifier elimination if we can show that quantifier elimination from a formula in our class can be reduced to the consideration of finitely many other such formulas with ***strictly lower degree.*** Sometimes we will need to transform a formula several times to make this true. Note also that the subproblems of lower-degree eliminations are not all independent. In fact the elimination of one quantifier may result in the production of several nested quantifiers, but the elimination of each one of these always involves a formula of strictly smaller degree.

Now we will look at the reduction procedures. These are somewhat different depending on whether there is an equation or not; and both generate intermediate results of the same kind, which we accordingly separate off into a third class.

5.3.5 Reduction of formulas without an equation

The key observation here is that, as a consequence of the continuity of polynomials, the set of points at which a polynomial (and by induction any finite set of polynomials as considered here) is strictly positive, or is nonzero, is *open* in the topological sense, i.e. given any point in the set, there is some nontrivial surrounding region that is also contained entirely in the set:

$$open(S) = \forall x \in S.\ \exists \delta > 0.\ \forall x'.\ |x' - x| < \delta \Rightarrow x' \in S$$

This means that if a set of polynomials are all positive at a point, they are all positive throughout a nontrivial open interval surrounding that point (and the converse is obvious). The idea behind the reduction step is that we can choose this interval to be as large as possible. There are four possibilities according to whether the interval extends to infinity in each direction. Clearly if the interval has a (finite) endpoint then one of the polynomials must be zero there, otherwise the interval could be properly extended. So we have:

$$\begin{array}{l}
(\exists x.\ \bigwedge_l q_l(x) > 0 \wedge \bigwedge_m r_m(x) \neq 0) \\
\Leftrightarrow (\forall x.\ \bigwedge_l q_l(x) > 0 \wedge \bigwedge_m r_m(x) \neq 0) \vee \\
\quad (\exists a.\ (\bigvee_l q_l(a) = 0 \vee \bigvee_m r_m(a) = 0) \wedge \\
\quad\quad \forall x.\ a < x \Rightarrow \bigwedge_l q_l(x) > 0 \wedge \bigwedge_m r_m(x) \neq 0) \vee \\
\quad (\exists b.\ (\bigvee_l q_l(b) = 0 \vee \bigvee_m r_m(b) = 0) \wedge \\
\quad\quad \forall x.\ x < b \Rightarrow \bigwedge_l q_l(x) > 0 \wedge \bigwedge_m r_m(x) \neq 0) \vee \\
\quad (\exists a.\ (\bigvee_l q_l(a) = 0 \vee \bigvee_m r_m(a) = 0) \wedge \\
\quad\quad \exists b.\ (\bigvee_l q_l(b) = 0 \vee \bigvee_m r_m(b) = 0) \wedge a < b \wedge \\
\quad\quad\quad \forall x.\ a < x < b \Rightarrow \bigwedge_l q_l(x) > 0 \wedge \bigwedge_m r_m(x) \neq 0)
\end{array}$$

We seem to have made a step towards greater complexity, but we shall see later how to deal with the resulting formulas.

5.3.6 Reduction of formulas with an equation

If there is an equation $p(x) = 0$ in the conjunction, then we can no longer use the open set property directly. Instead we distinguish three cases, according to the sign of the derivative $p'(x)$.

$$\begin{array}{l}
(\exists x.\ p(x) = 0 \wedge \bigwedge_l q_l(x) > 0 \wedge \bigwedge_m r_m(x) \neq 0) \\
\Leftrightarrow (\exists x.\ p'(x) = 0 \wedge p(x) = 0 \wedge \bigwedge_l q_l(x) > 0 \wedge \bigwedge_m r_m(x) \neq 0) \vee \\
\quad (\exists x.\ p(x) = 0 \wedge p'(x) > 0 \wedge \bigwedge_l q_l(x) > 0 \wedge \bigwedge_m r_m(x) \neq 0) \vee \\
\quad (\exists x.\ -p(x) = 0 \wedge -p'(x) > 0 \wedge \bigwedge_l q_l(x) > 0 \wedge \bigwedge_m r_m(x) \neq 0)
\end{array}$$

This results in a three-way case split. In the case $p'(x) = 0$, the derivative can be used for reduction (its leading coefficient is nonzero because it is a nonzero multiple of $p(x)$'s) and so we are reduced to considering formulas of lower degree. The other two branches are essentially the same, so we will only discuss the case $p'(x) > 0$. (We have written $-p(x) = 0$ rather than $p(x) = 0$ to emphasize the symmetry.)

Now if $\exists x. p(x) = 0 \wedge p'(x) > 0 \wedge \bigwedge_l q_l(x) > 0 \wedge \bigwedge_m r_m(x) \neq 0$, then we again have a largest interval on which $p'(x) > 0 \wedge \bigwedge_l q_l(x) > 0 \wedge \bigwedge_m r_m(x) \neq 0$; we don't use the equation. Supposing for the moment that the interval is finite, say (a, b), we must have $p(a) < 0$ and $p(b) > 0$, since $p(x)$ is strictly increasing over the interval and is zero somewhere within it.

But these two properties, conversely, are enough to ensure that $p(x) = 0$ somewhere inside the interval, by the intermediate value property. With a bit of care we can generalize this to semi-infinite or infinite intervals. For the $(-\infty, \infty)$ case we actually have the following generalization: if a polynomial has nonzero derivative everywhere then it must have a root. Indeed, every polynomial of odd (actual) degree has a root, so either the antecedent of this statement is trivially false, or the consequent trivially true. (Note that this is false for many non-polynomial functions, e.g. e^x has positive derivative everywhere but no root.) For the case where the interval is (a, ∞), we suppose that $p(a) < 0$ and $\forall x > a.\, p'(x) > 0$. If $p(x)$ is linear, the existence of a zero $> a$ is immediate; otherwise the derivative is nonconstant. The extremal behaviour of (nonconstant) polynomials is that $p(x) \to \pm\infty$ as $x \to \infty$, and we must have $p'(x) \to \pm\infty$ too (the leading coefficients, which eventually dominate, have the same signs). Therefore $p(x) \to -\infty$ is ruled out, and the result follows. The case of $(-\infty, b)$ is similar. So we have:

$$
\begin{array}{l}
(\exists x.\, p(x) = 0 \wedge p'(x) > 0 \wedge \bigwedge_l q_l(x) > 0 \wedge \bigwedge_m r_m(x) \neq 0) \\
\Leftrightarrow (\forall x.\, p'(x) > 0 \wedge \bigwedge_l q_l(x) > 0 \wedge \bigwedge_m r_m(x) \neq 0) \vee \\
\quad (\exists a.\, (p'(a) = 0 \vee \bigvee_l q_l(a) = 0 \vee \bigvee_m r_m(a) = 0) \wedge \\
\qquad p(a) < 0 \wedge \\
\qquad \forall x.\, a < x \Rightarrow p'(x) > 0 \wedge \bigwedge_l q_l(x) > 0 \wedge \bigwedge_m r_m(x) \neq 0) \vee \\
\quad (\exists b.\, (p'(b) = 0 \vee \bigvee_l q_l(b) = 0 \vee \bigvee_m r_m(b) = 0) \wedge \\
\qquad p(b) > 0 \wedge \\
\qquad \forall x.\, x < b \Rightarrow p'(x) > 0 \wedge \bigwedge_l q_l(x) > 0 \wedge \bigwedge_m r_m(x) \neq 0) \vee \\
\quad (\exists a.\, (p'(a) = 0 \vee \bigvee_l q_l(a) = 0 \vee \bigvee_m r_m(a) = 0) \wedge p(a) < 0 \wedge \\
\qquad \exists b.\, (p'(b) = 0 \vee \bigvee_l q_l(b) = 0 \vee \bigvee_m r_m(b) = 0) \wedge \\
\qquad\quad p(b) > 0 \wedge a < b \wedge \\
\qquad\quad \forall x.\, a < x < b \Rightarrow p'(x) > 0 \wedge \bigwedge_l q_l(x) > 0 \wedge \bigwedge_m r_m(x) \neq 0)
\end{array}
$$

5.3.7 Reduction of intermediate formulas

Now consider the universal formulas that arise from the above 'reduction' steps. These are all of one of the following forms (possibly including $\pm p'(x)$ among the $q(x)$'s).

- $\forall x.\, \bigwedge_l q_l(x) > 0 \wedge \bigwedge_m r_m(x) \neq 0$
- $\forall x.\, a < x \Rightarrow \bigwedge_l q_l(x) > 0 \wedge \bigwedge_m r_m(x) \neq 0$
- $\forall x.\, x < b \Rightarrow \bigwedge_l q_l(x) > 0 \wedge \bigwedge_m r_m(x) \neq 0$
- $\forall x.\, a < x < b \Rightarrow \bigwedge_l q_l(x) > 0 \wedge \bigwedge_m r_m(x) \neq 0$

Consider the first one, with the unrestricted universal quantifier, first. If a set of polynomials are strictly positive everywhere, then they are trivially nonzero everywhere. But conversely if they are nonzero everywhere, then by the intermediate value property, none of them can change sign; hence if we knew they were all positive at any convenient point, say $x = 0$, that would imply that they are all strictly positive everywhere. Thus:

$$\begin{aligned}&(\forall x.\ \textstyle\bigwedge_l q_l(x) > 0 \wedge \bigwedge_m r_m(x) \neq 0)\\ &\Leftrightarrow \textstyle\bigwedge_l q_l(0) > 0 \wedge\\ &\quad \neg\exists x.\ \textstyle\bigvee_l q_l(x) = 0 \vee \bigvee_m r_m(x) = 0\end{aligned}$$

Similar reasoning applies to the other three cases. We just need to pick a handy point inside each sort of interval. We choose $a+1$, $b-1$ and $\frac{(a+b)}{2}$ respectively, so we have:

$$\begin{aligned}&(\forall x.\ a < x \Rightarrow \textstyle\bigwedge_l q_l(x) > 0 \wedge \bigwedge_m r_m(x) \neq 0)\\ &\Leftrightarrow \textstyle\bigwedge_l q_l(a+1) > 0 \wedge\\ &\quad \neg\exists x.\ a < x \wedge (\textstyle\bigvee_l q(x) = 0 \vee \bigvee_m r_m(x) = 0)\end{aligned}$$

and

$$\begin{aligned}&(\forall x.\ x < b \Rightarrow \textstyle\bigwedge_l q_l(x) > 0 \wedge \bigwedge_m r_m(x) \neq 0)\\ &\Leftrightarrow \textstyle\bigwedge_l q_l(b-1) > 0 \wedge\\ &\quad \neg\exists x.\ x < b \wedge (\textstyle\bigvee_l q(x) = 0 \vee \bigvee_m r_m(x) = 0)\end{aligned}$$

and

$$\begin{aligned}&a < b \wedge\\ &(\forall x.\ a < x < b \Rightarrow \textstyle\bigwedge_l q_l(x) > 0 \wedge \bigwedge_m r_m(x) \neq 0)\\ &\Leftrightarrow a < b \wedge\\ &\quad \textstyle\bigwedge_l q_l(\frac{a+b}{2}) > 0 \wedge\\ &\quad \neg\exists x.\ a < x < b \wedge (\textstyle\bigvee_l q(x) = 0 \vee \bigvee_m r_m(x) = 0)\end{aligned}$$

Note that for the last theorem, the additional context $a < b$ is needed, otherwise the left would be vacuously true, the right not necessarily so. This context is available in the two theorems above; in fact (conveniently!) the very conjunction on the left of this equivalence occurs in both of them.

5.3.8 Proof of termination

The proof of termination is by induction on the formal degree. We assume that all existential formulas of degree $< n$ admit quantifier elimination by our method, and use this to show that formulas of degree n do too. Observe that each of the intermediate formulas has been transformed into a quantifier elimination problem of lower degree (we have an equation of the form $q_l(x) = 0$ or $r_m(x) = 0$). We may therefore assume by the inductive hypothesis that the algorithm will eliminate it. Even in branches that have introduced additional existential quantifiers for the endpoints of the interval, there is just such an equation for that, i.e. $q_l(a) = 0$ or $q_j(b) = 0$. Consequently, although we have generated three nested quantifier elimination problems in place of one, each of them is of lower degree. Hence the algorithm terminates. However it will display exponential complexity in the degree of the polynomials involved, which is not true of more sophisticated algorithms.

5.3.9 Comparison with Kreisel and Krivine

Kreisel and Krivine do not retain inequations $r(x) \neq 0$; instead, they split them into pairs of inequalities $r(x) < 0 \vee r(x) > 0$. This achieves significant formal simplification, but from our practical point of view, it's desirable to avoid this kind of splitting, which can rapidly lead to exponential blowups. Kreisel and Krivine also use an additional step in the initial simplification, so that instead of:

$$\exists x. \bigwedge_k p_k(x) = 0 \wedge \bigwedge_l q_l(x) > 0$$

they need only deal with a special case where the quantifier is bounded:

$$\exists x. a < x < b \wedge \bigwedge_k p_k(x) = 0 \wedge \bigwedge_l q_l(x) > 0$$

This uses the fact that:

$$\vdash (\exists y. P[y]) = (\exists u. 0 < u < 1 \wedge (\exists x. -1 < x < 1 \wedge P(u^{-1}x))$$

To see the truth of this, consider left-to-right and right-to-left implications, and pick witnesses for the antecedents. The right-to-left implication is trivial: set $y = u^{-1}x$. For the other direction, choose $u = 1/(|y|+2)$ and $x = y/(|y|+2)$.

Using the above theorem, an unbounded existential quantifier can be transformed into two bounded ones. The body of the inner quantifier (x) needs to be multiplied through by the appropriate power of u to avoid explicit use of division; since we have a context $0 < u$, that is easily done without affecting either equations or inequalities. From a theoretical point of view, this achieves a simplification in the presentation. Where we consider the possibility that the intermediate formulas will feature infinite or semi-infinite intervals, this is not the case for them; one merely gets the possibility that one or both endpoints are those of the overall interval. This simplification does not seem to be very great, and for our *practical* use, it is a bad idea to create two nested quantifiers, in view of the catastrophic complexity characteristics of the algorithm.

Kreisel and Krivine do not use the same reduction theorem for intermediate formulas:

$$\begin{aligned} &(\forall x. a < x < b \Rightarrow \textstyle\bigwedge_l q_l(x) > 0) \\ &\Leftrightarrow \textstyle\bigwedge_l q_l(\frac{a+b}{2}) > 0 \wedge \neg\exists x. a < x < b \wedge \bigvee_l q(x) = 0 \end{aligned}$$

Instead of $\bigwedge_l q_l(\frac{a+b}{2}) > 0$ they use the fact that the first nonzero derivative of each polynomial at the point a is positive. This works, but seems unnecessarily complicated. It was probably a hasty patch to the first edition, which incorrectly asserted that $\bigwedge q_l(a) \geq 0$ worked in its place.

Finally, to perform elimination with an *inequality* using an equation, rather than case-split over $a > 0 \vee a < 0$, they multiply through the inequality by a^2. Since $a \neq 0$, we have $0 < a^2$, so this is admissible. But while this avoids immediate case splits, it increases the degree of the other variables, and so can make additional eliminations more complex. In general, there are several trade-offs of this kind to be decided upon.

Otherwise we have followed their description quite closely, though to be pedantic they seem to confuse actual and formal degrees somewhat. Notably, they assert that the degree reduction step can reduce the degree of each polynomial in an inequality to below the degree of the lowest-degreed equation, suggesting that they use 'degree' for 'actual degree' (after all, a polynomial all of whose coefficients are zero is of no use in elimination). But then they say that if the leading coefficient is zero, deleting it reduces the degree, which suggests that they mean 'formal degree'. The presentation here, with a notion of context, is more precise and explicit about the question of coefficients being zero.

5.4 The HOL Implementation

When implementing any sort of derived rule in HOL, it is desirable to move as much as possible of the inference from 'run time' to the production of a few proforma theorems that can then be instantiated efficiently. To this end, we have defined encodings of common syntactic patterns in HOL which make it easier to state theorems of sufficient generality. The very first thing is to define a constant for $\neq$. This is merely a convenience, since then all the relations $x < y$, $x = y$, $x \neq y$ etc. have the same term structure, whereas the usual representation for inequations is $\neg(x = y)$.

5.4.1 Polynomial arithmetic

We define a constant poly which takes a list as an argument and gives a polynomial in one variable with that list of coefficients, where the head of the list corresponds to the constant term, and the last element of the list to the term of highest degree.

```
|- (poly [] x = &0) /\
   (poly (CONS h t) x = h + x * poly t x)
```

This immediately has the benefit of letting us prove quite general theorems such as 'every polynomial is differentiable' and 'every polynomial is continuous'.[6] Differentiation of polynomials can be defined as a simple recursive function on the list of coefficients:

```
|- (poly_diff_aux n [] = []) /\
   (poly_diff_aux n (CONS h t) =
       CONS (&n * h) (poly_diff_aux (SUC n) t))

|- poly_diff l = if l = [] then [] else poly_diff_aux 1 (TL l)
```

The operations of addition, negation and constant multiplication can likewise be defined in an easy way in terms of the list of coefficients. For example, the following clauses are an easy consequence of the definition of polynomial addition:

```
|- (poly_add [] m = m) /\
   (poly_add l [] = l) /\
   (poly_add (CONS h1 t1) (CONS h2 t2) =
        (CONS (h1 + h2) (poly_add t1 t2)))
```

and we have the theorems

```
|- !l x. --(poly l x) = poly (poly_neg l) x

|- !l x c. c * (poly l x) = poly (poly_cmul c l) x

|- !l m x. poly l x + poly m x = poly (poly_add l m) x
```

Apart from their main purpose of allowing us to state general theorems about polynomials, these encodings are actually useful in practice for keeping the coefficients well-organized. In general, the expressions manipulated involve several variables. During the elimination of a quantifier $\exists x. \ldots$, we want to single out x and treat the other variables as constants. However when performing arithmetic on the coefficients, we have to remember that these contain other variables which may be singled out in their turn.

The polynomial functions allow us to do this in a very natural way, instead of re-encoding the expressions for each new variable. For example, we can regard a polynomial in x, y and z as a polynomial in x whose coefficients are polynomials in y, whose coefficients are polynomials in z, whose coefficients, finally, are just rational constants. The variables are ordered according to the nesting of the quantifiers, since that is the order in which we want to consider them.

A set of conversions is provided to perform arithmetic on polynomials, that is, to add them, multiply them, and to multiply them by 'constants' (polynomials in 'lower' variables only). These accept and return polynomials

[6] Strictly speaking, we are really considering the functions $\mathbb{R} \to \mathbb{R}$ determined by polynomials, not the polynomials themselves. However as the underlying field $\mathbb{R}$ is infinite there is a one-one correspondence between them.

written using a single variable ordering; however they permit rational constants as degenerate instances of polynomials, and attempt to avoid redundant instances of `poly` in results. At the bottom level when the coefficients involve no variables, the conversions for rational numbers are used. There is also a conversion to 'apply' a polynomial at a particular argument.

Apart from being useful during the internal operation of the decision procedure, these functions are also used to perform the initial translation from arbitrary algebraic expressions into the canonical polynomial form. This is in conjunction with two conversions for the 'leaf' cases of variables and constants. A variable v is translated into `poly v [&0; &1]`, while a term not involving any variables is translated to its rational reduced form using the rational number conversions; if this fails then the term is not in the acceptable subset.

5.4.2 Encoding of logical properties

The reduction theorems have a recurring theme of 'for all polynomials in a finite list' or 'for some polynomial in a finite list'. Accordingly, we make the following general definitions:

```
|- (FORALL P [] = T) /\
   (FORALL P (CONS h t) = P h /\ FORALL P t)

|- (EXISTS P [] = F) /\
   (EXISTS P (CONS h t) = P h \/ EXISTS P t)
```

Now we need only the following extra definitions:

```
|- EQ x l = poly l x = &0

|- NE x l = poly l x /= &0

|- LE x l = poly l x <= &0

|- LT x l = poly l x < &0

|- GE x l = poly l x >= &0

|- GT x l = poly l x > &0
```

and we are in a position to state the reduction theorems actually at the HOL object level.

5.4.3 HOL versions of reduction theorems

The proforma theorems look even more overwhelming in their HOL form because of the use of the canonical polynomial format. However, one of them is rather simple:

```
|- (?x. FORALL (EQ x) [[b; a]] /\
        FORALL (GT x) [] /\ FORALL (NE x) []) =
   (a /= &0) \/ (b = &0)
```

For the others, we will begin by showing the main building blocks that are used to produce the final two proforma theorems. For formulas without an equation we have:

```
|- (?x. FORALL (GT x) l /\ FORALL (NE x) m) =
   (!x. FORALL (GT x) l /\ FORALL (NE x) m) \/
   (?a. EXISTS (EQ a) (APPEND l m) /\
        (!x. a < x ==> FORALL (GT x) l /\ FORALL (NE x) m)) \/
   (?b. EXISTS (EQ b) (APPEND l m) /\
        (!x. x < b ==> FORALL (GT x) l /\ FORALL (NE x) m)) \/
   (?a. EXISTS (EQ a) (APPEND l m) /\
        (?b. EXISTS (EQ b) (APPEND l m) /\
             a < b /\
             (!x. a < x /\ x < b
                  ==> FORALL (GT x) l /\ FORALL (NE x) m)))
```

The initial case-split for formulas with an equation is:

```
|- (?x. EQ x p /\ FORALL (GT x) l /\ FORALL (NE x) m) =
   (?x. FORALL (EQ x) [poly_diff p; p] /\
        FORALL (GT x) l /\ FORALL (NE x) m) \/
   (?x. EQ x p /\
        FORALL (GT x) (CONS (poly_diff p) l) /\
        FORALL (NE x) m) \/
   (?x. EQ x (poly_neg p) /\
        FORALL (GT x) (CONS (poly_diff (poly_neg p)) l) /\
        FORALL (NE x) m)
```

while the additional expansion (note that this applies twice to the above, with the sign of the polynomial occurring in the equation reversed) is:

```
|- (?x. EQ x p /\
        FORALL (GT x) (CONS (poly_diff p) l) /\
        FORALL (NE x) m) =
   (!x. FORALL (GT x) (CONS (poly_diff p) l) /\
        FORALL (NE x) m) \/
   (?a. EXISTS (EQ a) (APPEND (CONS (poly_diff p) l) m) /\
        LT a p /\
        (!x. a < x
             ==> FORALL (GT x) (CONS (poly_diff p) l) /\
                 FORALL (NE x) m)) \/
   (?b. EXISTS (EQ b) (APPEND (CONS (poly_diff p) l) m) /\
        GT b p /\
        (!x. x < b
             ==> FORALL (GT x) (CONS (poly_diff p) l) /\
                 FORALL (NE x) m)) \/
   (?a. EXISTS (EQ a) (APPEND (CONS (poly_diff p) l) m) /\
        LT a p /\
        (?b. EXISTS (EQ b) (APPEND (CONS (poly_diff p) l) m) /\
             GT b p /\
             a < b /\
             (!x. a < x /\ x < b
                  ==> FORALL (GT x) (CONS (poly_diff p) l) /\
                      FORALL (NE x) m)))
```

Finally, the intermediate formulas are tackled as follows:

```
|- (!x. FORALL (GT x) l /\ FORALL (NE x) m) =
   FORALL (GT (&0)) l /\ ~(?x. EXISTS (EQ x) (APPEND l m))

|- (!x. a < x ==> FORALL (GT x) l /\ FORALL (NE x) m) =
   FORALL (GT (a + &1)) l /\
   ~(?x. a < x /\ EXISTS (EQ x) (APPEND l m))

|- (!x. x < b ==> FORALL (GT x) l /\ FORALL (NE x) m) =
   FORALL (GT (b - &1)) l /\
   ~(?x. x < b /\ EXISTS (EQ x) (APPEND l m))

|- a < b /\
   (!x. a < x /\ x < b ==> FORALL (GT x) l /\ FORALL (NE x) m) =
   a < b /\
   FORALL (GT ((a + b) / &2)) l /\
   ~(?x. a < x /\ x < b /\ EXISTS (EQ x) (APPEND l m))
```

We will just show the final proforma theorem for the no-equation case; the one with an equation is similar but larger.

```
|- (?x. FORALL (EQ x) [] /\
        FORALL (GT x) l /\ FORALL (NE x) m) =
   FORALL (GT (&0)) l /\ ~(?x. EXISTS (EQ x) (APPEND l m)) \/
   (?a. EXISTS (EQ a) (APPEND l m) /\
        FORALL (GT (poly a [&1; &1])) l /\
        ~(?x. GT x [poly a [&0; --(&1)]; &1] /\
              EXISTS (EQ x) (APPEND l m))) \/
   (?b. EXISTS (EQ b) (APPEND l m) /\
        FORALL (GT (poly b [--(&1); &1])) l /\
        ~(?x. LT x [poly b [&0; --(&1)]; &1] /\
              EXISTS (EQ x) (APPEND l m))) \/
   (?a. EXISTS (EQ a) (APPEND l m) /\
        (?b. EXISTS (EQ b) (APPEND l m) /\
            GT b [poly a [&0; --(&1)]; &1] /\
            FORALL (GT (poly b [poly a [&0; &1 / &2];
                                &1 / &2])) l /\
            ~(?x. GT x [poly a [&0; --(&1)]; &1] /\
                  LT x [poly b [&0; --(&1)]; &1] /\
                  EXISTS (EQ x) (APPEND l m))))
```

The derivations of these theorems are not trivial, but follow quite closely the informal reasoning above. We first prove various properties of polynomials, e.g. the intermediate value property. Most of these follow easily from general theorems about continuous and differentiable functions, once we have proved the following, which is a reasonably easy list induction:

```
|- !l x. ((poly l) diffl (poly (poly_diff l) x))(x)
```

There is one theorem that is peculiar to polynomials.

```
|- !p a. poly a p < &0 /\
         (!x. a < x ==> poly (poly_diff p) x > &0)
         ==> ?x. a < x /\ (poly p x = &0)
```

Its proof is a bit trickier, but follows the lines of the informal reasoning given above, i.e. that the extremal behaviour of nonconstant polynomials is to tend to $\pm\infty$, and that the derivative's extremal sign is the same. The proof involves some slightly tedious details, e.g. 'factoring' a list into the significant part and a tail of zeros. Once the above theorem is derived, we can get the required 'mirror image':

```
|- !p b. poly b p > &0 /\
         (!x. x < b ==> poly (poly_diff p) x > &0)
         ==> ?x. x < b /\ (poly p x = &0)
```

by a slightly subtle duality argument, rather than by duplicating all the tedious reasoning. We make the additional definition:

```
|- (poly_aneg b [] = []) /\
   (poly_aneg b (CONS h t) =
      CONS (if b then --h else h) (poly_aneg (~b) t))
```

which is supposed to represent negation of the *argument*. Indeed, it is easy to prove by list induction that

```
|- !p x. (poly (poly_aneg F p) x = poly p (--x)) /\
         (poly (poly_aneg T p) x = --(poly p (--x)))
```

and

```
|- !p. (poly_diff (poly_aneg F p) =
           poly_neg (poly_aneg F (poly_diff p))) /\
       (poly_diff (poly_aneg T p) =
           poly_neg (poly_aneg T (poly_diff p)))
```

from which the required theorem follows by setting p to poly_aneg T p in the first theorem. These two together easily yield the 'bidirectional' version:

```
|- !p. (!x. poly (poly_diff p) x > &0) ==> ?x. poly p x = &0
```

The main reduction theorems are now derived mainly using the following general lemma, together with the easy facts that the set of points at which a finite set of polynomials are all strictly positive is open.

```
|- !P c.
       open(mtop mr1) P /\ P c
       ==> (!x. P x) \/
           (?a. a < c /\ ~P a /\ (!x. a < x ==> P x)) \/
           (?b. c < b /\ ~P b /\ (!x. x < b ==> P x)) \/
           (?a b. a < c /\ c < b /\ ~P a /\ ~P b /\
                  (!x. a < x /\ x < b ==> P x))
```

The property that is used for P is:

```
\x. FORALL (NE x) l /\ FORALL(NE x) m
```

Now the fact that $\neg P(x)$ immediately implies that one of the polynomials in the combined list is zero, whereas if FORALL (GT x) l were used directly, this would require some tedious reasoning with the intermediate value property. Now the theorem can have FORALL (GT x) l restored in place of FORALL (NE x) l by using slight variants of the reduction theorems for intermediate formulas.

5.4.4 Overall arrangement

An initial pass converts all atoms into standard form with a canonical polynomial on the left of each relation and zero on the right. The main conversion traverses the term recursively. When it reaches a quantifier, then, after using $(\forall x.\ P[x]) \Leftrightarrow \neg\exists x.\ \neg P[x]$ in the universal case, the conversion is called recursively on the body of the quantifier, which may thereafter be assumed quantifier-free. (Moreover, the list of variables giving the canonical order gets the additional quantified variable as its head during this suboperation). A few simplifications are applied to get rid of trivia like relations between rational constants. Then the body is placed in disjunctive normal form and the existential quantifier distributed over the disjuncts. Moreover, any conjuncts not containing the quantified variable are pulled outside. Then the conversion deals with each disjunct separately.

First, a combination of case-splitting and elimination using equations takes place, as in the abstract description above. Only after this stage is complete are non-strict inequalities expanded (e.g. $x \leq 0$ to $x < 0 \vee x = 0$), in order to maximize the benefits of elimination. When it does happen, this splitting may require a further distribution of the existential quantifier over the disjuncts. Finally, the formula is placed in canonical form using the additional constants like `EQ` and `FORALL`. The appropriate proforma theorem is used as a rewrite, these extra constants are expanded away in the result, along with instances of `APPEND`, `poly_neg` and `poly_diff`. After that, the main toplevel conversion is called again on the result to eliminate the nested existential quantifiers remaining.

Note that the final case-splits over the leading coefficients of polynomials remaining after elimination are actually done three-way, i.e. $a = 0 \vee a < 0 \vee a > 0$, rather than just $a = 0 \vee a \neq 0$ as in the abstract presentation. The reason is that otherwise the subsequent $a < 0 \vee a > 0$ split derived from $a \neq 0$ is done separately for each nested quantifier created. This is an unfortunate consequence of the bottom-up nature of the algorithm: the context of the inner quantified term is discharged at the upper level. A more intelligent organization would solve this problem, but it is more complicated. These additional case splits may be redundant in some cases, but that only becomes a serious problem where there are many conjuncts in the quantifier body. No case splits are performed when the coefficients are rational constants already, but otherwise no intelligence is used in relating different case splits.

5.5 Optimizing the linear case

The above algorithm is, as we shall see below, rather inefficient. To some extent this is inevitable, since deciding the theory is inherently difficult. However, motivated by the 'feeling that a single algorithm for the full elementary theory of **R** can hardly be practical' (van den Dries 1988) and the fact that many practical problems fall into a rather special class, let us see how to optimize some important cases. Probably the most satisfactory solution is to accumulate a large database of special cases that can be applied directly, by analogy with techniques used in computer algebra systems to find antiderivatives. However, we will consider some more 'algorithmic' optimizations. First, the case of $\exists x.\, p(x) = 0$ can be optimized in various ways, e.g. by formalizing Sturm's classical elimination strategy. In fact if $p(x)$ has odd formal degree, we can say at once:

$$\begin{aligned}
&(\exists x.\ a_n x^n + a_{n-1}x^{n-1} + \cdots + a_1 x + a_0 = 0)\\
&\Leftrightarrow a_n \neq 0 \lor\\
&a_n = 0 \land \exists x.\ a_{n-1}x^{n-1} + \cdots + a_1 x + a_0 = 0
\end{aligned}$$

while if $p(x)$ has even degree, we can use the fact that if the leading coefficient a_n is positive (resp. negative) then as $x \to \pm\infty$ we have $p(x) \to \infty$ (resp. $p(x) \to -\infty$). Therefore there is a root iff there is a negative (resp. positive) or zero turning point:

$$\begin{aligned}
(\exists x.\ p(x) = 0) \Leftrightarrow\ & a_n > 0 \land (\exists x.\ p'(x) = 0 \land p(x) \leq 0) \lor\\
& a_n < 0 \land (\exists x.\ p'(x) = 0 \land p(x) \geq 0) \lor\\
& a_n = 0 \land (\exists x.\ a_{n-1}x^{n-1} + \cdots + a_1 x + a_0 = 0)
\end{aligned}$$

This achieves a degree reduction. In fact a similar theorem is true if $\exists x.p(x) = 0$ is replaced by $\exists x.\ p(x) \geq 0$ and so on. Alternatively, the case of a single strict inequality can be dealt with as follows:

$$\begin{aligned}
&\exists x.\ p(x) > 0\\
&\Leftrightarrow\ (\forall x.\ p(x) > 0) \lor\\
&\qquad \exists x.\ p(x) = 0 \land (p'(x) \neq 0 \lor (p'(x) = 0 \land p''(x) \neq 0 \ldots)))
\end{aligned}$$

and then the first conjunct dealt with as in the main algorithm. This seems better than the main algorithm's reduction step, since it does not require any nested quantifiers to achieve a degree reduction. Such an approach generalizes to several inequalities, though the situation is slightly more complicated. It is not clear how to optimize the case with equations using the same techniques.

We do not actually implement any of these refinements. While they may be useful for academic examples, the most important *practical* problems are the linear ones, i.e. those where the variables to be eliminated occur with indices at most 1. A defect of the main algorithm is that, while linear equations yield elimination and an immediate result, linear inequalities are just as difficult as quadratic equations, and this difficulty is not negligible. Moreover, nonstrict inequalities are split; although the equality case leads to quick elimination, the resulting term blows up in size, which can be a serious problem for subsequent steps. It seems preferable to treat linear inequalities, strict and nonstrict, in an optimized way. Therefore we focus most of our energy on this special case.

5.5.1 Presburger arithmetic

A quantifier elimination procedure for linear arithmetic was demonstrated by Presburger (1930); an excellent exposition of this and other reducts of number theory is given by Enderton (1972). This was for the discrete structure $\mathbb{N}$, and in the case of the reals, many details become simpler because there are no difficult divisibility considerations. The reals make available alternative strategies, which we will note but do not explore. For example, reasoning much like that behind the main algorithm yields (except in the trivial case where there are no inequalities at all):

$$\begin{array}{l}(\exists x.\ \bigwedge_i a_i \leq x \wedge \bigwedge_j x \leq b_j)\\ \Leftrightarrow (\exists x.\ (\bigvee_i x = a_i \vee \bigvee_j x = b_j) \wedge \bigwedge_i a_i \leq x \wedge \bigwedge_j x \leq b_j)\end{array}$$

Integrated with the main algorithm, this yields a degree reduction. However if the nonstrict inequalities are replaced by strict ones, the corresponding formula becomes more complicated since it's possible for several polynomials to cut the x-axis at the same point, not necessarily with the same sign of derivative. The standard and most direct method, which we adopt, is based on the following:

$$(\exists x.\ \bigwedge_i a_i \leq x \wedge \bigwedge_j x \leq b_j) \Leftrightarrow \bigwedge_{i,j} a_i \leq b_j$$

This theorem generalizes to arbitrary combinations of strict and nonstrict orderings:

$$(\exists x.\ \bigwedge_i a_i \lhd_i x \wedge \bigwedge_j x \lhd_j b_j) \Leftrightarrow \bigwedge_{i,j} a_i \lhd_{i,j} b_j$$

where $\lhd_{i,j}$ is $<$ if either $\lhd_i$ or $\lhd_j$ is, and is $\leq$ if both $\lhd_i$ and $\lhd_j$ are. Moreover, since we do want to allow coefficients containing other variables but do not want to concern ourselves with rational functions, it's convenient to allow arbitrary coefficients of x which are assumed positive. It is in this generalized form that the theorem is proved in HOL. Once again, we use various special encodings to state the proforma theorems, starting with generalized strict/nonstrict inequalities determined by a Boolean flag.

```
|- LTE x (s,a,b) = if s then a * x + b < &0 else a * x + b <= &0
```

The theorem requires us to consider all pairs of inequalities from two lists, and to find the appropriate 'resolvent' of a pair of inequalities. These concepts are defined using:

```
|- (ALLPAIRS f [] l = T) /\
   (ALLPAIRS f (CONS h t) l = FORALL (f h) l /\ ALLPAIRS f t l)
```

and

```
|- GLI (s1,a1,b1) (s2,a2,b2) =
       (if s1 \/ s2 then (<) else (<=)) (a1 * b2) (a2 * b1)
```

The final theorem is as follows (the antecedent ensures all coefficients of x are positive):

```
|- FORALL (\p. FST(SND p) > &0) (APPEND l m) ==>
     ((?x. FORALL (GTE x) l /\ FORALL (LTE x) m) =
      ALLPAIRS GLI l m)
```

The proof of this is surprisingly tricky. The approach we use is to prove the version for nonstrict orderings first; this is a fairly straightforward double induction, using as a lemma the fact (itself an easy induction) that a nonempty list of reals has a maximum and minimum; the degenerate cases where one list or the other is empty are dealt with separately. Then the full theorem is approached by using:

$$
\begin{aligned}
& a+b<c \\
& \Leftrightarrow (\exists \epsilon > 0.\, a+(b+\epsilon) \leq c) \\
& \Leftrightarrow (\exists \epsilon > 0.\, \forall \delta.\, 0 \leq \delta \leq \epsilon \Rightarrow a+(b+\delta) \leq c)
\end{aligned}
$$

The existence of such an ϵ is preserved under conjunction; the form involving δ is used for most of the intermediate steps, since the following conveniently general lemma is easy to prove:

```
|- (?e. &0 < e /\ (!d. &0 <= d /\ d <= e ==> P1 d)) /\
   (?e. &0 < e /\ (!d. &0 <= d /\ d <= e ==> P2 d)) =
   (?e. &0 < e /\ (!d. &0 <= d /\ d <= e ==> P1 d /\ P2 d))
```

Using this, the existence of ϵ can be 'commuted' past the binary and listwise conjunctions in the above theorem, and hence the full theorem reduced to the nonstrict case.

The use of the theorem is fitted into the main algorithm just after the elimination phase, after the signs of the coefficients have been determined but before nonstrict inequalities have been split. It is used when there are no equations left and all inequalities are linear.

5.5.2 The universal linear case

In fact, the great majority of practical results fall into a still more restricted subset: a universal fact is to be proven, and all variables occur linearly with rational coefficients. In this case the full quantifier elimination procedure above is rather wasteful, and a separate optimized procedure has been coded. It is not a conversion that retains a logical equivalence at each stage, but rather a refutation procedure which derives a contradiction from a set of equations and inequalities. However the reasoning underlying it is closely related to the linear procedure mentioned above. In order to prove $\forall x_1, \ldots, x_n.\, P[x_1, \ldots, x_n]$, we attempt to refute $\neg P[x_1, \ldots, x_n]$ for free variables $x_1, \ldots, x_n$ (the reader may think of them as Skolem constants). This is done by deriving new inequalities using the same reasoning as leading from left to right in the general linear case. However now we map out an optimal route to the contradiction outside the logic, and deal with variables in an optimal order to reduce blowup, either of the number of derived facts or the sizes of the numerical coefficients. The result is about one order of magnitude faster on typical problems.

5.6 Results

First we will give results for eliminating a single quantifier from various formulas of 'degree 2' with the main algorithm.

$(\exists x.\ x^2 - x + 1 = 0) = \bot$	133.43
$(\exists x.\ x^2 - 3x + 1 = 0) = \top$	132.95
$(\exists x.\ x > 6 \wedge x^2 - 3x + 1 = 0) = \bot$	478.90
$(\exists x.\ 7x^2 - 5x + 3 > 0 \wedge x^2 - 3x + 1 = 0) = \top$	507.10

Sometimes a favourable elimination can yield a result very quickly in comparison, even when the formula appears more complicated. For example, the following takes just 18.83 seconds to reduce to falsity:

$$\exists x.\ 11x^3 - 7x^2 - 2x + 1 = 0 \wedge 7x^2 - 5x + 3 > 0 \wedge x^2 - 8x + 1 = 0$$

For another example of this phenomenon, consider the following well-known problem due to Davenport and Heinz:

$$\exists c.\ \forall b.\ \forall a.\ (a = d \wedge b = c) \vee (a = c \wedge b = 1) \Rightarrow aa = b$$

According to Loos and Weispfenning (1993), it is a case where Collins's original CAD algorithm performs badly. Even though it involves three nested quantifiers, it admits a favourable elimination, and our procedure takes only 26.38 seconds to reduce it to

$$-1 + d^4 = 0$$

A rather more interesting 'degree 2' example is the *general* quadratic equation:

$$\exists x.\ ax^2 + bx + c = 0$$

Our procedure takes a bit longer than for the corresponding examples with numerical coefficients: 532.57 seconds. This is as expected since now nontrivial polynomial elimination and determination of the signs of coefficients is necessary. The result is (intensionally!) much more complicated than the well-known solution given early in this chapter, but as can be seen from the answer below, the discriminant expression $b^2 - 4ac$ (usually multiplied by a) plays a pivotal role.

```
|- (?x. a * x pow 2 + b * x + c = &0) =
   (a = &0) /\ ((b = &0) /\ (c = &0) \/ b > &0 \/ b < &0) \/
   a > &0 /\
   ((--(b pow 2 * a) + &4 * c * a pow 2 = &0) \/
    --(b pow 2 * a) + &4 * c * a pow 2 < &0 /\
    &4 * a pow 2 > &0 \/
    --(b pow 2 * a) + &4 * c * a pow 2 > &0 /\
    --(&4 * a pow 2) > &0 \/
    b pow 2 * a + --(&4 * c * a pow 2) < &0 /\
    --(&4 * a pow 2) > &0 \/
    b pow 2 * a + --(&4 * c * a pow 2) > &0 /\
    &4 * a pow 2 > &0) \/
   a < &0 /\
   ((--(b pow 2 * a) + &4 * c * a pow 2 = &0) \/
    --(b pow 2 * a) + &4 * c * a pow 2 < &0 /\
    --(&4 * a pow 2) > &0 \/
    --(b pow 2 * a) + &4 * c * a pow 2 > &0 /\
    &4 * a pow 2 > &0 \/
    b pow 2 * a + --(&4 * c * a pow 2) < &0 /\
    &4 * a pow 2 > &0 \/
    b pow 2 * a + --(&4 * c * a pow 2) > &0 /\
    --(&4 * a pow 2) > &0)
```

This could be substantially improved given more intelligent (sometimes contextual) simplification; for example, $-4a^2 > 0$ is obviously false. Automation of such simplifications could be incorporated without great difficulty, but we do not explore this here since it is a practically endless project.

Larger nonlinear problems usually seem hard to do in a reasonable amount of time and space. This, and the complexity of some results, aren't simply peculiarities of our implementation; the state of the art is still quite restricted. For example, Lazard (1988) gives optimal solutions (those that are 'simplest' in a reasonable sense) obtained by hand for two classical examples, the non-negativity of the general quartic:

$$\forall x.\ ax^4 + bx^3 + cx^2 + dx + e \geq 0$$

and the so-called 'Kahan ellipse problem', which asks for conditions ensuring that a general ellipse lies entirely within the unit circle:

$$\forall x, y.\ \frac{(x-c)^2}{a^2} + \frac{(y-d)^2}{b^2} = 1 \Rightarrow x^2 + y^2 \leq 1$$

But he adds that no known general algorithm gives results of comparable simplicity; in fact according to Davenport, Siret, and Tournier (1988) no mechanized system had ever (in 1988) solved the ellipse problem at all, never mind elegantly, without some simplifying assumptions like $c = 0$.

For some further tractable test cases we consider the linear problems given by Loos and Weispfenning (1993). The first is derived from an expert system producing work plans for the milling of metal parts. It takes 189.75 seconds to eliminate the quantifiers here; in the case where the coefficients of x or y are zero in a branch of the case analysis, the linear procedure comes into play. Without that, the result would be substantially slower.

$$\exists x, y.\, 0 < x \wedge y < 0 \wedge xr - xt + t = qx - sx + s \wedge xb - xd + d = ay - cy + c$$

The next problem is from Collins and Johnson, and takes only 97.73 seconds.

$$\exists r. 0 < r \wedge r < 1 \wedge 0 < (1-3r)(a^2+b^2)+2ar \wedge (2-3r)(a^2+b^2)+4ar-2a-r < 0$$

We do not show the results of the last two examples, as they are both fairly large. The following arises from a planar transport problem; it is again entirely linear and the quantifiers can all be eliminated in 174.02 seconds.

$$\begin{array}{l}\exists x_{11}, x_{12}, x_{13}, x_{21}, x_{22}, x_{23}, x_{31}, x_{32}, x_{33}.\\ \quad x_{11} + x_{12} + x_{13} = a_1 \wedge x_{21} + x_{22} + x_{23} = a_2 \wedge \\ \quad x_{31} + x_{32} + x_{33} = a_3 \wedge x_{11} + x_{21} + x_{31} = b_1 \wedge \\ \quad x_{12} + x_{22} + x_{32} = b_2 \wedge x_{13} + x_{23} + x_{33} = b_2 \wedge \\ \quad 0 \le x_{11} \wedge 0 \le x_{12} \wedge 0 \le x_{13} \wedge \\ \quad 0 \le x_{21} \wedge 0 \le x_{22} \wedge 0 \le x_{23} \wedge \\ \quad 0 \le x_{31} \wedge 0 \le x_{32} \wedge 0 \le x_{33}\end{array}$$

with the final HOL theorem being:

```
|- (?x11 x12 x13 x21 x22 x23 x31 x32 x33.
          (x11 + x12 + x13 = a1) /\ (x21 + x22 + x23 = a2) /\
          (x31 + x32 + x33 = a3) /\ (x11 + x21 + x31 = b1) /\
          (x12 + x22 + x32 = b2) /\ (x13 + x23 + x33 = b2) /\
          &0 <= x11 /\ &0 <= x12 /\ &0 <= x13 /\
          &0 <= x21 /\ &0 <= x22 /\ &0 <= x23 /\
          &0 <= x31 /\ &0 <= x32 /\ &0 <= x33) =
   (--a2 <= &0 /\ --a3 <= &0 /\
    (--(&2 * b2) + --b1 + a3 + a2 + a1 = &0) /\
    --b2 <= &0 /\
    b2 + b1 + --a3 + --a2 + --a1 <= &0) /\
   --a1 <= &0 /\ --b1 <= &0 /\
   b1 + --a3 + --a2 + --a1 <= &0 /\
   --a3 + --a2 <= &0
```

The universal linear problems are the most important in practice, and our optimized linear procedure exhibits much better performance. Only when there are many instances of the absolute value function, whose elimination results in case splits, does the performance fall below what is acceptable in a typical interactive session.

$\vdash x + y = 0 \Leftrightarrow x = -y$	1.42
$\vdash w \leq x \wedge y \leq z \Rightarrow (w + y) \leq (x + z)$	0.72
$\vdash x \leq y \Rightarrow x < y + 1$	0.48
$\vdash -x \leq x \Leftrightarrow 0 \leq x$	0.50
$\vdash (a + b) - (c + d) = (a - c) + (b - d)$	1.07
$\vdash (x + y)(x - y) = xx - yy$	0.92
$\vdash \lvert x\rvert = 0 \Leftrightarrow x = 0$	1.22
$\vdash \lvert x - y\rvert = \lvert y - x\rvert$	4.55
$\vdash \lvert x - y\rvert < d \Rightarrow y < x + d$	1.57
$\vdash \lvert\lvert x\rvert - \lvert y\rvert\rvert \leq \lvert x - y\rvert$	19.10
$\vdash \lvert x\rvert \leq k \Leftrightarrow -k \leq x \wedge x \leq k$	1.40
$\vdash 11x \leq 15 \wedge 6y \leq 5x \Rightarrow 23y \leq 27$	2.56

We have only encountered one interesting linear problem in our own practice that is not universal, and the main linear procedure can prove it in a time that is acceptable (at least, comparable to a hand proof): 119.43 seconds.

$$\vdash \forall a, f, k.\ (\forall e.\ k < e \Rightarrow f < ae) \Rightarrow f \leq ak$$

5.7 Summary and related work

The full algorithm is clearly not ready for use as a general-purpose tool, but we believe this is a very interesting avenue of research. There is enormous scope for optimizing special cases; we have only sketched a few possibilities and implemented one. Moreover, when eliminating variables between formulas where they have coefficients a and b, one could, instead of multiplying by b and a respectively, multiply by $b/gcd(a, b)$ and $a/gcd(a, b)$, given some care over the signs. This might yield better performance when it comes to eliminating the other variables. The optimized linear procedure, though of modest range, *is* fast enough to be a very useful general-purpose tool. In fact, it was used incessantly throughout much of the theory development detailed in previous chapters, and used to derive similar procedures for the integers and naturals as special cases.

Numerous theorem provers (e.g. NQTHM, EHDM, EVES, Nuprl and PVS) include some decision procedure similar to the linear one described here, many similarly restricted to the universal fragment. Indeed, perhaps the first real 'theorem prover' ever implemented on a computer was a Presburger procedure by Davis (1957). The implementation in HOL by Boulton (1993) was a pioneering experiment in incorporating standard decision procedures into an LCF-style theorem prover. Our implementation of the optimized linear case was heavily influenced by his work. We are not aware of any other implementation of a decision procedure for the full elementary theory in a comparable context; most research in this line seems to take place in the computer algebra community. Our implementation makes no claims to match these for efficiency, but gives a good illustration of how sophisticated analytical reasoning can be embedded in proforma theorems which can then be applied reasonably quickly. The variant of the Kreisel and Krivine algorithm that we use is novel in some ways.

The universal linear fragment is just a degenerate case of linear programming:[7] we want merely to check that there is no feasible solution to a set of linear constraints, rather than optimize some objective function subject to those constraints. This special case is not much easier than full linear programming, but there are many efficient algorithms for the latter. The classic simplex method (Dantzig 1963) often works well in practice, and recently new algorithms have been developed that have polynomial complexity; the first was due to Khachian (1979) and a version that looks practically promising is given by Karmarkar (1984). The variable elimination method used here cannot compete with these algorithms on large examples. It's questionable whether very large linear systems are likely to arise in typical mathematical or verification applications, though Corbett and Avrunin (1995) discuss the use of integer programming in a verification application to avoid exhaustive enumeration. In any case, it's possible to reduce tautology checking, which *is* of considerable practical significance, to integer programming. A fascinating survey of the connections between tautology checking and integer programming is given by Hooker (1988).

Acknowledgements

Thanks to Konrad Slind for first pointing out to me the decidability of this theory, and to James Davenport for getting me started with some pointers to the literature.

[7] Or integer programming in the case of $\mathbb{N}$ and $\mathbb{Z}$. In linear programming terminology our derived decision procedure for the integers, mentioned in passing above, solves integer problems by considering the real-number 'LP relaxation'.

6. Computer Algebra Systems

We contrast computer algebra systems and theorem provers, pointing out the strengths and weaknesses of each, and suggest a simple way to achieve a synthesis of some of the best features of both. Our method is based on the systematic separation of search for a solution and checking the solution, using a physical connection between systems. We describe the separation of proof search and checking, another key LCF implementation technique, in some detail and relate it to proof planning and to the complexity class NP. Finally, the method is illustrated by some concrete example of computer algebra results proved formally in HOL: the evaluation of trigonometric integrals.

6.1 Theorem provers vs. computer algebra systems

Computer algebra systems (CASs) have already been mentioned in the introduction. Superficially they seem similar to computer theorem provers: both are computer programs for helping people with formal symbolic manipulations. However in practice there is surprisingly little common ground between them, either as regards the internal workings of the systems themselves or their respective communities of implementors and users. A table of contrasts might include the following points. Computer algebra systems:

- Are used by (mostly applied) mathematicians, scientists and engineers.
- Perform mainly multiprecision arithmetic, operations on polynomials (usually over $\mathbb{R}$) and classical 'continuous' mathematics such as differentiation, integration and series expansion.
- Are easy to use, so much so that they are increasingly applied in education (though this is controversial).
- Work very quickly.
- Have little real concept of logical reasoning, and are often ill-defined or imprecise.
- Make mistakes, often as a result of deliberate design decisions rather than bugs (though certainly it is unlikely that such large and complex pieces of code are bug-free).

By contrast, theorem provers:

- Are mainly used by computer scientists interested in systems verification, or by logically-inclined mathematicians interested in formalization of mathematics or experimenting with new logics.
- Perform logical reasoning first and foremost, sometimes backed up by special proof procedures for particular domains such as linear arithmetic over the natural numbers or integers; they are typically biased towards 'discrete' mathematics. (Mizar is an exception here.)
- Are difficult to use. This is true in varying degrees; for example in the present author's opinion, Mizar is quite easy whereas HOL is quite difficult. Nevertheless none of them seem to approach the ease of use of CASs. Major systems, with Mizar again a notable exception (Szczerba 1989), are almost never used for education, though there are some 'toy' provers like Jape[1] specifically designed for that purpose.
- Work slowly. Again, this varies in degree, but they are much less competent at really big mathematical problems than CASs.
- Are fundamentally based on logic, and demarcate correct logical reasoning.
- Are rather reliable. This is especially true of LCF-style systems like HOL, where the design methodology keeps the critical core of the inference engine extremely small compared with the size of the whole system.

An obvious result of these contrasts is that computer theorem provers are much less popular than computer algebra systems. CASs can handle bread and butter problems in all branches of applied, and sometimes even pure, mathematics. By contrast, computer theorem provers focus on rather 'purist' forms of reasoning, whose details are not widely understood even by pure mathematicians. (Or are rejected by mathematicians — Brouwer for example actively opposed the formalization of mathematics.) However, since theorem provers do have notable advantages, it seems a pity to neglect them. Indeed, let's look at the defects of computer algebra systems in a little more detail.

As remarked by Corless and Jeffrey (1992), the typical computer algebra system supports a rather limited style of interaction. The user types in an expression E; the CAS cogitates, usually not for very long, before returning another expression E'. (If E and E' are identical, that usually means that the CAS was unable to do anything useful. Unfortunately, as we shall see, the converse does not always hold!) The implication is that we should accept the theorem $\vdash E = E'$. Occasionally some slightly more sophisticated data may be returned, e.g. a condition on the validity of the equation, or even a set of possible expressions $E'_1, \ldots, E'_n$ with corresponding conditions on validity, e.g.

$$\sqrt{x^2} = \begin{cases} x & \text{if } x \geq 0 \\ -x & \text{if } x \leq 0 \end{cases}$$

[1] See the Jape Web page
`http://www.comlab.ox.ac.uk/oucl/users/bernard.sufrin/jape.html`.

However, the simple equational style of interaction is by far the most usual. Certainly, CASs are almost never capable of expressing really sophisticated logical dependencies as theorem provers are.

Now consider the claim that CASs are 'ill-defined'. Well, what of these purported equational theorems that the CAS tries to convince us of? After our previous stress on the many interpretations of equality with respect to undefinedness, we can obviously wonder what the precise interpretation of equality is. For example, if the CAS claims $\frac{d}{dx}(1/x) = -1/x^2$, is it assuming an interpretation 'either both sides are undefined or both are defined and equal'? Or is it simply making a mistake and forgetting the condition $x \neq 0$? Very often this is not clear. There are other ambiguities too. For example, when a CAS says $(x^2 - 1)/(x - 1) = x + 1$, we might assume that it is either assuming an interpretation of equality 'where both sides are defined, they are equal' or just ignoring sideconditions. But the very meaning of expressions like $(x^2-1)/(x-1)$ is open to question. One can interpret such an expression in at least two ways. Most obviously, it is just an expression built from arithmetic operators on $\mathbb{R}$, containing one free variable x. But another interpretation is that it is to be regarded as denoting a rational function in one variable over $\mathbb{R}$, that is, a member of $\mathbb{R}(x)$, defined as the field of fractions of the polynomial ring $\mathbb{R}[x]$.[2] Here x does not really denote a free variable; it is just a notational convenience. And under this interpretation the above equation holds strictly: $x - 1$ is not the zero polynomial, so division by it is perfectly admissible.

Even when a CAS can be relied upon to give a result that admits a precise mathematical interpretation, that doesn't mean that its answers are always right. For example, a recent version of Maple[3] evaluates:

$$\int_{-1}^{1} \sqrt{x^2}\, dx = 0$$

What seems to happen is that the simplification $\sqrt{x^2} = x$ is applied, regardless of the sign of x. In general, CASs tend to perform simplifications fairly aggressively, even if they aren't strictly correct in all circumstances. The policy is to try always to do *something*, even if it isn't absolutely sound. After all, it often happens that ignoring a few singularities in the middle of a calculation does make no difference to the result. This policy may also be a consequence of the limited equational style of interaction that we have already drawn attention to. If the CAS has only two alternatives, to do nothing or to return an equation that is true only with a few provisos, it might be felt that it's better to do the latter. By contrast, designers of theorem provers try

---

[2] Equivalently, we can consider it as a member of the field resulting from adjoining an element x that is transcendental over the ground field.

[3] Maple V Release 2. Maple and Maple V are registered trademarks of Waterloo Maple Software.

hard to ensure that they do not make wrong inferences, even if this leads to its being hard to make their systems do anything useful at all.

We have already described a reasonably extensive theory of real analysis in HOL. Therefore it seems we have partly eliminated one defect of our theorem prover: its ability to tackle just discrete mathematics. Of course we haven't considered complex analysis, multivariate calculus, matrices, and many other topics. But we have made a reasonable start, and in general it seems clear that the typical discrete mathematics bias of theorem provers arises from the nature of existing verification efforts, or the lack of enthusiasm for the hard work of theory development, rather than any intrinsic difficulty. So the question arises: can we use our work to try to combine the best features of theorems provers and CASs? Below we describe just such a project, where CAS-type results are provided in HOL, but stated with logical precision and mediated by strict formal inference rules.

Now many computer algebra systems include complicated algorithms and heuristics for various tasks. Implementing these directly in the LCF style would be a major undertaking, and it seems unlikely that the results would be anything like as efficient. However one often sees, at least when one is especially looking, that many of the answers found may be *checked* relatively easily. The CAS can arrive at the result in its usual way, and need not be hampered by the need to produce any kind of formal proof. The eventual checking may then be done rigorously à la LCF, with proportionately little extra difficulty. To integrate finding and checking, we can physically link the prover and the CAS. In what follows, these themes appear several times, so we begin by discussing at length the issues that arise.

6.2 Finding and checking

Classical deductive presentations of mathematics, the style of which goes back to Euclid, often show little trace of how the results and the proofs were arrived at. Sometimes the process of discovery is very different, even in some cases arising via a complicated process of evolution, as shown in the study of Euler's theorem on polyhedra by Lakatos (1976). For example, Newton is popularly believed to have arrived at most of the theorems of *Principia* using calculus, but to have translated them into a purely geometric form so that they would be more easily understood, or more readily accepted as rigorous, by his contemporaries. Often the reasons are connected with the aesthetics of the deductive method; Gauss compared other considerations besides the deductive proof to the scaffolding used to construct a beautiful building, which should be taken down when the building is finished.

From the perspective of computer theorem proving, there are similarly interesting differences between proof finding and proof checking. For example, it is very straightforward and cheap to multiply together two large prime numbers on a computer, e.g.:

$$3490529510847650949147849619903898133417764638493387843990820577$$

and

$$32769132993266709549961988190834461413177642967992942539798288533$$

It's not even prohibitively hard to do it by hand. However going from the product (which we will call r to save space) back to the above factors seems, without prior knowledge of those factors, difficult. The security of certain cryptographic schemes depends on that (though perhaps not *only* on that). In fact the above factorization was set as a challenge ('RSA129'), and was eventually achieved by a cooperative effort of around a thousand users lavishing spare CPU cycles on the task.

6.2.1 Relevance to our topic

There are two contrasts between the tasks of finding the factorization and checking it, both significant for the business of implementation in computer theorem provers. The first is in computational complexity. We've already discussed the *practical* complexity. From a theoretical point of view, multiplying n-digit numbers even in the most naive way requires only n^2 operations. But factorizing an n-digit number is not even known to be polynomial in n, and certainly seems likely to be worse that n^2.[4] The second contrast is one of implementation complexity. Writing an adequate multiprecision arithmetic routine is not a very challenging programming exercise. But present-day factorization methods are rather complex — it's a hot research topic — and often rely for their justification on fairly highbrow mathematics.

The crucial point is that even under the LCF strictures, a result can be arrived at it any way whatsoever provided that it is *checked* by a rigorous reduction to primitive inferences. This idea has already been used (following Boulton) in the optimized linear arithmetic decision procedure, where the proof is found using efficient ad hoc data structures before being reduced to HOL primitives. Work on first order automation in HOL, e.g. that of Kumar, Kropf, and Schneider (1991), uses the same techniques: the search for a proof is conducted without HOL inferences, and when this (usually the speed-critical part) is finished, the proof (normally short) can be translated back to HOL.

In general, we want the search stage to produce some kind of 'certificate' that allows the result to be arrived at by proof with acceptable efficiency.

[4] The problem is known to be in P if the Extended Riemann Hypothesis holds. Also, it's generally not as hard to prove compositeness nonconstructively, e.g. it's pretty quick to check that $2^{r-1} \not\equiv 1 \pmod r$, so by Fermat's little theorem, r is composite.

In the case of factorization, the certificate was simply the factors. Often the certificate can be construed simply as the 'answer' and the checking process a confirmation of it. But as we shall see, other certificates are possible. Bundy's 'proof plans', for example, essentially use a complete proof as the certificate, clearly a uniquely convenient one for checking by inference. The earlier example of first order automation in HOL is similar, though there the proof search is computationally intensive, whereas in proof planning, the main difference is that the proof search involves sophisticated AI techniques. Indeed according to Bundy, Harmelen, Hesketh, and Smaill (1991), checking proof plans seems *slower* than finding them, though it is much easier to implement. In fact they report that 'it is an order of magnitude less expensive to find a plan than to execute it', though this may be due in part to a badly implemented inference engine and the relatively limited problem domain for the planner (inductive proofs).

6.2.2 Relationship to NP problems

The classic definition of the complexity class NP is that it is the class of problems solvable in polynomial time by a nondeterministic Turing machine (one that can explore multiple possibilities in parallel, e.g. by replicating itself). However, many complexity theory texts give another definition: it is the class of problems whose solutions may be *checked* in polynomial time on a *deterministic* Turing machine. Now when they are framed as decision problems, as they usually are, there is no 'solution' to the problems beyond yes/no; checking that is no different from finding it. But in general there exists for each problem a key piece of data called a *certificate* that can be used in polynomial time to confirm the result. Often this *is* the 'answer' to the problem if the problem is rephrased as 'find an x such that $P[x]$' rather than 'is there an x such that $P[x]$?'. But in general, the certificate can be some other piece of data. Indeed, to prove that the two characterizations of NP are equivalent, one uses the fact that the execution trace of a nondeterministic Turing machine can be used as the certificate; checking this can be done simply by interpreting it. The other way is easy: the NDTM can explore all possibilities, running the checking procedure on each.

The equivalence of the two definition is strongly reminiscent of Kleene's normal form theorem in recursive function theory. That says that unbounded search need only be done in one place; here we say that nondeterminism can be concentrated in one place. Indeed, there is a similar *logical* (or 'descriptive') version of both results: Kleene's theorem states that any recursive predicate can be expressed as a first order existential statement with primitive recursive, indeed Δ_1^0, body (Σ_1^0), while Fagin (1974) proves that NP problems are precisely those expressible as existential statements in second order logic over finite structures (Σ_1^1).

The close similarity with our wish for efficient proof checking should now be clear. We are interested in cases where a certificate can be produced by an algorithm, and this easily checked. Our version of the idea 'easily checkable' is less pure and more practical, since in the assessment of what can be checked 'easily' we include a number of somewhat arbitrary factors such as the nature of the formal system at issue and the mathematical and programming difficulty underlying the checking procedure. (For example, even if factoring numbers turns out to be in P, it will almost certainly be dramatically harder than multiplying the factors out again.) But the analogy is still strikingly close.

The complementary problems to the NP ones are the co-NP ones. Here it is *negative* answers that can be accompanied by a certificate allowing easy checking. A good example of a co-NP problem is tautology checking, the dual of the NP-complete problem of Boolean satisfiability. Boolean satisfiability admits an easily checked certificate, viz, a satisfying valuation, but it seems that no such certificate exists for tautologies. We may expect, therefore, that our analogs of co-NP complete problems will be harder to support with an efficient checking process. From a theoretical point of view this is almost true by definition, but the practical situation is not so clear. It may be that algorithms that are used with reasonable success to perform search in practice could produce a certificate that allows easy checking.

For example, a problem that looks intuitively complementary to the problem of factorization is primality testing. However as shown by Pratt (1975), short certificates are possible and so the problem is not only in co-NP but also in NP.[5] An especially strong form of this result is due to Pomerance (1987), who shows that every prime has an $O(log\ p)$ certificate, or more precisely that 'for every prime p there is a proof that it is prime that requires for its verification $(\frac{5}{2}+o(1))log_2p$ multiplications mod p'. Whether useful primality testing algorithms can naturally produce such certificates is another matter, but a related idea has been explored in practice by Elbers (1996).

6.2.3 What must be internalized?

The separation of proof search and proof checking offers an easy way of incorporating sophisticated algorithms, computationally intensive search techniques and elaborate heuristics, without compromising either the efficiency of search or the security of proofs eventually found. It is interesting to enquire which algorithms can, in theory and in practice, provide the appropriate certificates. If formal checkability is considered important, it may lead to a shift in emphasis in the development and selection of algorithms for mathematical computations.

We have placed in opposition two extreme ways of implementing an algorithm as an LCF derived rule: to implement it entirely inside the logic, justified by formal inference at each stage, or to perform an algorithm with-

[5] As already remarked, it's probably in P.

out any regard to logic, yet provide a separate check afterwards. However, there are intermediate possibilities, depending on what is required.

For example, consider the use of Knuth-Bendix completion to derive consequences from a set of algebraic laws. Slind (1991) has implemented this procedure in HOL, where at each stage the new equations are derived by inference. However the fact that any particular rewrite system resulting is canonical is *not* proved inside the logic. This could be done either specially for each particular system concerned, or by internalizing the algorithm and proving its correctness. Either would require much more work, and cost much more in efficiency. And if all we want is to prove *positive* consequences of the rewrites, this offers no benefits. On the other hand to prove *negative* results, e.g. that a group exists that does not satisfy a certain equation, then this kind of internalization would be necessary. Such a theme often appears in HOL, where the steps in an algorithm may all be justified by inference, but the overall reasoning justifying its usefulness, completeness, efficiency or whatever are completely external (one might say informal). We shall give an example below where the correctness of a procedure is easy to see, but its completeness requires slightly more substantial mathematics.

6.3 Combining systems

The general issue of combining theorem provers and other symbolic computation systems has recently been attracting more attention. As well as our own experiments with a computer algebra system, detailed below, HOL has for example been linked to other theorem provers (Archer, Fink, and Yang 1992) and to model checkers (Seger and Joyce 1991). Methodologies for cooperation between systems are classified by Calmet and Homann (1996) according to several different properties. For example, if more than two systems are involved, the network topology is significant: are there links between each pair or is all communication mediated by some central system? A related issue is which, if any, systems in the network act as master or slave. In our case, we use a system with just two components, HOL and Maple, and HOL is clearly the master. It would be interesting to extend the arrangement with multiple CASs; the intention would still be that HOL is the master, but some additional auction mechanism for prioritizing results from the CASs would be required.

6.3.1 Trust

One of the most interesting categorizations of such arrangements is according to *degree of trust*. For example, our work does not involve trusting Maple at all, since all its results are rigorously checked. However one might, at the other end of the scale, trust all Maple's results completely: if when given an expression E, Maple returns E', then the theorem $\vdash E = E'$ is accepted. Such an arrangement, exploiting a link between Isabelle and Maple, is described by Ballarin, Homann, and Calmet (1995). This runs the risk of importing into the theorem prover all the defects in correctness of the CAS, which we have already discussed. However it may, if used only for problems in a limited domain, be quite acceptable. For example, despite our best efforts, arithmetic by inference is very slow in HOL, and the results of CASs are generally pretty reliable. So one might use such a scheme, restricted to the evaluation of ground terms, perhaps making explicit in the HOL theorem, in the case of irrational numbers, the implied accuracy of the CAS's result. For example if '`evalf(Pi,20)`' in Maple returns `3.14159265358979323855`, we may assert the theorem:

$$\vdash |\pi - 3.1415926535897932385| < 10^{-18}$$

An interesting way of providing an intermediate level of trust was proposed by Mike Gordon.[6] This is to tag each theorem $\vdash \psi$ derived by trusting an external tool with an additional assumption logically equivalent to falsity. We can define a new constant symbol for this purpose, bearing the name of the external tool concerned; `MAPLE` in our case. The theorem `MAPLE` $\vdash \psi$ is, from a logical point of view, trivially true. But pragmatically it is quite appealing. First, it has a natural reading 'assuming Maple is sound, then ψ'. Moreover, any derived theorems that use this fact will automatically inherit the assumption `MAPLE` and any others like it, so indicating clearly the dependence of the theorem on the correctness of external tools.[7]

Finally, another possible method is to perform checking yet *defer* it until later, e.g. batching the checks and running them all overnight. This fits naturally into the framework of lazy theorems proposed by Boulton (1992). Of course, there is the defect that if one of the checks fails overnight, then the day's work might be invalidated, but one hopes that the external tool will generally give correct answers.

6.3.2 Implementation issues

There are various low-level details involved in linking systems. First, it is necessary to provide a translation between the concrete syntaxes used by the prover and CAS, which are generally different. In a heterogeneous system containing many systems, there is obviously a strong practical argument for a single accepted interlingua, since then only n translators need to be written instead of $n^2/2$. There have been a number of attempts to arrive at a standard language and translation system; recently many of these have been unified

[6] Message to info-hol mailing list on 13 Jan 93, available on the Web as `ftp://ftp.cl.cam.ac.uk/hvg/info-hol-archive/09xx/0972`.

[7] A variant of this idea is implemented as the 'oracles' mechanism in the latest version of Isabelle (Paulson 1994).

in an ambitious project called 'OpenMath'.[8] Time will tell whether this will be a success. We used our own ad hoc translation between HOL and Maple syntax.

As far as systems for managing the connection go, our approach follows the same lines as the CAS/PI system, which was designed by Kajler (1992) as a general system for interfacing and interconnecting symbolic computation systems. Like Kajler, we use important parts of the standard Centaur system from INRIA. This works very well, but Centaur is rather heavyweight, so in the future it might be worth exploring other alternatives. Perhaps now the most obvious candidate is Expect (Libes 1995), which can be used in a rather straightforward way to link programs and systems. Our arrangement is along the same lines as discussed by Clément, Montagnac, and Prunet (1991). The organization involves three different processes: HOL, Maple, and a bridge. Communication between them is by broadcasting messages. HOL and Maple can send and receive messages with strings representing formulas in their own syntax. For example, $(\sin x + \cos x)'$ is represented as `diff(sin(x)+cos(x),x)` in Maple but as `deriv x.(sin x)+(cos x)` in HOL. The bridge performs this data coercion automatically. Communicating by broadcasting makes the prover completely independent of the CAS: HOL just requests an answer from an oracle. This means that it would be quite possible to connect a different CAS without any visible change on the prover side. Moreover Maple acts as a server, so several HOL sessions can share the same Maple session.[9] The HOL session can interact with the CAS via a single function `call_CAS` whose type is *term* → *string* → *term*. Its first argument is the term to transform, and the second is the transformation to apply, e.g. `SIMPLIFY` or `FACTORIZE`.

6.4 Applications

Let us now see how some typical features of computer algebra can be soundly supported in our combined system. The most elementary use of computer algebra systems is to perform arbitrary-precision integer and rational arithmetic. (Though elementary, the author has talked to a physicist who said this is all he uses CASs for!) We've already seen how this can be supported in HOL. Moreover, we have seen how real number approximation can be handled in HOL too; although CASs often also have the ability to deal with radicals like $\sqrt{7}$ or even general algebraic numbers in some situations. For example we can ask Maple to factorize $x^3 + 5$ in the algebraic extension field $\mathbb{Q}(\sqrt[3]{5})$,[10] and get the result $(x^2 - \sqrt[3]{5}x + (\sqrt[3]{5})^2)(x + \sqrt[3]{5})$. We do not provide any special facilities for algebraic numbers in HOL, though it does not seem

[8] See the OpenMath Web page, `http://www.openmath.org/`.

[9] The interaction is stateless on the CAS side.

[10] The polynomial ring $\mathbb{Q}[x]$, modulo the polynomial $x^3 - 5$.

to be difficult in principle to do so. Perhaps it's better done over $\mathbb{C}$ rather than $\mathbb{R}$, but that also presents no difficulty except for the pragmatic problem of a further profusion of number system types.

Despite their emphasis on 'continuous' mathematics, most CASs have a number of algorithms for dealing with divisibility properties of integers, e.g. primality testing, factorization and the finding of GCDs. We will not discuss this at length here for three reasons: (1) we have already used factorization and primality testing in our general discussion of finding vs. checking; (2) this is rather off the main topic of our book; and (3) many of the same issues arise in a more interesting form with polynomials, which we treat below. We will just note a couple of points. First, it would be interesting from our point of view to have better facilities for providing certificates of primality wherever possible than are provided by current systems. Another interesting issue is that many CASs also provide a 'probabilistic' primality test, whose result is not guaranteed, and it would be interesting to see what, if any, formal reading in HOL can be derived from such a statement.

6.4.1 Polynomial operations

Strictly speaking, one should distinguish carefully between polynomials as objects (members of $\mathbb{R}[x]$), their associated function ($\mathbb{R} \to \mathbb{R}$) and the value of the function for a particular x. Such ambiguities are especially insidious since many statements, e.g. factorizations like $x^2 - 1 = (x - 1)(x + 1)$, can be read in any of these ways, though as we have already noted, in the case of rational functions there is a subtle distinction. But when one wishes to consider the primality of a polynomial or the GCD of a set of polynomials, these statements only really make sense when the polynomials are regarded as objects of the ring $\mathbb{R}[x]$. We have already seen how polynomials, regarded as real number expressions, can be dealt with in HOL. Let us now examine briefly how polynomials as objects are formalized in HOL, since it involves a rather subtle trick.

Our theory of polynomials is generic over arbitrary rings whose carrier is a whole type α (though in the applications that follow, α is always real). The corresponding type of polynomials is $(\alpha)poly$. This means that, although we only deal directly with univariate polynomials, one can get polynomials in several variables by iterating the polynomial type constructor. The obvious representation for polynomials (found in many algebra texts) is as functions $f : \mathbb{N} \to \alpha$ such that for all sufficiently large n we have $f(n) = 0$. The special role of 0 is a problem: HOL has no dependent types, so the type constructor cannot be parametrized by the zero element of the ring. We get round this by using the ε operator to yield a canonical element of each type, so we define the type with $\varepsilon x.\ \top$ playing the role of the zero element. This and the zero element are then automatically swapped by pseudo type bijections parametrized by the zero of the ring.

Now let us look at how some polynomial properties can be proved in the combined HOL-Maple system. The most straightforward is the case of polynomial factorization. Just as with the example of integer factorization, any answer given by the CAS can be checked easily in HOL. It is simply necessary to multiply out the factors and prove that the two results are equal by collecting together similar terms. This latter operation can be done in two different ways, corresponding to the view of a polynomial as a real-valued expression or a member of the polynomial ring. Both are straightforward; for the former we use the tools used in the decision procedure for canonical polynomial expressions. For example, we can easily get theorems such as:

```
|- x pow 4 - y pow 4 = (x - y) * (x + y) * (x pow 2 + y pow 2)
```

If a polynomial is reducible, then its factors are an ideal certificate. Hence a small variant of the above scheme suffices to prove reducibility. However the converse is not true. When Maple, given a query '`irreduc(x ** 2 + y ** 2 - 1)`' responds 'true', that gives us no help at all in checking the result. It is an interesting question, which we do not investigate here, whether a convenient certificate *could* be given, by analogy with Pratt's certificates for prime numbers. Cantor (1981) proves that polynomial-time checkable certificates exist for univariate polynomials over the integers, though it isn't clear whether practical algorithms can find them. In the absence of some certificate, it seems the only way to prove an irreducibility theorem in HOL is to execute some standard algorithm inside the logic, by proof. For example, it's fairly easy to prove the above example by trying all possible factors, which necessarily have lower degree. It might not even be hard to prove Kronecker's criterion. However, it would not be quite so straightforward to implement more sophisticated algorithms.

Between these two extremes of checkability lies the interesting example of finding GCDs. If we ask Maple to find the GCD of $x^2 - 1$ and $x^5 + 1$ using its `gcd` function, for example, it responds with $x + 1$. How can this result be checked? Well, it's certainly straightforward to check that this is *a* common divisor. If we don't want to code polynomial division ourselves in HOL, we can call Maple's `divide` function, and then simply verify the product as above. But how can we prove that $x + 1$ is a *greatest* common divisor?[11] At first sight, there is no easy way, short of replicating something like the Euclidean algorithm inside the logic (though that isn't a really difficult prospect).

However, a variant of Maple's GCD algorithm, called `gcdex` will, given polynomials p and q, produce not just the GCD d, but also two other polynomials r and s such that $d = pr + qs$. Indeed, the coefficients in this sort of Bezout identity follow easily from the Euclidean GCD algorithm. For example, applied to $x^2 - 1$ and $x^5 + 1$ we get the following equation:

[11] The use of 'greatest' is a misnomer: in a general ring we say that a is a GCD of b and c iff it is a common divisor, and any other common divisor of b and c divides a. For example, both 2 and -2 are GCDs of 8 and 10 over $\mathbb{Z}$.

$$(-x^3 - x)(x^2 - 1) + 1(x^5 + 1) = x + 1$$

This again can be checked easily, and from that, the fact that $x + 1$ is the *greatest* common divisor follows by an easily proved theorem, since any common factor of $x^2 - 1$ and $x^5 + 1$ must, by the above equation, divide $x + 1$ too. So here, given a certificate slightly more elaborate than simply the answer, easy and efficient checking is possible.

Groebner bases (Weispfenning and Becker 1993) give rise to a number of interesting CAS algorithms. Buchberger's algorithm, applied to a set of polynomials defining an ideal, derives a Groebner basis, which is a canonical set of polynomials (subject to some appropriate ordering among the variables) that describes the same ideal. Crudely speaking, it is a generalization of Euclidean division to the multivariate case; it also has a close relationship to Knuth-Bendix completion of a set of rewrite rules. Groebner bases give a way of solving various equality and membership problems for polynomial ideals.[12] The possibility of separating search from checking for Buchberger's algorithm is quite interesting. It *is* much easier to show that a given set is a Groebner basis than to calculate it, but to prove that the Groebner basis corresponds to the same ideal would seem to require something like the sequence of divisions used by the algorithm be copied inside the logic. However these are not too difficult, and at least the correctness of Buchberger's algorithm need not be justified in the theorem prover.[13] Not surprisingly, this is closely related to the completion example that we have already cited.

6.4.2 Differentiation

We have already mentioned that we found it convenient to provide an automatic conversion, `DIFF_CONV`, for proving results about the derivatives of particular expressions. This is not very difficult. It is well-known that there are systematic approaches to differentiation; such methods are taught in schools. One has rules for differentiating algebraic combinations, i.e. sums, differences, products and quotients, as well as certain basic functions like x^n, $sin(x)$ and e^x. Using the chain rule, these may be plugged together to give the derivative of the result. Just such an algorithm has been implemented in HOL. It retains a set of theorems for composing derivatives, which the user may augment to deal with any new functions. Initially, it contains theorems for derivatives of sums, products, quotients, inverses, negations and powers. When the user adds a new theorem to the set, it is first processed into a compositional form, using the chain rule. For example the theorem for differentiating *sin*:

---

[12] It can be used to solve a limited range of quantifier elimination problems for the reals. But in contrast to algebrically closed fields, there is no simple relationship over $\mathbb{R}$ between ideal membership and the roots of the polynomials involved.

[13] In fact Théry (1997) has recently verified a version of Buchberger's algorithm in the Coq system.

```
|- !x. (sin diffl cos(x))(x)
```

becomes:

```
|- (g diffl m)(x) ==> ((\x. sin(g x)) diffl (cos(g x) * m))(x)
```

This set of theorems is indexed by term nets, to allow efficient lookup.[14] To find the derivative of an expression $\lambda x. t[x]$, the function first checks if $t[x]$ is just x, in which case the derivative is 1, or does not have x free, in which case the derivative is 0. Otherwise, it attempts to find a theorem for the head operator of the term, and backchains through this theorem. Any resulting hypotheses are split into two sets: those that are themselves derivative assertions (head operator `diffl`) and those that are not. The former group are attacked by a recursive call, the latter group accumulated in the assumptions. The recursion yields some additional variable instantiations and the results follow. If no derivative theorem for the relevant operator is available, then a new variable is introduced as a postulated derivative. Finally, if the original expression is not a lambda expression, then an η-expansion is performed automatically. For example, the expression 'sin' is then acceptable.

Here are some examples. If we don't include the basic theorem about the derivative of sin, then a derivative l is postulated:

```
#DIFF_CONV '\x. sin x + x';;
|- !l x.
    ((\x. sin x) diffl l)(x)
    ==> ((\x. sin x + x) diffl (l + &1))(x)
```

However once we include the theorem `DIFF_SIN` in the basic derivatives, we get the answer directly:

```
#DIFF_CONV '\x. sin x + x';;
|- !x. ((\x. sin x + x) diffl (cos x * &1 + &1))(x)
```

Note that we get a trivial multiple of 1, because for the sake of regularity, the procedure treats $sin(x)$ as a degenerate instance of the chain rule, so multiplies the result by x's derivative! However, it is easy to eliminate most of these trivia by a simple rewrite of the resulting theorem. A few basic simplification strategies are packaged up as `DIFF_SIMP_CONV`. As a final example, note how the appropriate side-conditions are derived automatically:

```
#DIFF_SIMP_CONV '\x. sin(x) + (&1 / cos(x))';;
   |- !x. ~(cos x = &0)
          ==> ((\x. (sin x) + ((&1) / (cos x))) diffl
               ((cos x) + ((sin x) / ((cos x) pow 2))))(x)
```

[14] Term nets are a well-known indexing method for tree structures, introduced into Cambridge LCF's rewriting by Paulson (1987).

If we chose, we could manually simplify the condition using the theorem COS_ZERO:

```
|- !x. (cos x = &0) =
       (?n. ~EVEN n /\ (x = (&n) * (pi / (&2)))) \/
       (?n. ~EVEN n /\ (x = --((&n) * (pi / (&2)))))
```

6.4.3 Integration

It is well-known that integration is more difficult than differentiation. There are systematic rules of transformation such as integration by parts, but these cannot always be applied in a mechanical way to find integrals for arbitrary expressions. Instead, one is usually taught to rely on knowledge of a large number of particular derivatives, together with a few special tricks. (For example, faced with the prospect of integrating $1/(1+x^2)$, one is hardly likely to think of the arctangent function, unless one already knows what its derivative is.) Many integrals can then be reduced to these well-known archetypes by processes of transformation, some systematic, like the use of partial fractions, others ad hoc and even based on guesswork.

It is not widely appreciated that algorithms *do* exist that can solve certain classes of integration problems in a completely mechanical way. For example, Davenport (1981) describes an algorithm that suffices for arbitrary rational functions. However there are still classes for which no systematic technique is known, and many CASs rely on a formalization of typical human tricks.

Now, for indefinite integrals, there is rather a simple checking procedure, namely differentiating the result. Strictly, we should distinguish between finding indefinite integrals and finding antiderivatives. However the majority of everyday integration problems can be solved by finding an antiderivative. Moreover, since our formalization of the integral obeys the Fundamental Theorem of Calculus, we know conversely that it is sufficient to find an antiderivative. If we were basing our work on the Lebesgue or Riemann integral, we would also need to prove that the function concerned is actually integrable, e.g. is of bounded variation. For example, let us try to find the integral:

$$\int_0^x sin(u)^3 \, du$$

If we ask Maple, it tells us that the result is $-\frac{1}{3}sin(x)^2cos(x)-\frac{2}{3}cos(x)+\frac{2}{3}$, which we will write as $f(x)$. Now if we could prove that $\frac{d}{dx}f(x) = sin(x)^3$, then by the Fundamental Theorem of Calculus, we would have:

$$\int_0^x sin(u)^3 \, du = f(x) - f(0)$$

and since we also have $f(0) = 0$ (this amounts to checking that the right 'constant of integration' has been used) Maple's result would be confirmed. There is certainly no difficulty in differentiating $f(x)$ inside HOL, using DIFF_CONV. We get the theorem:[15]

$$\vdash \frac{d}{dx} f(x) = -\frac{1}{3}(2sin(x)cos(x)cos(x) - sin(x)^3) + \frac{2}{3}sin(x)$$

Unfortunately, even after routine simplification, we have not derived $sin(x)^3$. In general, our scheme of using checking *does* rely on the simplification steps being powerful enough to prove that we have the result we wanted, even if differentiation has left it in a slightly different form. Here our simplification is not powerful enough. This is not just a defect of our toy system; Maple itself gives more or less the same result when asked to perform the differentiation. We need something domain-specific.

It is not hard to give a simplification procedure that suffices for proving that a polynomial in $sin(x)$ and $cos(x)$ is identically zero.[16] The idea is that if the polynomial has a factor $sin(x)^2 + cos(x)^2 - 1$ it is certainly zero, and moreover the reverse is true: if the polynomial is identically zero then it has such a factor. Indeed $\forall x.\ p(sin(x), cos(x)) = 0$ iff $\forall u, v.\ u^2 + v^2 = 1 \Rightarrow p(u, v) = 0$, because these different set of variables parametrize the same values. Considering this over $\mathbb{C}[u, v]$, where $u^2 + v^2 - 1$ is still irreducible and therefore squarefree, the Hilbert Nullstellensatz tells us that $u^2 + v^2 - 1$ divides $p(u, v)$; but the coefficients in the quotient must be rational.[17]

What's more, this procedure nicely illustrates the previous application of Maple to factorization problems. If we ask Maple to divide $-\frac{1}{3}(2uvv - u^3) + \frac{2}{3}u - u^3$ by $u^2 + v^2 - 1$ and check the result in HOL, we get a theorem:

$$\vdash -\frac{1}{3}(2uvv - u^3) + \frac{2}{3}u - u^3 = -\frac{2}{3}u(u^2 + v^2 - 1)$$

which contains the required factor. From this we get the result we wanted, which in HOL notation is:

```
|- Dint(&0,x) (\u. sin(u) pow 3)
               (--(&1 / &3) * (sin x) pow 2 * cos x
               - (&2 / &3) * cos x + &2 / &3)
```

15 As usual we actually deal with the relational form in HOL, but we write it this way for familiarity's sake.

16 Alternatively, as pointed out to the author by Nikolaj Bjørner, writing $cos(x) = (e^{ix} + e^{-ix})/2$ etc. allows a fairly direct simplification strategy, given some basic properties of *complex* numbers.

17 An alternative direct proof was shown to the author by G. K. Sankaran. Consider the polynomials concerned as polynomials in u, i.e. keep v fixed. We can divide $p(u, v)$ by $u^2 + (v^2 - 1)$ and the remainder will be linear in u; say $p(u, v) = q(u, v)(u^2 + v^2 - 1) + g(v)u + h(v)$. Moreover $g(v)u + h(v)$ is by hypothesis zero wherever $u^2 + v^2 - 1$ is. But there are infinitely many such pairs (u, v) with v rational and u irrational, and $g(v)$ must be zero for all those values. A polynomial can only have finitely many zeros, so $g(v)$ must be the zero polynomial, and hence so is $h(v)$.

Here are some runtimes for the evaluation of similar integrals. Note that the most costly part is the subsequent algebraic simplification, rather than the differentiation. Partly this is because of the use of a rather crude technique,[18] partly because the expressions get quite large and require a certain amount of rational arithmetic. For example, the integration of $sin^{10}x$ requires a proof of:

$$\begin{aligned}
&-((((9u^8)v)v - (uu^9))\tfrac{1}{10})- \\
&(((7u^6)v)v - (uu^7))\tfrac{9}{80} - \\
&(((5u^4)v)v - (uu^5))\tfrac{21}{160} - \\
&(((3u^2)v)v - (uu^3))\tfrac{21}{128} - \\
&(vv - (uu))\tfrac{63}{256} + \tfrac{63}{256} - u^{10} \\
&= (-\tfrac{9}{10}u^8 - \tfrac{63}{80}u^6 - \tfrac{21}{32}u^4 - \tfrac{63}{128}u^2 - \tfrac{63}{256})(u^2 + v^2 - 1)
\end{aligned}$$

Function to integrate	Differentiation time	Simplification time
$sin\ x$	0.06	0.96
$sin^2 x$	0.38	4.17
$sin^3 x$	0.63	7.33
$sin^4 x$	0.75	14.08
$sin^5 x$	1.12	20.67
$sin^6 x$	1.48	26.33
$sin^7 x$	1.60	38.37
$sin^8 x$	1.80	42.53
$sin^9 x$	1.65	49.03
$sin^{10} x$	1.93	70.00
$sin\ x\ cos\ x$	0.23	2.30
$sin^2 x\ cos\ x$	0.21	2.41
$sin^6 x\ cos^4 x$	1.98	45.73

In fact, it is now suggested (e.g. by Fateman) that the most inclusive and reliable method for integration is simply the use of very large lookup tables, of the kind that used to be employed extensively in the days before computer algebra. Einwohner and Fateman (1995) are accumulating such results in machine-readable form, and even experimenting with optical character recognition (OCR) to scan in published tables. They remark:

> We recognize the inevitability that some published entries are outright flawed. We hope to be able to check the answers as we enter them. Unfortunately some of the table entries, *as well as some algorithmically derived answers*, are erroneous principally in missing essential restrictions on the parameters of the input and output.

[18] We use the tools for manipulating canonical polynomial expressions from the decision procedure. Apart from being unoptimized for this application, powers of a variable are evaluated highly inefficiently and many common subexpressions are transformed separately.

An interesting application for theorem proving would be to prove the correctness of such tables of results once and for all, perhaps using human guidance where necessary. The techniques described above are quite limited, in that in general they apply only to indefinite integrals. (Though there are some special circumstances where one can achieve similar checking by differentiating with respect to free variables in the body of the integral, leading to the popular trick (Almkvist and Zeilberger 1990) of 'differentiating under the integral sign'.) But in general there seems no reason why we could not undertake such checking in a system like HOL.

6.4.4 Other examples

We will just note some other instances in computer algebra where checking is relatively easy. The first is in solving all kinds of equations. Indeed, the integration problem is a trivial differential equation, and the same techniques should work for more complicated differential equations. Ordinary algebraic equations, including simultaneous equations, admit the same general strategy; indeed since the verification part often involves calculation with ground terms only, it is generally easier. However to check the solution of some algebraic equations expressed in terms of radicals, superior methods for manipulating algebraic numbers would be useful. At present we would be obliged to use approximations.

Another interesting example is summation in finite terms. This process is closely analogous to integration, and the problem is similarly difficult to solve algorithmically; again people usually rely on guesswork and a few standard tricks. However just as indefinite integrals may be checked by differentiation, summations with a variable as the upper limit of summation may be checked by finite differences. To verify that $\Sigma_{i=1}^{n} f(i) = F(n)$, we simply need to check that for arbitrary n, $F(n) - F(n-1) = f(n)$ (analogous to differentiation), as well as that $F(0) = 0$ (analogous to checking the constant of integration). The result then follows by induction.

6.5 Summary and related work

The most substantial attempt to create a sound and reliable computer algebra system is probably the work of Beeson (1992) on Mathpert. This is a computer algebra system designed mainly for educational use, and the intended use dictates two important features. First, it attempts to perform only logically sound steps. Second, it tries to justify its reasoning instead of producing *ex cathedra* pronouncements. Since it has not yet been used extensively, it's hard to judge how successful it is. By contrast, our effort is relatively modest, but gets quite a long way for relatively little implementation difficulty.

Conversely, the most convincing example of importing real logical expressiveness and theorem proving power into computer algebra is the work of

Clarke and Zhao (1991) on Analytica. Here a theorem prover is coded in the Mathematica[19] system. It is capable of proving some remarkably complicated theorems, e.g. some expressions due to Ramanujan, completely automatically. However, it still relies on Mathematica's native simplifier, so it is does yet provide such a high level of rigour as our LCF approach.

Our theme of checkability has been stressed by a number of researchers, notably Blum (1993). He suggests that in many situations, checking results may be more practical and effective than verifying code. This argument is related to, in some sense a generalization of, arguments by Harrison (1995b) in favour of the LCF approach to theorem proving rather than so-called 'reflection'. Mehlhorn et al. (1996) describe the addition of result checking to routines in the LEDA library of C++ routines for computational geometry (e.g. finding convex hulls and Voronoi diagrams). Our interest is a little different in that it involves checking according to a formal deductive calculus. However it seems that many of the same issues arise. For instance, they remark that 'a convex hull program that delivers a triangulation of the hull is much easier to check than a program that only returns the hull polytope', which parallels our example of a certificate for the GCD consisting of more than just the answer. Out of all the applications of this idea, perhaps the closest to our interests is the work of Clarke and Zhao (1991), who prove certain summations by verifying Mathematica's answers using induction.

Acknowledgements

Much of the work described in this chapter was done in collaboration with Laurent Théry. He implemented the physical connection, as well as inspiring many of the important intellectual themes. The connection with NP problems was pointed out to me by Konrad Slind, who in addition gave me some useful advice regarding the literature. Thanks also to Gilles Kahn for pointing me at Fateman's work on integral tables, and to Norm Megill for making me aware of the work on prime certificates.

[19] Mathematica is a registered trademark of Wolfram Research Inc.

7. Floating Point Verification

One of the most promising application areas for theorem proving is the verification of floating point hardware, a topic that has recently attracted some attention. We explain why a theorem prover equipped with a theory of real numbers is a good vehicle for this kind of application, showing in particular how it allows a natural specification style. We discuss different ways of specifying the accuracy of basic floating-point calculations, and as an illustration, verify simple algorithms for evaluating square roots and natural logarithms.

7.1 Motivation

The correctness of floating point arithmetic operations is a topic of some current concern. A flaw in Intel's flagship Pentium processor's floating-point division instruction was discovered by a user and became public on 30th October 1994 — a technical analysis of the bug is given by Pratt (1995). After considerable vacillation, Intel eventually (on 21st December 1994) agreed to a policy of no-questions-asked replacement, and wrote off $306 million to cover the costs. This is a good illustration of how hardware correctness, even when not a matter of life and death, can be of tremendous financial, and public relations, significance.

Theorem proving seems a promising approach to verifying floating point arithmetic, at least when the theorem prover is equipped with a good theory of real numbers. We have two reasons in mind.

7.1.1 Comprehensible specifications

Floating-point numbers correspond to certain real numbers. This is the whole raison d'être of floating point arithmetic, and it is on this basis, rather than in terms of bitstrings, that one would like to specify the intended behaviour of floating-point operations. Suppose F represents the set of floating point numbers. There is a natural valuation function $v : F \to \mathbb{R}$ (for the sake of simplicity, we ignore special values like infinities and NaNs), and using this we may specify the intended behaviour of floating-point operations.

Consider a mathematical function of one argument, say $f : \mathbb{R} \to \mathbb{R}$; examples might include unary negation, square root and sin. Suppose we are interested in specifying the behaviour of a floating-point counterpart $f^* : F \to F$. An obvious way is to demand that for each $a \in F$, the value $v(f^*(a))$ is 'close to' the true mathematical value $f(v(a))$. One might like to express this by saying that a corresponding diagram 'almost commutes':

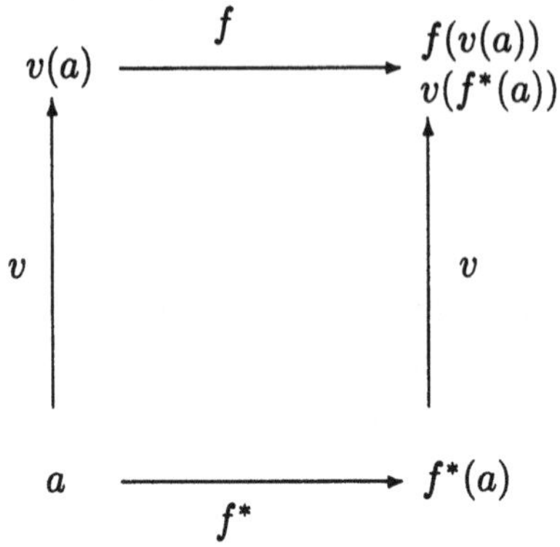

Similarly, for a function g of n arguments we can consider the relationship between $g(v(a_1), \ldots, v(a_n))$ and $v(g^*(a_1, \ldots, a_n))$. Of course we need to be precise about what we mean by 'close to'; this point is considered in detail later. But certainly, the above style of specification seems the most natural, and the most satisfactory for relating floating point computations to the real number calculations they are intended to approximate.

7.1.2 Mathematical infrastructure

The correctness of more complex floating-point algorithms often depends on some quite sophisticated mathematics. One of the attractions of using a theorem prover is that this can be integrated with the verification itself. For example Archer and Linz (1991) remark, regarding verification of higher-level numerical algorithms:

> As with the verification of non-numerical programs, automated support for the proof process, such as a verification condition generator, can greatly help in maintaining the correct assertions, which often become complex. [...] Ideally, one wishes to augment such support with the ability to check proofs of assertions in the underlying theory.

In particular using a theorem prover:

- One can avoid *mathematical* errors in the assumptions underlying the algorithm's correctness or efficiency.
- One can reliably generate any necessary precomputed constants by justifying them inside the theorem prover.

Often, transcendental functions are approximated using Taylor series, Chebyshev polynomials, rational functions or some more sophisticated technique. Proofs that these techniques give the desired level of accuracy tend to be nontrivial. For example, one might need to justify the algorithm due to Remes (1934) for finding coefficients in 'optimal' rational number approximations — see Fike (1968) for a presentation.[1]. Moreover, one might wish to calculate the constants with a high level of assurance with proven error bounds. Typically, availability of cheap memory and increasing levels of miniaturization mean that large lookup tables of precomputed constants are an increasingly common way of improving floating point performance in software and hardware implementations.[2] And it was an error in just such a lookup table that caused the Pentium bug.

7.2 Floating point error analysis

Because of the finite limits of floating-point numbers, mathematical operations on them are usually inexact. An important aspect of numerical programming is keeping the errors within reasonable bounds. In fixed point computation, we are usually interested in absolute errors, i.e. the difference $\epsilon = x^* - x$ between the approximate value calculated, x^*, and the true mathematical value x. However floating point values fluctuate so widely in magnitude that this is not usually significant; instead we are more interested in the *relative* error, δ, where $x^* = x(1 + \delta)$. (Sometimes one even sees sophisticated combinations of the two.) An alternative to relative error which is often more natural is to measure 'units in the last place' (ulps). Roughly speaking, one *ulp* of a floating point number is the value of its least significant bit. In fact, it is often preferable to define one *ulp* in terms of the exact real number being approximated, as the distance between the two closest floating point numbers to it. This makes round-to-nearest correspond to a maximum error of $0.5ulp$.

Whatever measure of error we use, there are several different ways of analyzing how it propagates through expressions. The most obvious is to express the error in the result as a function of error in the input argument(s). These results may then be composed according to the actual sequence of computations performed. An ingenious alternative is to proceed *backwards*; that is, given an error in the output, to calculate the perturbation in the input that would yield the same result for the exact mathematical function. As shown by Wilkinson (1963), this 'backward error analysis' turns out to give much less pessimistic bounds in many important numerical algorithms, e.g. the finding of eigenvalues, where a forward error analysis suggests, contrary to experience, that the accuracy easily becomes hopelessly bad.

A rather radical alternative, proposed by Sutherland (1984) in the context of program verification, is not to attempt numerical estimation of errors at

[1] Actually, in recent work, we have found it better to do post-hoc proofs of the quality of approximations derived by this algorithm, rather than justify the algorithm itself — see Appendix B

[2] Though one needs to be careful that this does not cause cache misses.

all. Instead, it is merely ensured that as the accuracy of individual operations tends to infinity, so does the accuracy of the result. This can be formalized using the notion of infinitesimal from Nonstandard Analysis. Although such an analysis cannot yield any real quantitative information about error bounds, it is rather easy to apply and as reported by Hoover and McCullough (1993), can discover many bugs in software. This is because various functions exhibit discontinuities (e.g. the square root function becomes undefined below zero) which will cause the asymptotic result to fail unless they are properly taken account of by the algorithm.

7.3 Specifying floating point operations

Our proposal above was to specify the correctness of floating point operations by comparing the approximate floating point result with the true mathematical result, using the valuation function $v : F \to \mathbb{R}$ to mediate between the realms of floating point and real numbers. However there are quite a few different ways in which this can be done.

7.3.1 Round to nearest

It seems that the most stringent specification we can give is that the computed result is the closest representable floating-point number to the true mathematical answer. For example, for a multiplication operation MUL this means:

$$\forall a_1, a_2 \in F. \neg\exists a' \in F. |v(a') - v(a_1)v(a_2)| < |v(\mathtt{MUL}(a_1, a_2)) - v(a_1)v(a_2)|$$

Actually, though, this is too lax to specify the result of a floating point operation completely, since it may happen that there are two equally close representable values. Humans are usually taught to round 0.5000... up to 1, but the IEEE (1985) standard for binary floating point arithmetic mandates a (default) rounding mode of 'round to even':

> An implementation of this standard shall provide round to nearest as the default rounding mode. In this mode the representable value nearest to the infinitely precise result shall be delivered; if the two nearest representable values are equally near, the one with its least significant bit zero shall be delivered.

Fixing the choice between such alternatives has the merit that operations will behave identically on all implementations, even if they use quite different (correct!) algorithms. The IEEE Standard demands that the operations of addition, subtraction, multiplication, division, and square root be performed as if done with full accuracy then rounded using this scheme or whichever of the others is in force (see later). This approach based on the exact mathematical result ensures that the operations share important characteristics of the abstract counterparts. For example, multiplication is:

- Symmetric, i.e. $\texttt{MUL}(a,b) = \texttt{MUL}(b,a)$
- Monotone, i.e. if $0 \leq v(a) \leq v(a')$ and $0 \leq v(b) \leq v(b')$ then we also have $v(\texttt{MUL}(a,b)) \leq v(\texttt{MUL}(a',b'))$.

Empirical studies suggest that it also avoids a tendency for floating point results to drift systematically. Using the 'human style' rounding, there is a tendency to drift upwards, presumably because the situation of being midway between two representable values happens quite often. For example, when adding normalized numbers with the same sign and identical exponents, exactly one bit, which is often 1, must be discarded. (By contrast, subtraction of such pairs of numbers is always exact.)

7.3.2 Bounded relative error

The above correctness criterion is sometimes unrealistically stringent for other functions such as the transcendentals *sin*, *cos*, *exp*, *ln* etc; this may be why the IEEE standard does not discuss such functions. The difficulty is known as the 'table maker's dilemma', and arises because being able to approximate a real number arbitrarily closely does *not* in general mean that one can decide the correctly rounded digits in a positional expansion. For example, a value x one is approximating may be exactly the rational number 3.15. This being the case, knowing for any given $n \in N$ that $|x - 3.15| < 10^{-n}$ does not help to decide whether 3.1 or 3.2 is the correctly rounded result to one decimal place. For similar reasons, the original definition of 'computable real number' by Turing (1936), based on a computable decimal expansion, turned out to be inadequate, and was subsequently modified, because the sum of two computable numbers may be uncomputable in this sense.

Now, if one knows that x is irrational, then for any troublesomely close rational q, one must eventually be able to find n such that $|x - q| > 10^{-n}$ and so decide the decimal expansion. The only trouble is, one does not know *a priori* that a number one is concerned with is irrational.[3] For example, it is still unknown whether Euler's constant:

$$\gamma = lim_{n \to \infty}(1 + \frac{1}{2} + \cdots + \frac{1}{n} - ln(n))$$

[3] It's easy to dress up the Halting Problem as a question 'is this computable number rational?'. Define the nth approximant to be zero if the machine is still going after n steps, otherwise an approximant to some known irrational like π. Though if x is rational it has a trivially computable decimal expansion. This shows one must distinguish carefully between a function's being computable and having a computable graph.

is rational. In the case of the common transcendental functions like *sin*, there are results of number theory assuring us that for nontrivial rational arguments the result is irrational.[4] And all floating-point values *are* rational of course, at least in conventional representations, though not in novel schemes like the exponential towers proposed by Clenshaw and Olver (1984). However the appropriate bounds on the evaluation accuracy required to ensure correct rounding in all cases may be impractically hard to find analytically. Exhaustive search is hardly an option for double precision, though perhaps more systematic ways are feasible.[5] Even if the evaluation accuracy bounds are found, they may be very much larger than the required accuracy in the result. Goldberg (1991) gives the illustrative example of:

$$e^{1.626} = 5.083499996273\ldots$$

To round the result correctly to 4 decimal places, one needs to approximate it to within 10^{-9}.[6] In summary then, it is usually appropriate to settle for a weaker criterion. For example if `SIN` : $F \times F \to F$ is a floating point `SIN` function, we might ask, for some suitable small δ that (assuming f is a nonzero floating point number):

$$\left|\frac{v(\mathtt{SIN}(f))}{sin(v(f))} - 1\right| < \delta$$

An alternative is to say that the result is *one of the two* closest representable values to the true mathematical result. However the above seems at least as useful practically, and can give sharper error bounds; in general the second closest representable value might be almost 1*ulp* (unit in the last place) different from the true mathematical value.

7.3.3 Error commensurate with likely input error

Even guaranteeing small relative errors, while quite possible, can be rather difficult. For example, consider the evaluation of $sin(x)$ where x is just below the largest representable number in IEEE double precision, say about $2^{1024} \approx 1.8 \times 10^{308}$. Most underlying algorithms for *sin*, e.g. Taylor series,

---

4 In fact for nonzero *algebraic* $x \in \mathbb{C}$ it follows from the work of Lindemann (1882) that all the following are *transcendental*: e^x, $sin(x)$, $cos(x)$, $tan(x)$, $sinh(x)$, $cosh(x)$, $sin^{-1}(x)$, and for $x \neq 1$ too, $cos^{-1}(x)$ and $ln(x)$. Baker (1975) gives a proof.

5 There are results in transcendental number theory, e.g. those due to Mahler (1953), that can bound the distance between a transcendental and a rational approximation. However these tend to be very general — for example we are only concerned with rationals of the form $\frac{p}{2^q}$ rather than general rationals — and would probably need substantial further work to give bounds sharp enough for practical purposes.

6 On naive probabilistic grounds one would expect to need in general something like twice the apparent accuracy.

only work, or only converge reasonably quickly, for fairly small arguments. Therefore the usual first step is to perform an appropriate range reduction, e.g. finding an x' with $-\pi \leq x' < \pi$ and $x' - x = 2n\pi$ for $n \in \mathbb{Z}$. However in this case, performing the range reduction accurately is not straightforward. Simply evaluating $x/(2\pi)$, rounding this to an integer n and then evaluating $x' = x - 2n\pi$, where the operations are performed with anything like normal accuracy, is obviously going to return 0, since x and $n\pi$ are going to be identical down to about the 300th decimal place, far more than is representable. If accurate rounding is required, it's necessary to store $\frac{1}{\pi}$ or some such number to over a thousand bits, and perform the range reduction calculation to that accuracy (Payne and Hanek 1983).

Since this sort of super-accurate computation need only be kicked in when the argument is large, a situation that one hopes will, in the hands of a good numerical programmer, be exceptional, it need not affect average performance. However in a hardware implementation in particular, there may be a significant cost in chip area which might be put to better use. It seems that many designers do not make the required effort. Ng (1992) showed the huge disparities between (then) current computing systems on $sin(10^{22})$: only a very few systems gave the right answer.

One can certainly defend the policy of giving inaccurate answers in such situations, and this leads us to a new notion of correctness. Floating point calculations are generally not performed in number-theoretic applications. The *inputs* to floating point calculations are usually inexact, either because they are necessarily approximate measures of physical quantities, or because they are the rounded-off results of previous floating point calculations. One might expect that the average floating point value is inaccurate by at least $0.5ulp$. Accordingly, we may say that a function is correct if its disparity from the true mathematical answer could be explained by a very small (say $0.5ulp$) perturbation of the input:

$$\exists \eta.\ |\eta| < 0.5ulp \wedge f(v(x)(1+\eta)) = v(f^*(x))$$

There is an obvious analogy between this approach and backward error analysis. It has the merit of offering a simple criterion that is not sensitive to the 'condition' of the problem, i.e. the relative swings in output with input. Nevertheless, as pointed out by Kahan,[7] one sometimes wants the appropriate 'input perturbations' for various functions to be correlated in some way. For example, when calculating:

$$f(x) = \begin{cases} \frac{1}{2} & \text{if } x = 1 \\ -atn(ln(x))/acos(x)^2 & \text{if } x < 1 \\ atn(ln(x))/acos(x)^2 & \text{if } x > 1 \end{cases}$$

[7] See, e.g. the notes for CS 267, available on the Web as `http://HTTP.CS.Berkeley.EDU/~wkahan/ieee754status/cs267fp.ps`.

replacing $ln(x)$ and $acos(x)$ by $ln(x')$ and $acos(x'')$ for close but uncorrelated x' and x'' can lead to grave inaccuracy as $x \to 1$, even though the function as a whole is well-behaved there.

7.4 Idealized integer and floating point operations

We will illustrate our discussion with a couple of examples of HOL-based verification. We assume without further analysis that n-bit integer arithmetic operations (signed and unsigned), are available for any given n, and show how to implement floating point operations using these as components. We are not really interested in the hardware level here, so representations in terms of bit strings seem a gratuitous complication. Instead we simply use natural numbers to represent the n-bit values. Whatever the value of n, the representing type is simply `:num`; in one sense it is artificial to mix up all the values like this, but in the absence of dependent types, it seems the most straightforward approach. In any case, it allows the extension of an m-bit value to an n-bit value ($n \geq m$) without any explicit coercion function.

The arithmetic operators are intended to model the usual truncating operations on n-bit numbers, in the signed case, interpreting the numbers in 2s complement fashion. Several operations are the same regardless of whether they are regarded as signed or unsigned, namely addition (**add**), negation (**neg**) and subtraction (**sub**)

```
|- add n x y = (x + y) MOD (2 EXP n)

|- neg n x = 2 EXP n - x MOD (2 EXP n)

|- sub n x y = add n x (neg n y)
```

There are unsigned strict (`ult`) and nonstrict (`ule`) comparisons, together with left and right unsigned ('logical') shift operations `sll` and `srl`, together with a function **umask** to mask out all but the bottom b bits:

```
|- ult n x y = x MOD (2 EXP n) < y MOD (2 EXP n)

|- ule n x y = x MOD (2 EXP n) <= y MOD (2 EXP n)

|- srl n b x = (x MOD (2 EXP n)) DIV (2 EXP b)

|- sll n b x = (x * 2 EXP b) MOD (2 EXP n)

|- umask n b x = (x MOD 2 EXP b) MOD (2 EXP n)
```

There are corresponding signed versions called `slt`, `sle`, `sra` and `sla`, whose definition we will not show here. Finally, there is a function to regard an n-bit value as a binary fraction, and return its real number value:

```
|- mval n x = &(x MOD (2 EXP n)) / &2 pow n
```

In our work with binary fractions of value m, we will assume that inputs obey $\frac{1}{2} \leq m < 1$; in other words the top bit of m is set. Such floating point values are said to be *normalized*. By using normalized numbers we make the maximum use of the bitfield available to the mantissa.[8] On the other hand when the exponent drops below the minimum representable value e_{min}, the number cannot be represented at all (whereas it could, albeit to lower accuracy, by relaxing the normalization condition). We also cannot represent 0 directly as a normalized number, so in practice one allocates a normally unused value for the exponent to represent zero. In fact the IEEE standard includes both positive and negative zeros, as well as positive and negative infinities and NaN's (NaN = not a number) to represent exceptional conditions in a way that (usually) propagates through a calculation.

The algorithms we choose to verify are for the square root and natural logarithm functions. We give quantitative error bounds via systematic proofs in HOL that the algorithms preserve appropriate invariants. In such floating point operations, we can separate three sources of error:

1. Error in the initial range reduction.
2. Error because of the essentially approximate nature of the main algorithm, even assuming ideal operations.
3. Error because of rounding error in the implementation of the main algorithm.

In the cases of the functions we consider, the initial range reduction is particularly simple, and we discuss it only briefly. The main effort is involved in quantifying errors of the second and third kind.

7.5 A square root algorithm

First we explain the verification of a *natural number* square root algorithm and then show how to adapt it to our floating point situation. The algorithm is a binary version of a quite well-known technique for extracting square roots by hand, analogous to performing long division. The algorithm is iterative; at each step we feed in two more bits of the input (starting with the most significant end), and get one more bit of the output (ditto). More precisely, we maintain three numbers, x_n, y_n and r_n, all zero for $n = 0$. At each stage we claim the following invariant property holds:

$$x_n = y_n^2 + r_n \wedge r_n \leq 2y_n$$

[8] Since the top mantissa bit is always 1 in a normalized number, it is redundant, and can be used, e.g. to store the sign. Actually the IEEE standard interprets a mantissa as $1 + m$, not $(1 + m)/2$.

This means that $y_n^2 \leq x_n < (y_n + 1)^2$, the latter inequality because $x_n < y_n^2 + 2y_n + 1$ is equivalent to $x_n \leq y_n^2 + 2y_n$, i.e. $r_n \leq 2y_n$ (remember that we are in the domain of the natural numbers). That is, y_n is the truncation of the square root of x_n to the natural number below it, and r_n is the remainder resulting from this truncation. Accordingly, when the full input has been fed in, y_n will hold a good approximation to the square root of the intended value x. The iteration step is as follows, where s_n is the value (considered as a 2-bit binary integer) of the next two bits shifted in. We always set $x_{n+1} = 4x_n + s_n$, which amounts to shifting in the next two input bits. Also:

- If $4y_n + 1 \leq 4r_n + s_n$ then $y_{n+1} = 2y_n + 1$ and $r_{n+1} = (4r_n + s_n) - (4y_n + 1)$
- Otherwise $y_{n+1} = 2y_n$ and $r_{n+1} = 4r_n + s_n$.

It is not hard to see that this step does preserve the invariant property. Consider the two cases separately:

1. If $4y_n + 1 \leq 4r_n + s_n$ then we have

$$\begin{aligned} y_{n+1}^2 + r_{n+1} &= (2y_n + 1)^2 + ((4r_n + s_n) - (4y_n + 1)) \\ &= 4y_n^2 + 4y_n + 1 + 4r_n + s_n - 4y_n - 1 \\ &= 4y_n^2 + 4r_n + s_n \\ &= 4(y_n^2 + r_n) + s_n \\ &= 4x_n + s_n \end{aligned}$$

   and furthermore

$$\begin{aligned} r_{n+1} \leq 2y_{n+1} &\Leftrightarrow (4r_n + s_n) - (4y_n + 1) \leq 2(2y_n + 1) \\ &\Leftrightarrow 4r_n + s_n \leq 8y_n + 3 \\ &\Leftrightarrow 4r_n + s_n \leq 4(2y_n) + 3 \end{aligned}$$

   But this is true because $r_n \leq 2y_n$ and $s_n \leq 3$ (since s_n is only 2 bits wide).
2. Otherwise we have $4y_n + 1 > 4r_n + s_n$, so

$$\begin{aligned} y_{n+1}^2 + r_{n+1} &= (2y_n)^2 + (4r_n + s_n) \\ &= 4y_n^2 + 4r_n + s_n \\ &= 4(y_n^2 + r_n) + s_n \\ &= 4x_n + s_n \end{aligned}$$

   and furthermore, using the above hypothesis:

$$\begin{aligned} r_{n+1} \leq 2y_{n+1} &\Leftrightarrow 4r_n + s_n \leq 2(2y_n) \\ &\Leftrightarrow 4r_n + s_n \leq 4y_n \\ &\Leftrightarrow 4r_n + s_n < 4y_n + 1 \end{aligned}$$

since we are dealing with natural numbers; but this is true by hypothesis.

This shows that the basic algorithm works as claimed. The corresponding proof can be rendered in HOL without much difficulty. We assume that the inputs and desired outputs are n-bit values; to ensure no overflow occurs in intermediate calculations, we find it is necessary to store r and y as $n+2$ bit values. The stepwise algorithm is specified as follows:

```
|- SQRT_STEP n k x (y,r) =
     let s = if 2 * SUC k <= n
             then umask n 2 (srl n (n - 2 * SUC k) x)
             else 0 in
     let r' = add (n + 2) (sll (n + 2) 2 r) s in
     let y' = add (n + 2) (sll (n + 2) 2 y) 1 in
     if ule (n + 2) y' r'
     then add n (sll n 1 y) 1,sub (n + 2) r' y'
     else sll n 1 y,r'
```

Thus, all operations are done by shifting and masking. There are now a series of slightly tedious but relatively easy proofs showing that under certain assumptions, no overflow will occur, and the above assignments therefore correspond to their idealized mathematical counterparts. There is an additional lemma proving that the rather intricate assignments of s above do indeed build up the number $2^n x$ from the top, two bits at a time:

```
|- EVEN n /\ k < n
   ==> (((2 EXP PRE n * x) DIV 4 EXP (n - SUC k)) MOD 4 =
        if 2 * SUC k <= n
        then (x DIV 2 EXP (SUC n - 2 * SUC k)) MOD 4
        else if 2 * k = n then (2 * x) MOD 4 else 0)
```

Putting all the parts together, and defining the full algorithm as an n times iteration of the above step:

```
|- (SQRT_ITER n 0 x (y,r) = y,r) /\
   (!k. SQRT_ITER n (SUC k) x (y,r) =
        SQRT_STEP n k x (SQRT_ITER n k x (y,r)))
```

we get the final correctness theorem by induction:

```
|- !n. EVEN n /\ x < 2 EXP n /\ (y,r = SQRT_ITER n n x (0,0))
       ==> y < 2 EXP n /\
           (2 EXP n * x = y * y + r) /\
           r <= 2 * y
```

In order to extend this to a floating point algorithm, it is merely necessary to fail on negative inputs, and halve the exponent, so not much interesting detail arises here. We have:

$$\sqrt{2^{2e}\frac{m}{2^n}} = 2^e\frac{\sqrt{2^n m}}{2^n}$$

and therefore our earlier algorithm to approximate $\sqrt{2^n x}$ for an n-bit value x is exactly what's needed. However if the exponent is *odd*, then the above operation needs to be modified. We have:

$$\sqrt{2^{2e+1}\frac{m}{2^n}} = \sqrt{2^{2e+2}\frac{m}{2^{n+1}}} = 2^{e+1}\frac{\sqrt{2^{n-1}m}}{2^n}$$

Therefore we have an alternative version of the algorithm which will approximate the square root of $2^{n-1}m$ rather than $2^n m$. Its stepwise behaviour is as follows:

```
|- SQRT_STEP' n k x (y,r) =
      let s = if 2 * SUC k <= n
              then umask n 2 (srl n (SUC n - 2 * SUC k) x)
              else if 2 * k = n then umask n 2 (sll n 1 x)
              else 0 in
      let r' = add (n + 2) (sll (n + 2) 2 r) s in
      let y' = add (n + 2) (sll (n + 2) 2 y) 1 in
      if ule (n + 2) y' r'
      then add n (sll n 1 y) 1,sub (n + 2) r' y'
      else sll n 1 y,r'
```

and it yields the corresponding correctness theorem:

```
|- !n. EVEN n /\ x < 2 EXP n /\ (y,r = SQRT_ITER' n n x (0,0))
      ==> y < 2 EXP n /\
          (2 EXP PRE n * x = y * y + r) /\
          r <= 2 * y
```

It is possible to refine the algorithm so that it yields the closest value to the true square root, i.e. rounds to nearest rather than downwards. It is simply necessary to add 1 to the result iff $y \leq r$ (the proof is not hard). However in the case of $2^{n-1}m$, this may lead to a carry and the necessity of renormalization, which we don't want to concern ourselves with. However, it is easy to give a correctness assertion in terms of the actual real number square root. Observe that:

$$\left(\frac{\sqrt{x/2^n}}{y/2^n}\right)^2 = \frac{2^n x}{y^2} = 1 + \frac{r}{y^2}$$

But it's easy to see that $y \geq 2^{n-1}$ provided $x \geq 2^{n-2}$, and so since $r \leq 2y$, the above is $\leq 1 + 2/2^{n-1}$. Now since:

$$0 < d \wedge 0 \leq x \wedge 1 \leq x^2 \wedge x^2 \leq 1 + 2d \Rightarrow 1 \leq x \wedge x < 1 + d$$

this relative error is halved in the square root. In HOL, the final theorem yielding the relative error is:

```
|- !n. EVEN(n) /\
       2 EXP (n - 2) <= x /\
       x < 2 EXP n /\
       (y,r = SQRT_ITER n n x (0,0))
       ==> 2 EXP (n - 1) <= y /\
           y < 2 EXP n /\
           ?d. &0 <= d /\ d < inv(&2 pow (PRE n)) /\
               (sqrt(mval(n) x) = mval(n) y * (&1 + d))
```

It is worth noting that assumptions easily overlooked in informal practice (e.g. that n is even) are fully brought out in this formal treatment.

7.6 A CORDIC natural logarithm algorithm

The CORDIC (Co-Ordinate Rotation DIgital Computer) technique, invented by Volder (1959) and developed further by Walther (1971), provides a simple scheme for calculating a wide range of transcendental functions. It is an iterative algorithm which at stage k requires multiplications only by 1 ± 2^{-k}, which can be done efficiently by a shift and add. Logarithms and exponentials work in a particularly direct and simple way; trigonometric and inverse trigonometric functions are not much harder.[9] The algorithm relies on fairly small precomputed constant tables, typically of the function concerned applied to arguments 1 ± 2^{-k} for k ranging from 0 up to at least the number of bits required in the result. We have already seen how such tables may be generated in HOL.

Here is a CORDIC algorithm to find the natural logarithm of x, which we shall suppose to be in the range $\frac{1}{2} \leq x < 1$, evidently the case for the mantissa of a normalized floating point number. We start off with $x_0 = x$ and $y_0 = 0$. At each stage:

- If $x_k(1+2^{-(k+1)}) < 1$ then $x_{k+1} = x_k(1+2^{-(k+1)})$ and $y_{k+1} = y_k + ln(1+2^{-(k+1)})$.
- Otherwise $x_{k+1} = x_k$ and $y_{k+1} = y_k$.

[9] The standard CORDIC algorithm for the trigonometric functions needs to calculate $sin(x)$ and $cos(x)$ together. However this is often useful, since empirical studies of code show that the majority of instances of $sin(x)$ are accompanied by a nearby instance of $cos(x)$.

Now it is easy to establish by induction on k that at stage k we have $x_k < 1$ but $x_k(1+2^{-k}) \geq 1$, and that $y_k = ln(x_k) - ln(x)$. For example, if we know $x_k(1+2^{-k}) \geq 1$, then either:

- We have $x_{k+1} = x_k(1+2^{-(k+1)}) < 1$, and

$$\begin{aligned} x_{k+1}(1+2^{-(k+1)}) &= x_k(1+2^{-(k+1)})^2 \\ &= x_k(1+2^{-k}+2^{-2(k+1)}) \\ &\geq x_k(1+2^{-k}) \\ &\geq 1 \end{aligned}$$

- We have $x_k(1+2^{-(k+1)}) \geq 1$ and $x_{k+1} = x_k$, so $x_{k+1}(1+2^{-(k+1)}) \geq 1$ as required.

So, using the monotonicity of ln (for a positive argument) we find that at stage k we have $ln(x_k) + ln(1+2^{-k}) \geq 0$. Now we use the following theorem, which will be applied frequently in what follows:

$$\forall x.\, 0 \leq x \Rightarrow ln(1+x) \leq x$$

This is derived in HOL from $\forall x.\ 1+x \leq e^x$, which itself follows easily by truncation of the power series for the exponential function. This yields $-2^{-k} \leq ln(x_k) < 0$. Since $y_k = ln(x_k) - ln(x)$ this yields $|y_k + ln(x)| \leq 2^{-k}$, so by a suitable number of iterations, we can approximate $ln(x)$ (actually $-ln(x)$) as closely as we please.

The above was based on an abstract mathematical description of the algorithm. However a real implementation will introduce additional errors, because the right shift will lose bits, and the stored logarithm values will be inexact. In our verification we must take note of these facts. We parametrize the verification by two numbers n, the number of bits used for the x_k, and m, the number of bits used for the y_k. Accordingly, the stepwise behaviour of the algorithm is specified as follows:

```
|- CORDIC_STEP n m logs k (x,y) =
      let x' = srl n (SUC k) x in
      let xn = neg n x in
      if ult n x' xn
      then add n x x',add m y (logs (SUC k))
      else x,y
```

Note that in order to test whether $x_k(1+2^{-(k+1)}) > 1$ we need to test whether the expression on the left causes overflow. For simplicity, we actually perform an unsigned comparison of x_k and $-x_k 2^{-(k+1)}$. Here $logs(k)$ is supposed to represent the stored natural number approximation to $2^m ln(1+2^{-k})$; assumptions about this function appear later as conditions in the correctness assertions. The full algorithm is specified as follows; it simply iterates the above step.

```
|- (CORDIC_ITER n m logs 0 (x,y) = x,y) /\
   (!k. CORDIC_ITER n m logs (SUC k) (x,y) =
        CORDIC_STEP n m logs k (CORDIC_ITER n m logs k (x,y)))
```

For convenience we separate off the x_k and y_k components using the following additional definitions:

```
|- CORDIC_X n m logs k x = FST (CORDIC_ITER n m logs k (x,0))

|- CORDIC_Y n m logs k x = SND (CORDIC_ITER n m logs k (x,0))
```

The first stage in the verification is to move from the truncating 'machine' operations and express the behaviour of the algorithm in terms of natural number arithmetic. This amounts to verifying that overflow never occurs in any of the calculations. For the x_k this is true per construction, so the proof is easy; for the y_k it's a little tricker. We make the additional assumption that $\forall i.\ 2^i logs(i) \leq 2^m$; since $ln(1+2^{-i}) \leq 2^{-i}$, the logarithm approximations can be chosen so that this is true. Given that, we have by induction that $2^k(\Sigma_{i=0}^k logs(i+1)) \leq 2^m(2^k - 1)$, and so overflow never occurs. This yields the following theorems:

```
|- ~(x = 0) /\ x < 2 EXP n
   ==> (CORDIC_X n m logs 0 x = x) /\
       (!k. CORDIC_X n m logs (SUC k) x =
            if CORDIC_X n m logs k x
               + CORDIC_X n m logs k x DIV 2 EXP (SUC k)
               < 2 EXP n
            then CORDIC_X n m logs k x +
                 CORDIC_X n m logs k x DIV (2 EXP (SUC k))
            else CORDIC_X n m logs k x)

|- ~(x = 0) /\ x < 2 EXP n /\ (!i. 2 EXP i * logs i <= 2 EXP m)
   ==> (CORDIC_Y n m logs 0 x = 0) /\
       (!k. CORDIC_Y n m logs (SUC k) x =
            if CORDIC_X n m logs k x
               + CORDIC_X n m logs k x DIV (2 EXP (SUC k))
               < 2 EXP n
            then CORDIC_Y n m logs k x + logs (SUC k)
            else CORDIC_Y n m logs k x)
```

Given that, the only remaining task is to transcribe the following reasoning into HOL. This is a little tedious, but not really difficult. The abstract mathematical analysis above needs two modifications. The calculation of $x_k(1+2^{-(k+1)})$ includes a truncation which we denote by ϵ_k, and the logarithm values, while they do not overflow, are inaccurate by δ_k. Constants (parametrized by x and various other variables) are used in the HOL proofs to denote these errors. We can easily prove from the above that $0 \leq \epsilon_k < 2^{-n}$, and we assume $|\delta_i| < 2^{-m}$ for all i up to the number of iterations, k. The step phase of the algorithm becomes:

- If $x_k(1+2^{-(k+1)}) - \epsilon_k < 1$ then $x_{k+1} = x_k(1+2^{-(k+1)}) - \epsilon_k$ and $y_{k+1} = y_k + ln(1+2^{-(k+1)}) - \delta_k$.
- Otherwise $x_{k+1} = x_k$ and $y_{k+1} = y_k$.

Clearly we still have $x_k < 1$. However the other properties become more complicated. We find that it is convenient to assume that $k+2 \leq n$, i.e. that n is a little more than the maximum number of iterations used. On that basis we find that:

$$x_k(1+2^{-k}) \geq (1 - k2^{-n})$$

Certainly this is true for $k = 0$ (it just says $x \geq \frac{1}{2}$). So suppose it is true for k; we will prove it for $k+1$. There are two cases to consider.

1. If $x_k(1+2^{-(k+1)}) - \epsilon_k < 1$, then we have

$$\begin{aligned} x_{k+1}(1+2^{-(k+1)}) &= (x_k(1+2^{-(k+1)}) - \epsilon_k)(1+2^{-(k+1)}) \\ &= x_k(1+2^{-k}) + x_k 2^{-2(k+1)} - \epsilon_k(1+2^{-(k+1)}) \\ &\geq (1-k2^{-n}) + (\frac{1}{2})2^{-2(k+1)} - 2^{-n}(1+2^{-(k+1)}) \\ &= (1-(k+1)2^{-n}) + (\frac{1}{2})2^{-2(k+1)} - 2^{-n}2^{-(k+1)} \end{aligned}$$

   It suffices, then, to show that $2^{-n}2^{-(k+1)} \leq (\frac{1}{2})2^{-2(k+1)}$. But this is equivalent to $k+2 \leq n$, true by hypothesis.
2. Otherwise we have $x_k(1+2^{-(k+1)}) - \epsilon_k \geq 1$ and $x_{k+1} = x_k$, so

$$\begin{aligned} x_{k+1}(1+2^{-(k+1)}) &= x_k(1+2^{-(k+1)}) \\ &\geq x_k(1+2^{-(k+1)}) - \epsilon_k \\ &\geq 1 \\ &\geq 1-(k+1)2^{-n} \end{aligned}$$

As far as the accuracy of the corresponding logarithm we accumulate is concerned, we claim:

$$|y_k - (ln(x_k) - ln(x))| \leq k(4\,2^{-n} + 2^{-m})$$

Again this is trivially true for $k = 0$, so consider the two cases.

1. If $x_k(1+2^{-(k+1)}) - \epsilon_k < 1$, then we have for the overall error $E = |y_{k+1} - (ln(x_{k+1}) - ln(x))|$:

$$\begin{aligned} E &= |(y_k + ln(1+2^{-(k+1)}) + \delta_k) \\ &\quad -(ln(x_k(1+2^{-(k+1)}) - \epsilon_k) - ln(x))| \\ &= |(y_k - (ln(x_k) - ln(x))) + ln(1+2^{-(k+1)}) + ln(x_k) \\ &\quad -ln(x_k(1+2^{-(k+1)}) - \epsilon_k) + \delta_k| \\ &\leq |y_k - (ln(x_k) - ln(x))| + |ln\left(\frac{x_k(1+2^{-(k+1)})}{x_k(1+2^{-(k+1)}) - \epsilon_k}\right)| + |\delta_k| \\ &\leq k(4\,2^{-n} + 2^{-m}) + |ln\left(1 + \frac{\epsilon_k}{x_k(1+2^{-(k+1)}) - \epsilon_k}\right)| + 2^{-m} \\ &\leq k(4\,2^{-n}) + (k+1)2^{-m} + \frac{\epsilon_k}{x_k(1+2^{-(k+1)}) - \epsilon_k} \\ &\leq k(4\,2^{-n}) + (k+1)2^{-m} + \frac{2^{-n}}{(\frac{1}{2}) - 2^{-n}} \\ &\leq k(4\,2^{-n}) + (k+1)2^{-m} + \frac{2^{-n}}{\frac{1}{2} - \frac{1}{4}} \\ &= (k+1)(4\,2^{-n} + 2^{-m}) \end{aligned}$$

(Of course the bound on $\frac{2^{-n}}{(\frac{1}{2})-2^{-n}}$ could be sharpened if, as is likely in practice, n is much larger than 2.)

2. Otherwise $x_{k+1} = x_k$ and $y_{k+1} = y_k$, so since $k(4\,2^{-n} + 2^{-m}) \leq (k+1)(4\,2^{-n} + 2^{-m})$ the result follows.

Finally we can analyze the overall error bound after k iterations. Since $|y_k + ln(x)| \leq |y_k - (ln(x_k) - ln(x))| + |ln(x_k)|$, we just need to find a bound for $|ln(x_k)|$. Because

$$1 \geq x_k \geq \frac{1 - k2^{-n}}{1 + 2^{-k}}$$

we have:

$$\begin{aligned} |ln(x_k)| &\leq ln\left(\frac{1+2^{-k}}{1-k2^{-n}}\right) \\ &\leq ln\left(\frac{(1+2^{-k})(1+2k2^{-n})}{(1-k2^{-n})(1+2k2^{-n})}\right) \\ &= ln\left(\frac{(1+2^{-k})(1+2k2^{-n})}{1+k2^{-n}-2k^2 2^{-2n}}\right) \\ &= ln(1+2^{-k}) + ln(1+2k2^{-n}) - ln(1+k2^{-n}-2k^2 2^{-2n}) \\ &\leq 2^{-k} + 2k2^{-n} - ln(1+k2^{-n}-2k^2 2^{-2n}) \end{aligned}$$

If we introduce the additional assumption that $k \leq 2^{n-1}$, hardly a stringent requirement since in practice n will be at least 20, then we find that $ln(1+k2^{-n} - 2k^2 2^{-2n}) \geq ln(1) = 0$, so we have $|ln(x_k)| \leq 2^{-k} + 2k2^{-n}$. We get our grand total error bound:

$$|y_k + ln(x)| \leq k(6\,2^{-n} + 2^{-m}) + 2^{-k}$$

This expression is rather complicated, and would have become still more so if certain error bounds had been sharpened. However if we have a desired accuracy (say N bits), it's easy to find appropriate n, m and k to make sure it is met. Note that the assumptions about the accuracy of the logarithm approximations are in exactly the form that we can generate automatically for any particular values.

```
|- inv(&2) <= mval n x /\
   mval n x < &1 /\
   k + 2 <= n /\
   k <= 2 EXP (n - 1) /\
   (!i. 2 EXP i * logs i <= 2 EXP m) /\
   (!i. i <= k ==>
         abs(&(logs(SUC i))
             - &2 pow m * ln(&1 + inv(&2 pow SUC i))) < &1)
   ==> abs(mval m (CORDIC_Y n m logs k x) + ln (mval n x))
       <= &k * (&6 * inv(&(2 EXP n)) + inv(&(2 EXP m))) +
          inv(&(2 EXP k))
```

We do not analyze the range reduction by adding $e\,ln(2)$ (where e is the exponent and $ln(2)$ is also a prestored constant). It does not, given a reasonable multiplication and addition operation, make any substantial difference to the accuracy of the result, and it would oblige us to concern ourselves with various other floating point operations like alignment and renormalization; such an analysis would be quite straightforward, but add nothing of interest.

However the final range reduction can make an important difference to the provable error bounds. The *absolute* error is essentially unaffected, but since the magnitude of the result may change dramatically, the relative error can be correspondingly affected. Let us suppose that $e = 0$ (so the original number is actually equal to m) and $m \approx 1$, or alternatively that $e = 1$ and $m \approx \frac{1}{2}$ when the same phenomenon will arise after range reduction. We have seen that the *absolute* error in the main part of the algorithm can be quite tightly bounded by appropriate choices of k, n and m. However, if $m \approx 1$, the resulting logarithm is very close to zero. Therefore the *relative* error, after the result is renormalized, could be very large. There are essentially two ways to deal with this:

1. When the original number $1-x$ is close to 1, use an alternative algorithm. One could choose m quite a bit bigger than the number of bits required

in the mantissa, say N_3 larger. Now if x is at least 2^{-N_3}, we are OK. Otherwise an alternative algorithm can be kicked in, which is adequate for x below 2^{-N_3}. For example, one might evaluate the first one or two terms of the Taylor series for $-ln(1-x) = x + \frac{x^2}{2} + \frac{x^3}{3} + \cdots$, which if x is small converges quickly.

2. One can accept an error specification of the third kind we discussed above, i.e. 'commensurate with the error in the input'. If our final error is ϵ, the necessary relative perturbation δ in the argument x satisfies $y_k = -ln(x(1+\delta))$, and so

$$-ln(x(1+\delta)) = -ln(x) + \epsilon$$

Therefore $-ln(1+\delta) = \epsilon$ and so $\delta = e^{-\epsilon} - 1$. For small ϵ, we have $\delta \approx -\epsilon$; certainly $|\delta| \leq 2|\epsilon|$ for any reasonable ϵ. Consequently, the error in this form can be very tightly bounded even without extensions of the algorithm.

7.7 Summary and related work

We have illustrated how the current version of the HOL system contains ample mathematical infrastructure to verify floating point algorithms and derive precise error bounds. We believe that such proofs, precisely because they are rather messy and intricate, are difficult for humans to get right, and because they demand substantial mathematical infrastructure, difficult to tackle with tools like model checkers that are often useful in hardware verification.

The two examples chosen were quite simple, and we ignored precise details of the floating point format (e.g. representation of zero). However the gap between these examples and real designs is quantitative, not qualitative. We also neglected the details of how the algorithms are represented in hardware (or software). This is deliberate, since we want to focus on algorithms rather than the details of implementation. However, it might be more attractive to describe algorithms in something closer to the traditional Pascal-style pseudocode rather than as a HOL recursive function. There are already several HOL embeddings of such languages together with verification environments, e.g. the work of von Wright, Hekanaho, Luostarinen, and Långbacka (1993). A few of the other verification efforts we discuss below get closer to the hardware level.

The IEEE standard for binary floating point arithmetic has been formalized in Z by Barratt (1989). The radix-indpendent IEEE standard 854, which is similar in the main ideas, has been formalized by Miner (1995), while Wichmann (1989) describes a similar project in VDM for the more abstract 'Brown model' of floating point. There have been a number of hand proofs of correctness of floating point algorithms; notably, Barratt gives one for the INMOS Transputer's floating point unit. Only recently have there been many mechanized proofs; we are aware of none that involve transcendental functions. Some work on integer arithmetic operations is relevant too, e.g. the verification in NQTHM of a divider by Verkest, Claesen, and Man (1994) and in particular the square root example in Nuprl by O'Leary, Leeser, Hickey, and Aagaard (1994), which is quite close to the integer core of our first example. Recently, Moore, Lynch, and Kaufmann (1996) describe the verification of a division algorithm. Because of the nature of the underlying logic in the ACL2 prover (quantifier-free first order arithmetic), they found it necessary to use rational numbers; therefore it would seem hard to extend these techniques to transcendental functions. All the examples we have cited use theorem proving. However Bryant (1995) shows how it is at least possible to verify single iterations of an SRT divider using model-checking techniques, while the verification of a floating-point multiplier by Aagaard and Seger (1995) uses the Voss system, which combines theorem proving and model checking to good effect.

Acknowledgements

Thanks to Tim Leonard and others at Digital Equipment Corporation in Boston for valuable help on floating point arithmetic.

8. Conclusions

The arrangement of previous chapters has more or less corresponded to a systematic walk through the code and theory development, and then our applications. However this was done with the aim of bringing out as many *general* points as possible. Sometimes implementation issues were discussed or not discussed, not on the grounds of their intrinsic interest or lack of it, but because they were or were not a convenient peg from which to hang general reflections. While it is of course always desirable to provide concrete illustrations of abstract phenomena, there is a danger that these general points have been submerged under the mass of detail. Accordingly, we will now recapitulate some of the themes that we consider to be important.

8.1 Mathematical contributions

This book was mainly concerned with theorem proving technology and its application. However we believe some parts of our work are of purely mathematical interest. In particular, Chapter 2 gives the only detailed comparison we know of different reals constructions and places them in perspective. Moreover, the mathematical details of the construction we use appear new, and it helps to clarify the otherwise rather puzzling notion of 'nearly additive' functions. The later development of mathematical analysis seems novel in some of the details, e.g. the approach to the transcendental functions.[1]

8.2 The formalization of mathematics

In general, the exigencies of computer formalization make us more careful about exactly which proof to choose, and help to give a more objective idea of just what is 'obvious'. (Even though this standard of obviousness doesn't always coincide with human intuition.) In this way, we tend either to invent

[1] In such a long-established branch of mathematics, it is difficult to claim with certainty that things are completely new. At least, we invented them independently and have not been able to find them in the literature, except where otherwise stated.

new notions ourselves (e.g. the approach to the transcendental functions) or find useful ideas in the literature (e.g. the Carathéodory derivative).

We believe our work also sheds interesting light on the connection between informal and formal mathematics. In particular, we have pointed out the subtleties over partial functions and the apparently uncontroversial matter of how to read equations $s = t$. We have also showed that in some cases formalization is not an uninteresting and artificial process (as for example the identification of (x, y) with $\{\{x\}, \{x, y\}\}$ in set theory arguably is). In particular, our analysis of bound variables is rather attractive.

Partial functions aside, our elementary analysis seems to work quite well in the HOL logic, more or less bearing out the remark by Hilbert and Ackermann (1950) that 'the calculus of order ω is the appropriate means for expressing the modes of inference of mathematical analysis'. In particular the analysis of all variable binding into λ-calculus is very elegant and clarifying. However, the formal separateness of $\mathbb{N}$ and $\mathbb{R}$ (not to mention $\mathbb{Z}$ and $\mathbb{C}$ ...) is something of an irritant. (IMPS, as well as its sophisticated support for partial functions, has a mechanism for subtypes which avoids these difficulties.) For multivariate calculus, it would be convenient to have at least a few very simple dependent types, such as n-ary Cartesian products for variable n. This would allow natural expression, for example, of theorems about functions $\mathbb{R}^m \to \mathbb{R}^n$, which at present would have to be handled by means of explicit set constraints. The author has been told that IMPS, which does not have dependent types, can nevertheless handle such examples adequately by using arbitrary types as the domains (in HOL, one could naturally use polymorphic types) but adding hypotheses about their dimension. This works particularly well if analysis is stepped up to more abstract Euclidean spaces.

New issues may be raised by formalizing different branches of mathematics. In particular, we feel that modern abstract algebra is likely to pose problems not only for type theories such as HOL's,[2] but even for more sophisticated ones. The most effective way to assess the difficulties is always to try it. For example Huet and Saïbi (1994) have been conducting an interesting investigation of category theory, which is notoriously hard to formalize even in set theory, in Coq. (Of course, one has to separate any difficulties arising from the use of types from those arising because of constructivity.) Perhaps the right solution, dispiriting though it may be to most theoretical computer scientists, is to use traditional set theory. Mizar for example uses ZF set theory plus the Tarski-Grothendieck axiom of universes;[3] there is a type system built on top but that has no foundational role. Gordon (1994) describes some ideas about combining the merits of set theory and type the-

[2] Even the definition of polynomials described in Chapter 6 needed some trickery to work nicely in HOL!

[3] This asserts that every set is contained in a universe set, i.e. a set closed under the usual generative principles. It was introduced by Tarski (1938), and subsequently popularized by Grothendieck in the 60s — SGA 4 (Grothendieck, Artin, and Verdier 1972) has an appendix on this topic attributed to 'N. Bourbaki'.

ory, and Agerholm (1994) has constructed the D_∞ model of λ-calculus in Gordon's combined system, something hard to do in a direct way in (at least simple) type theory.

8.3 The LCF approach to theorem proving

We have drawn attention on occasion to the usefulness of programmability. The development often included trivial nonce programs to automate tiresome bits of reasoning, and the ability to do this is very welcome. But it is even more important to be able to write substantial derived rules to automate tasks that, by hand, would be almost unbearably tedious, e.g.

- Defining quotient types
- Differentiating expressions
- Deciding formulas of elementary arithmetic

In a non-LCF system, such an extension would require insecure internal modification of the prover's code. The 'honest toil' of systematically developing the theory has certainly been hard work, but only needed to be done once. We can now have complete confidence in the soundness of the resulting theory.

At first sight the insistence on reduction to primitives might appear hopelessly impractical, but we believe that this work shows quite the reverse. Efficiency has not been a significant concern; we have found no indication that any proofs likely to arise in related fields of mathematics or verification would be infeasible for HOL. Certainly it is not possible to do arithmetic very efficiently, but we have shown that the system is still adequate for the uses we make of it. In fact both chapters 5 and 6 can be seen as particularly striking illustrations of the two main techniques for writing efficient LCF-style proof procedures: the use of proforma theorems, and the separation of search from inference. Both of these have been used by HOL experts for a long time, but our work is arguably the most sophisticated application to date. Boulton (1993) gave the first detailed analysis of the separation of proof search and inference; our work simply adds the new twist of performing search in a completely separate system. Much of the development we have described, in particular chapter 5, shows the power of encoding inferences in proforma theorems. The systematic adoption of this technique gives good reason for confidence that most theorem proving tasks can be implemented à la LCF with adequate efficiency. A more detailed exposition of some of the general lessons is given by Harrison (1995b). This includes for example a discussion of the importance of efficient equality testing of pointer-equivalent structures in order to make the 'proforma theorem' approach generally applicable. This has influenced some changes in the primitive 'prelogic' operations in the latest versions of HOL.

8.4 Computer algebra systems

We have seen that theorem provers and computer algebra systems offer complementary strengths, which it seems appealing to combine. Of course, whether a synthesis of the two styles is really *useful* remains to be seen. Apparently not many users of CASs are troubled by their logical inexpressiveness, still less by their incorrectness or imprecision. (Contrast the storm of protest over the Pentium floating point bug with the widespread indifference to the mathematical horrors lurking inside most CASs!) And it may be that the injection of mathematical rigour makes the systems much more difficult to use — rigour may mean rigor mortis. More practical experience is needed to determine this. If so, it may drive the invention of new ideas, or the resurrection of old ones, which bring the rigorous deductive mathematics and the freeswinging intuitive methods closer together; Nonstandard Analysis seems a promising possibility.

At the very least, however, we can say that computer algebra and theorem proving communities have a lot to learn from each other, and importing certain features of CASs into theorem provers seems an attractive project. Developing real computer algebra facilities inside a theorem prover is a major undertaking which could occupy a large research team for many years. Our work is modest in comparison, but gets a lot of mileage out of some fairly straightforward implementation work. It also highlights the general issue of 'finding vs checking' as applied to symbolic computation. It would be interesting to catalogue the algorithms currently used for various kinds of symbolic computation, analyzing whether they allow some kind of easy or efficient checking process. Where formal checkability is important, this could provide the central criterion for the selection of one algorithm over another.

8.5 Verification applications

We hope that the potential for theorem proving techniques in verification has been demonstrated. In particular, floating point verification seems an ideal application area, especially in view of current interest. It is only with access to theories of elementary analysis that a truly integrated mechanical proof of algorithms for the transcendental functions becomes possible. However we have shown that new theoretical difficulties then emerge over which form of specification provides the right balance between usefulness and practical implementability. As far as we know, these rather subtle issues have never been completely resolved. Such ideas will surely have to be explored by the inevitable committees which will attempt to standardize the behaviour of transcendental function implementations.

Whichever formal specification method is chosen, there seems no doubting the competence of present day theorem proving technology to establish correctness. These correctness proofs are a mixture of some fairly high-level mathematics with detailed consideration of overflow and the evaluation of precomputed constants. These respective components make them hard for model checkers and hard to do accurately by hand, so we believe that theorem provers like HOL are the ideal vehicle. The proofs we have given are based on relatively high-level algorithm descriptions, and we have ignored very low-level details of the arrangement of bitfields inside the machine. However there seems no difficulty in extending this sort of verification right down to the gate level, if desired.

8.6 Concluding remarks

Perhaps, like the dog that did not bark in the night, the most striking feature of our work is the wealth of possibilities that we have *not* considered. We could try formalizing many interesting and relevant branches of mathematics such as complex analysis, differential equations, integral transforms, approximation methods and classical dynamics. As for applications, we could for example use our work to link high-level verification efforts with analogue signal-level details (Hanna 1994). Thus there is the welcome, if ironic, possibility that although the use of the reals was motivated by the formal specification/informal intentions gap we drew attention to in the introduction, it could narrow the formal model/actual behaviour gap too! There are many other interesting targets for verification, including DSP chips and hybrid systems. Even the sample we have given is enough, we hope, to show how the real numbers open up new horizons in theorem proving.

A. Logical foundations of HOL

Here we will discuss the basics of HOL's types, terms and deductive system. Gordon and Melham (1993) give a discussion that is both more leisurely and more precise, but for an older version of HOL. The work in this thesis was done using our own HOL Light system, and the deductive foundations of this version have been significantly simplified, with fewer basic logical constants, simpler primitive inference rules and fewer axioms.

Terms and types

HOL's logic is based on λ-calculus, a formalism invented by Alonzo Church. In HOL, as in λ-calculus, there are only four kinds of term:

- Constants, e.g. $[]$ (the empty list), $\top$ (true) and $\bot$ (false). The set of constants is extensible by constant definition, which we discuss later.
- Variables, e.g. n, x, p. We assume some arbitrary denumerable set of variables; in HOL a variable may have any string as its name.
- Applications, e.g. $f(x)$. This represents the evaluation of a function f at an argument x; any terms may be used in place of f and x. The brackets are often omitted, e.g. $f\ x$.
- Abstractions, e.g. $\lambda x.\ t[x]$. This example represents 'the function of x that yields $t[x]$'. Any term may be used for the body; x need not appear free in it.

Abstractions are not often seen in informal mathematics, but they have at least two merits. First, they allow one to write anonymous function-valued expressions without naming them (occasionally one sees $x \mapsto t[x]$ used for this purpose), and since our logic is avowedly higher order, it's desirable to place functions on an equal footing with first-order objects in this way. Secondly, they make variable dependencies and binding explicit; by contrast in informal mathematics one often writes $f(x)$ in situations where one really means $\lambda x.\ f(x)$. *Lambda-calculus* is, as its name suggests, a formal deductive system based on the above syntax, namely a system of rules for generating equations $\vdash s = t$ (read the 'turnstile' symbol $\vdash$ as 'it is derivable that ...'). There are rules for the reflexivity and substitutivity of equality, as well as a few special lambda-calculus rules:

- Alpha-conversion means consistently changing the name of the variable in a λ-abstraction. It permits the deduction of equations like $\vdash (\lambda x.\ t[x]) = (\lambda y.\ t[y])$. On the intuitive semantics of lambda-expressions, this is obviously valid.
- Beta-conversion expresses the intention that abstraction and application are converse operations; it allows one to deduce equations like $\vdash (\lambda x.\ t[x])s = t[s]$.
- Eta-conversion incorporates a kind of extensionality principle, but expresses it purely in terms of the equation calculus. It allows the deduction of $\vdash (\lambda x.\ t\ x) = t$, where x is not free in t.

Church's original idea was to use λ-calculus as the core for a logical system, adding constants and additional rules for logical operations. For example, one can represent predication by function application, and truth by equality with the constant '$\top$'. Unfortunately this turned out to be inconsistent. For example, if N is a negation operation, one can derive the Russell paradox about the set of all sets that do not contain themselves (think of $P\ x$ as $x \in P$):

$$\vdash (\lambda x.\ N(x\ x))(\lambda x.\ N(x\ x)) = N((\lambda x.\ N(x\ x))(\lambda x.\ N(x\ x)))$$

Accordingly, Church (1940) augmented λ-calculus with a theory of types, simplifying Russell's system from Principia Mathematica and giving what is often called 'simple type theory'. HOL follows this system quite closely. Every term has a unique *type* which is either one of the basic types or the result of applying a type constructor to other types. The only basic types in HOL are initially the type of booleans, *bool* and the infinite type of individuals *ind*; the only type operator is the function space constructor $\rightarrow$. HOL extends Church's system by allowing also 'type variables' which give a form of polymorphism. Examples of HOL types then, include *ind* and $\alpha \rightarrow bool$ (where α is a type variable). We write $t : \gamma$ to indicate that a term t has type γ. Readers familiar with set theory may like to think of types as sets within which the objects denoted by the terms live, so $t : \gamma$ can be read as $t \in \gamma$. Note that the use of the colon is already standard in set theory when used for function spaces, i.e. one typically writes $f : A \rightarrow B$ rather than $f \in A \rightarrow B$.

Just as in typed programming languages, functions may only be applied to arguments of the right type; only a function of type $f : \gamma \rightarrow \ldots$ may be applied to an argument of type γ. This restriction is decidable and applied at the level of the term syntax. In fact, when a term is written down, even with no type annotations at all, HOL is capable not only of deciding whether it has a type, but inferring a most general type for it if it does. Essentially the same form of type inference goes on in the ML programming language; both use an algorithm given by Milner (1978).[1]

[1] Actually, the presence of overloaded operators, either in HOL or ML, complicates the most general type property. ML also features so-called `let`-polymorphism which has no counterpart in HOL.

Primitive inference rules

The HOL formal system allows the deduction of arbitrary *sequents* of the form $\phi_1, \ldots, \phi_n \vdash \psi$ (read as 'if ϕ_1 and ... and ϕ_n then ψ') where the terms involved have type *bool*; they need not simply be equations. (Where there are no assumptions it is customary to write just $\vdash \psi$.) There are no additional logical constants involved in the basic deductive system. The derivable sequents are those that can be generated by the following inference rules:

$$\frac{}{\vdash t = t}\ \texttt{REFL}$$

This rule says that equality is reflexive.

$$\frac{\Gamma \vdash s = t \quad \Delta \vdash t = u}{\Gamma \cup \Delta \vdash s = u}\ \texttt{TRANS}$$

This rule says that equality is transitive. It is of course necessary to include in the conclusion theorem any assumption that may have played a role in deducing the top two theorems.

$$\frac{\Gamma \vdash s = t \quad \Delta \vdash u = v}{\Gamma \cup \Delta \vdash s(u) = t(v)}\ \texttt{MK\_COMB}$$

This says that equal functions applied to equal arguments give equal results. We have assumed without comment that the types agree, e.g. $s : \sigma \to \tau$, $t : \sigma \to \tau$, $u : \sigma$ and $v : \sigma$.

$$\frac{\Gamma \vdash s = t}{\Gamma \vdash (\lambda x.\, s) = (\lambda x.\, t)}\ \texttt{ABS}$$

This rule requires that x is not a free variable in any of the assumptions Γ. It says that if, without using any special properties of x, we deduced that two expressions involving x are equal, then the functions that take x to those values are equal.

$$\frac{}{\vdash (\lambda x.\, t)x = t}\ \texttt{BETA}$$

This expresses the fact that combination and abstraction are converse operations, i.e. 'the function that takes an argument x to t', applied to an argument x, gives t.

$$\frac{}{\{p\} \vdash p}\ \texttt{ASSUME}$$

This says simply that from any p we can deduce p. Of course, p must have type *bool*.

$$\frac{\Gamma \vdash p = q \quad \Delta \vdash p}{\Gamma \cup \Delta \vdash q}\ \texttt{EQ\_MP}$$

This connects equality with deduction, saying that if p and q are equal, and we can deduce p, then we can deduce q (from the appropriately combined assumptions).

$$\frac{\Gamma \vdash p \quad \Delta \vdash q}{(\Gamma - \{q\}) \cup (\Delta - \{p\}) \vdash p = q} \text{ DEDUCT\_ANTISYM\_RULE}$$

This rule also connects equality and deduction, effectively saying that equality on the boolean type represents logical equivalence. Ignoring extra hypotheses for a moment, it says that if we can deduce p from q and q from p, then p and q are equal, under the accumulated assumptions.

$$\frac{\Gamma[x_1, \ldots, x_n] \vdash p[x_1, \ldots, x_n]}{\Gamma[t_1, \ldots, t_n] \vdash p[t_1, \ldots, t_n]} \text{ INST}$$

This rule expresses the fact that variables are to be interpreted as schematic, i.e. if p is true for variables $x_1, \ldots, x_n$, then we can replace those variables by any terms of the same type and still get something true. Note that the substitution is also applied to all hypotheses.

$$\frac{\Gamma[\alpha_1, \ldots, \alpha_n] \vdash p[\alpha_1, \ldots, \alpha_n]}{\Gamma[\gamma_1, \ldots, \gamma_n] \vdash p[\gamma_1, \ldots, \gamma_n]} \text{ INST\_TYPE}$$

This is the same, but for substitution of type variables rather than term variables.

Some readers may find certain aspects of the above discussion too imprecise or informal. For example, we have not defined precisely what a free variable is, nor the tricky process of substituting for term or type variables. Moreover, we have not given a detailed justification of why this particular axiomatization, a natural deduction system based on equality alone, was chosen. The short answer is that it seems a good compromise between simplicity and practical usability.

Definitions

All theorems in HOL are deduced using just the above rules, starting from a small set of *axioms*, which we will discuss shortly. Mathematics in HOL is derived just from these very basic axioms. However there is a special rule of definition, which allows the addition of new constants and corresponding new axioms provided they are purely definitional in character.[2] If $t : \tau$ is any term without free (term or type) variables, and $c : \tau$ an unused constant,

[2] From a logical point of view, we may say that HOL is actually an evolving sequence of logical systems, each a conservative extension of previous ones.

then $c : \tau$ may be added to the stock of constants, and the axiom $\vdash c = t$ included as a theorem.[3]

One can also define new types and type constructors in HOL. Given any subset of a type γ, marked out by its characteristic predicate $P : \gamma \to \mathit{bool}$, then given a theorem asserting that P is nonempty, one can define a new type (or type operator if γ contains type variables) in bijection with this set. Both these definitional principles give a way of producing new mathematical theories without compromising soundness: one can easily prove that these principles are consistency-preserving.

Derived rules

HOL's logic is then built up by including constants for the usual logical operations. An attractive feature is that these do not need to be postulated: it has been known since Henkin (1963) how to define all logical constants in terms of equality, at least from a classical point of view. We do things in an 'intuitionistic' manner, giving useful deductive rules before we later assert the Law of the Excluded Middle, i.e. that every Boolean term is either true or false. While it is more typical (Prawitz 1965) to take a few additional logical constants such as $\forall$ and $\Rightarrow$ as primitive, our approach is very similar to the usual definitions of the internal logic of a topos; see e.g. Lambek and Scott (1986).

We will now show how all the logical constants are defined. These are $\top$ (true), $\wedge$ (and), $\Rightarrow$ (implies), $\forall$ (for all), $\exists$ (there exists), $\vee$ (or), $\bot$ (false) $\neg$ (not) and $\exists!$ (there exists a unique). What we write as $\forall x.\, P[x]$ is a syntactic sugaring of $\forall(\lambda x.\, P[x])$. Using this technique, quantifiers and the Hilbert ε operator can be used as if they bound variables, but with all binding implemented in terms of λ-calculus. There are several examples in this book.

$$
\begin{aligned}
&\top = (\lambda x.\, x) = (\lambda x.\, x)\\
&\wedge = \lambda p.\, \lambda q.\, (\lambda f.\, f\; p\; q) = (\lambda f.\, f \top \top)\\
&\Rightarrow = \lambda p.\, \lambda q.\, p \wedge q = p\\
&\forall = \lambda P.\, P = \lambda x.\, \top\\
&\exists = \lambda P.\, \forall Q.\, (\forall x.\, P(x) \Rightarrow Q) \Rightarrow Q\\
&\vee = \lambda p.\, \lambda q.\, \forall r.\, (p \Rightarrow r) \Rightarrow (q \Rightarrow r) \Rightarrow r\\
&\bot = \forall P.\, P\\
&\neg = \lambda t.\, t \Rightarrow \bot\\
&\exists! = \lambda P.\, \exists P \wedge \forall x.\, \forall y.\, P\; x \wedge P\; y \Rightarrow (x = y)
\end{aligned}
$$

[3] HOL actually has a slightly more general principle of definition of which the above is a special case, but this is not relevant to this book.

From the definitions and the primitive rules, it is then possible to define derived inference rules that give convenient ways of manipulating logical formulas without explicitly taking everything back to the definitions. Because HOL is a programmable system in the LCF style, these can all be encapsulated as ML functions that look to the user the same as primitive rules.

Classical axioms

That concludes the logic proper, and in fact quite a bit of interesting mathematics, e.g. infinitary inductive definitions, can be developed just from that basis (Harrison 1995a). But for general use we adopt three more axioms. First there is an axiom of extensionality, which we encode as an η-conversion theorem: $\vdash (\lambda x.\, t\; x) = t$. Then we introduce one new primitive logical constant ε, of polymorphic type $(\alpha \to \mathit{bool}) \to \alpha$, the so-called Hilbert choice operator. It is accompanied by a new axiom giving the basic property of ε, namely that it picks out something satisfying P whenever there is something to pick:

$$\vdash \forall x.\, P(x) \Rightarrow P(\varepsilon x.\, P(x))$$

This is a form of the Axiom of (global) Choice. Rather surprisingly, it also makes the logic classical, i.e. allows us to prove the theorem $\vdash \forall p.\, p \vee \neg p$; see Beeson (1984) for the proof we use. Finally there is an axiom asserting that the type *ind* is infinite. the Dedekind/Peirce definition of 'infinite' is used:

$$\vdash \exists f : \mathit{ind} \to \mathit{ind}.(\forall x_1, x_2.(f(x_1) = f(x_2)) \Rightarrow (x_1 = x_2)) \wedge \neg(\forall y.\exists x.y = f(x))$$

From that simple foundation, all the HOL mathematics and applications, including those described here, is developed by definitional extension.

B. Recent developments

The main body of this book was written as our PhD thesis in the summer of 1996. Since then, we have continued to work in closely related areas, in particular completing a large verification (Harrison 1997a) of an algorithm due to Tang (1989) for calculating floating-point exponentials. This work represents a natural continuation of the last chapter, whose closing summary anticipated several of the main features.

First, this verification was based not on an ad hoc floating point format, but on the IEEE (1985) standard for binary floating point arithmetic. This wasn't done in the thesis partly for reasons of simplicity and partly because it did not seem necessary to get the main points across. However it is obviously important for verifying algorithms in an industrial situation. This required the HOL formalization of the IEEE standard, but that generally presented few difficulties. The standard has reasonable mathematical properties, though it requires us to deal in many situations with a few special cases such as infinities and NaNs that we managed to avoid before.

Secondly, the algorithm was not expressed as a recursive function in the HOL logic, but using an embedded imperative programming language. This seems much more natural and intuitive, in that it corresponds quite closely to the typical pseudocodes often used to describe algorithms. Moreover, our little language can naturally be seen as a subset either of programming languages like C or Ada, or of high-level hardware description languages such as Verilog, VHDL and Hardware C; hence it corresponds quite directly to implementations either in software or hardware. There are projects at the University of Cambridge Computer Laboratory looking at formal HOL-based semantics for the C programming language (Norrish 1997) and the Verilog hardware description language (Gordon 1995), as well as a new project concerned with Handel (Page 1996). We hope in due course to make a more formal connection with at least some of these efforts.

This verification required some additional work (Harrison 1997c) that makes an interesting supplement to several other book chapters. The algorithm uses a low-order polynomial approximation to the exponential function, and proving in a formal HOL way that this approximation has a sufficiently good error bound turned out to be the hardest part of the verification, in fact the only part that gave any real difficulty. We were able to reduce the problem to finding roots of a polynomial, and proving that they had all been found. For the latter part, we needed to prove Sturm's theorem in HOL, which forms a natural extension (or contraction!) of the work on decision procedures for the reals. Moreover, when we came to apply the theorem to the case in hand, we relied on the Maple computer algebra system to find squarefree decompositions, Sturm sequences, and sets of isolating intervals for the roots of polynomials, as well as to perform polynomial division. All these results were checked in HOL, following the approach given in Chapter 6 of the book. Finally, the verification involved a certain amount of explicit calculation, performed using the approaches indicated in Chapter 5. Whether this sort of approach is entirely satisfactory when such large numbers are involved is still not completely clear.

A significant omission in the main body of this book is any detailed discussion of how the HOL proofs look when doing formalized mathematics and/or verification applications. We sometimes indicated how long they are, how much time they took to construct, and other significant properties, but didn't pay much attention to their style or structure. In fact, we have come to believe that for mathematics at least the highly procedural tactic-based approach of HOL can probably be improved using some more declarative proof language such as the one used by Mizar (Trybulec 1978). These issues are considered rather discursively in a recent paper (Harrison 1997b).

Bibliography

Aagaard, M. D. and Seger, C.-J. H. (1995) The formal verification of a pipelined double-precision IEEE floating-point multiplier. In *Proceedings of the 1995 International Conference on Computer-Aided Design*, San Jose, CA.

Abian, A. (1979) An ultimate proof of Rolle's theorem. *The American Mathematical Monthly*, **86**, 484–485.

Abian, A. (1981) Calculus must consist of the study of real numbers in their decimal representation and not of the study of an abstract complete ordered field or nonstandard real numbers. *International Journal of Mathematical Education in Science and Technology*, **12**, 465–472.

Agerholm, S. (1994) Formalising a model of the λ-calculus in HOL-ST. Technical Report 354, University of Cambridge Computer Laboratory, New Museums Site, Pembroke Street, Cambridge, CB2 3QG, UK.

Almkvist, G. and Zeilberger, D. (1990) The method of differentiating under the integral sign. *Journal of Symbolic Computation*, **10**, 571–591.

Andersen, F., Petersen, K. D., and Pettersson, J. S. (1993) Program verification using HOL-UNITY. See Joyce and Seger (1993), pp. 1–15.

Archer, M., Fink, G., and Yang, L. (1992) Linking other theorem provers to HOL using PM: Proof manager. See Claesen and Gordon (1992), pp. 539–548.

Archer, M., Joyce, J. J., Levitt, K. N., and Windley, P. J. (eds.) (1991) *Proceedings of the 1991 International Workshop on the HOL theorem proving system and its Applications*, University of California at Davis, Davis CA, USA. IEEE Computer Society Press.

Archer, M. and Linz, P. (1991) On the verification of numerical software. In Kaucher, E., Markov, S. M., and Mayer, G. (eds.), *Computer Arithmetic: scientific computation and mathematical modelling*, pp. 117–131. J. C. Baltzer AG Scientific Publishing Co.

Argonne National Laboratories (1995) A summary of new results in mathematics obtained with Argonne's automated deduction software. Available on the Web: `http://www.mcs.anl.gov/home/mccune/ar/new_results/`.

Arthan, R. D. (1996) Undefinedness in Z: Issues for specification and proof. In Kerber, M. (ed.), *CADE-13 Workshop on Mechanization *of Partial Functions.* Workshop proceedings available on the Web in `ftp://ftp.cs.bham.ac.uk/pub/authors/M.Kerber/96-CADE-WS`.

Artmann, B. (1988) *The Concept of Number: From Quaternions to Monads and Topological Fields.* Ellis Horwood series in Mathematics and its Applications. Ellis Horwood. Original German edition, 'Der Zahlbegriff', published in 1983 by Vandenhoeck and Rupprecht, Göttigen. Translated with additional exercises and material by H.B. Griffiths.

Baker, A. (1975) *Transcendental Number Theory.* Cambridge University Press.

Ballantyne, A. M. and Bledsoe, W. W. (1977) Automatic proofs of theorems in analysis using non-standard techniques. *Journal of the ACM*, **24**, 353–374.

Ballarin, C., Homann, K., and Calmet, J. (1995) Theorems and algorithms: An interface between Isabelle and Maple. See Levelt (1995), pp. 150–157.

Barratt, M. (1989) Formal methods applied to a floating-point system. *IEEE Transactions on Software Engineering*, **15**, 611–621.

Beeson, M. (1992) Mathpert: Computer support for learning algebra, trig, and calculus. In Voronkov, A. (ed.), *Logic programming and automated reasoning: international conference LPAR '92*, Volume 624 of *Lecture Notes in Computer Science*, St. Petersburg, Russia, pp. 454–456. Springer-Verlag.

Beeson, M. J. (1984) *Foundations of constructive mathematics: metamathematical studies*, Volume 3 of *Ergebnisse der Mathematik und ihrer Grenzgebiete.* Springer-Verlag.

Behrend, F. A. (1956) A contribution to the theory of magnitudes and the foundations of analysis. *Mathematische Zeitschrift*, **63**, 345–362.

Bishop, E. and Bridges, D. (1985) *Constructive analysis*, Volume 279 of *Grundlehren der mathematischen Wissenschaften.* Springer-Verlag.

Blum, M. (1993) Program result checking: A new approach to making programs more reliable. In Lingas, A., Karlsson, R., and Carlsson, S. (eds.), *Automata, Languages and Programming, 20th International Colloquium, ICALP93, Proceedings*, Volume 700 of *Lecture Notes in Computer Science*, Lund, Sweden, pp. 1–14. Springer-Verlag.

Boehm, H. J., Cartwright, R., O'Donnel, M. J., and Riggle, M. (1986) Exact real arithmetic: a case study in higher order programming. In *Conference Record of the 1986 ACM Symposium on LISP and Functional Programming*, pp. 162–173. Association for Computing Machinery.

Boulton, R. (1992) A lazy approach to fully-expansive theorem proving. See Claesen and Gordon (1992), pp. 19–38.

Boulton, R. et al. (1993) Experience with embedding hardware description languages in HOL. In Stavridou, V., Melham, T. F., and Boute, R. T. (eds.), *Proceedings of the IFIP TC10/WG 10.2 International Conference on Theorem Provers in Circuit Design: Theory, Practice and Experience*, Volume A-10 of *IFIP Transactions A: Computer Science and Technology*, Nijmegen, The Netherlands, pp. 129–156. North-Holland.

Boulton, R. (1993) Efficiency in a fully-expansive theorem prover. Technical Report 337, University of Cambridge Computer Laboratory, New Museums Site, Pembroke Street, Cambridge, CB2 3QG, UK. Author's PhD thesis.

Bourbaki, N. (1966) *General topology*, Volume 1 of *Elements of mathematics*. Addison-Wesley. Translated from French 'Topologie Genérale' in the series 'Eléments de mathématique', originally published by Hermann in 1966.

Bowen, J. P. and Gordon, M. J. C. (1995) A shallow embedding of Z in HOL. *Information and Software Technology*, **37**, 269–276.

Boyer, R. S. and Moore, J. S. (1979) *A Computational Logic*. ACM Monograph Series. Academic Press.

Brent, R. P. (1976) Fast multiple-precision evaluation of elementary functions. *Journal of the ACM*, **23**, 242–251.

de Bruijn, N. G. (1976) Defining reals without the use of rationals. *Indagationes Mathematicae*, **38**, 100–108.

de Bruijn, N. G. (1980) A survey of the project AUTOMATH. In Seldin, J. P. and Hindley, J. R. (eds.), *To H. B. Curry: Essays in Combinatory Logic, Lambda Calculus, and Formalism*, pp. 589–606. Academic Press.

Bryant, R. E. (1986) Graph-based algorithms for Boolean function manipulation. *IEEE Transactions on Computers*, **C-35**, 677–691.

Bryant, R. E. (1995) Bit-level analysis of an SRT divide circuit. Technical Report CMU-CS-95-140, School of Computer Science, Carnegie Mellon University, Pittsburgh, PA 15213.

Bundy, A., Harmelen, F. v., Hesketh, J., and Smaill, A. (1991) Experiments with proof plans for induction. *Journal of Automated Reasoning*, **7**, 303–323.

Burkill, J. C. (1962) *A first course in mathematical analysis*. Cambridge University Press. New printing 1978.

Burkill, J. C. (1965) *The Lebesgue Integral*, Volume 44 of *Cambridge Tracts in Mathematics and Mathematical Physics*. Cambridge University Press.

Burkill, J. C. and Burkill, H. (1970) *A second course in mathematical analysis*. Cambridge University Press. New printing 1980.

Burrill, C. W. (1967) *Foundations of Real Numbers*. McGraw-Hill.

Calmet, J. and Homann, K. (1996) Classification of communication and cooperation mechanisms for logical and symbolic computation systems. In Baader, F. and Schulz, K. U. (eds.), *Proceedings of the First International Workshop 'Frontiers of Combining Systems' (FroCoS'96)*, Kluwer Series on Applied Logic, Munich, pp. 133–146. Kluwer.

Camilleri, A. J. (1990) Mechanizing CSP trace theory in higher order logic. *IEEE Transactions on Software Engineering*, **16**, 993–1004.

Cantor, D. G. (1981) Irreducible polynomials with integer coefficients have succinct certificates. *Journal of Algorithms*, **2**, 385–392.

Carnap, R. (1937) *The Logical Syntax of Language*. International library of psychology, philosophy and scientific method. Routledge & Kegan Paul. Translated from 'Logische Syntax der Sprache' by Amethe Smeaton

(Countess von Zeppelin), with some new sections not in the German original.

Chirimar, J. and Howe, D. J. (1992) Implementing constructive real analysis: Preliminary report. In Myers, J. P. and O'Donnell, M. J. (eds.), *Constructivity in Computer Science: Proceedings of Summer Symposium*, Volume 613 of *Lecture Notes in Computer Science*, San Antonio, TX, pp. 165–178. Springer-Verlag.

Church, A. (1940) A formulation of the Simple Theory of Types. *Journal of Symbolic Logic*, **5**, 56–68.

Claesen, L. J. M. and Gordon, M. J. C. (eds.) (1992) *Proceedings of the IFIP TC10/WG10.2 International Workshop on Higher Order Logic Theorem Proving and its Applications*, Volume A-20 of *IFIP Transactions A: Computer Science and Technology*, IMEC, Leuven, Belgium. North-Holland.

Clarke, E. and Zhao, X. (1991) Analytica — a theorem prover for Mathematica. Technical report, School of Computer Science, Carnegie Mellon University.

Clarke, E. M. and Emerson, E. A. (1981) Design and synthesis of synchronization skeletons using branching-time temporal logic. In Kozen, D. (ed.), *Logics of Programs*, Volume 131 of *Lecture Notes in Computer Science*, Yorktown Heights, pp. 52–71. Springer-Verlag.

Clément, D., Montagnac, F., and Prunet, V. (1991) Integrated software components: a paradigm for control integration. In Endres, A. and Weber, H. (eds.), *Software development environments and CASE technology: European symposium*, Volume 509 of *Lecture Notes in Computer Science*, Königwinter, pp. 167–177. Springer-Verlag.

Clenshaw, C. W. and Olver, F. W. J. (1984) Beyond floating point. *Journal of the ACM*, **31**, 319–328.

Cohen, L. W. and Ehrlich, G. (1963) *The Structure of the Real Number System*. The University Series in Undergraduate Mathematics. Van Nostrand.

Cohen, P. J. (1969) Decision procedures for real and p-adic fields. *Communications in Pure and Applied Mathematics*, **22**, 131–151.

Collins, G. E. (1976) Quantifier elimination for real closed fields by cylindrical algebraic decomposition. In Brakhage, H. (ed.), *Second GI Conference on Automata Theory and Formal Languages*, Volume 33 of *Lecture Notes in Computer Science*, Kaiserslautern, pp. 134–183. Springer-Verlag.

Conway, J. H. (1976) *On Numbers and Games*, Volume 6 of *L. M. S. Monographs*. Academic Press.

Coquand, T. (1992) An intuitionistic proof of Tychonoff's theorem. *Journal of Symbolic Logic*, **57**, 28–32.

Corbett, J. C. and Avrunin, G. S. (1995) Using integer programming to verify general safety and liveness properties. *Formal Methods in System Design*, **6**, 97–123.

Corless, R. M. and Jeffrey, D. J. (1992) Well... it isn't quite that simple. *SIGSAM Bulletin*, **26**(3), 2–6.

Dalen, D. v. and Monna, A. F. (1972) *Sets and Integration: an Outline of the Development.* Wolters-Noordhoff.

Dantzig, G. B. (1963) *Linear Programming and Extensions.* Princeton University Press.

Davenport, J. H. (1981) *On the integration of algebraic functions*, Volume 102 of *Lecture Notes in Computer Science.* Springer-Verlag.

Davenport, J. H., Siret, Y., and Tournier, E. (1988) *Computer algebra: systems and algorithms for algebraic computation.* Academic Press.

Davis, M. (1957) A computer program for Presburger's algorithm. In *Summaries of talks presented at the Summer Institute for Symbolic Logic, Cornell University*, pp. 215–233. Institute for Defense Analyses, Princeton, NJ. Reprinted in Siekmann and Wrightson (1983), pp. 41–48.

Dedekind, R. (1872) *Stetigkeit und Irrationalzahlen.* Braunschweig.

Denjoy, A. (1912) Une extension de l'intégrale de M. Lebesgue. *Comptes Rendus de l'Académie des Sciences, Paris*, **154**.

DePree, J. and Swartz, C. (1988) *Introduction to Real Analysis.* Wiley.

Dijkstra, E. W. (1976) *A Discipline of Programming.* Prentice-Hall.

van den Dries, L. (1988) Alfred Tarski's elimination theory for real closed fields. *Journal of Symbolic Logic*, **53**, 7–19.

Dutertre, B. (1996) Elements of mathematical analysis in PVS. In von Wright, J., Grundy, J., and Harrison, J. (eds.), *Theorem Proving in Higher Order Logics: 9th International Conference, TPHOLs'96*, Volume 1125 of *Lecture Notes in Computer Science*, Turku, Finland, pp. 141–156. Springer-Verlag.

Ebbinghaus, H.-D. et al. (1990) *Numbers*, Volume 123 of *Graduate Texts in Mathematics.* Springer-Verlag. Translation of the 2nd edition of 'Zahlen', 1988.

Ehrlich, P. (ed.) (1994) *Real numbers, Generalizations of the Reals, and Theories of Continua*, Volume 242 of *Synthese Library.* Kluwer.

Einwohner, T. H. and Fateman, R. J. (1995) Searching techniques for integral tables. See Levelt (1995), pp. 133–139.

Elbers, H. (1996) Construction of short formal proofs of primality. Preprint.

Enderton, H. B. (1972) *A Mathematical Introduction to Logic.* Academic Press.

Engeler, E. (1993) *Foundations of Mathematics: Questions of Analysis, Geometry and Algorithmics.* Springer-Verlag. Original German edition *Metamathematik der Elementarmathematik* in the *Series Hochschultext.*

Engelking, R. (1989) *General Topology*, Volume 6 of *Sigma series in pure mathematics.* Heldermann Verlag.

Erdös, P. and Szekeres, G. (1935) On a combinatorial problem in geometry. *Compositio Mathematica*, **2**, 463–470.

Ernst, G. W. and Hookway, R. J. (1976) The use of higher order logic in program verification. *IEEE Transactions on Computers*, **C-25**, 844–851.

Fagin, R. (1974) Generalized first-order spectra and polynomial-time recognizable sets. In Karp, R. M. (ed.), *Complexity of Computation*, Volume 7 of *SIAM-AMS Proceedings*, pp. 43–73. American Mathematical Society.

Faltin, F., Metropolis, N., Ross, B., and Rota, G.-C. (1975) The real numbers as a wreath product. *Advances in Mathematics*, **16**, 278–304.

Farmer, W., Guttman, J., and Thayer, J. (1990) IMPS: an interactive mathematical proof system. In Stickel, M. E. (ed.), *10th International Conference on Automated Deduction*, Volume 449 of *Lecture Notes in Computer Science*, Kaiserslautern, Federal Republic of Germany, pp. 653–654. Springer-Verlag.

Farmer, W. M. and Thayer, F. J. (1991) Two computer-supported proofs in metric space topology. *Notices of the American Mathematical Society*, **38**, 1133–1138.

Feferman, S. (1964) *The Number Systems: Foundations of Algebra and Analysis.* Addison-Wesley Series in Mathematics. Addison-Wesley.

Fike, C. T. (1968) *Computer Evaluation of Mathematical Functions.* Series in Automatic Computation. Prentice-Hall.

Forester, M. B. (1993) Formalizing constructive real analysis. Technical Report CORNELLCS:TR93-1382, Cornell University Department of Computer Science.

Freyd, P. J. and Scedrov, A. (1990) *Categories, allegories.* North-Holland.

Gabbay, D. (1973) The undecidability of intuitionistic theories of algebraically closed fields and real closed fields. *Journal of Symbolic Logic*, **38**, 86–92.

Goldberg, D. (1991) What every computer scientist should know about floating point arithmetic. *ACM Computing Surveys*, **23**, 5–48.

Gordon, M. J. C. (1985) Why higher-order logic is a good formalism for specifying and verifying hardware. Technical Report 77, University of Cambridge Computer Laboratory, New Museums Site, Pembroke Street, Cambridge, CB2 3QG, UK.

Gordon, M. J. C. (1994) Merging HOL with set theory: preliminary experiments. Technical Report 353, University of Cambridge Computer Laboratory, New Museums Site, Pembroke Street, Cambridge, CB2 3QG, UK.

Gordon, M. J. C. (1995) The semantic challenge of Verilog HDL. In *Proceedings of the Tenth Annual IEEE Symposium on Logic in Computer Science*, San Diego, CA, USA, pp. 136–145. IEEE Computer Society Press.

Gordon, M. J. C. (1989) Mechanizing programming logics in higher order logic. In Birtwistle, G. and Subrahmanyam, P. A. (eds.), *Current Trends in Hardware Verification and Automated Theorem Proving*, pp. 387–439. Springer-Verlag.

Gordon, M. J. C. (1996) From LCF to HOL and beyond. Festschrift for Robin Milner, to appear.

Gordon, M. J. C. and Melham, T. F. (1993) *Introduction to HOL: a theorem proving environment for higher order logic.* Cambridge University Press.

Gordon, M. J. C., Milner, R., and Wadsworth, C. P. (1979) *Edinburgh LCF: A Mechanised Logic of Computation*, Volume 78 of *Lecture Notes in Computer Science*. Springer-Verlag.

Grothendieck, A., Artin, M., and Verdier, J. L. (1972) *Théorie des Topos et Cohomologie Étale des Schemas (SGA 4), vol. 1*, Volume 269 of *Lecture Notes in Mathematics*. Springer-Verlag.

Haggarty, R. (1989) *Fundamentals of Mathematical Analysis*. Addison-Wesley.

Hanna, F. K. and Daeche, N. (1986) Specification and verification using higher-order logic: A case study. In Milne, G. and Subrahmanyam, P. A. (eds.), *Formal Aspects of VLSI Design: Proceedings of the 1985 Edinburgh Workshop on VLSI*, pp. 179–213.

Hanna, K. (1994) Reasoning about real circuits. In Melham, T. F. and Camilleri, J. (eds.), *Higher Order Logic Theorem Proving and Its Applications: Proceedings of the 7th International Workshop*, Volume 859 of *Lecture Notes in Computer Science*, Valletta, Malta, pp. 235–253. Springer-Verlag.

Harrison, J. (1991) The HOL reduce library. Distributed with HOL system.

Harrison, J. (1994) Constructing the real numbers in HOL. *Formal Methods in System Design*, **5**, 35–59.

Harrison, J. (1995a) Inductive definitions: automation and application. In Windley, P. J., Schubert, T., and Alves-Foss, J. (eds.), *Higher Order Logic Theorem Proving and Its Applications: Proceedings of the 8th International Workshop*, Volume 971 of *Lecture Notes in Computer Science*, Aspen Grove, Utah, pp. 200–213. Springer-Verlag.

Harrison, J. (1995b) Metatheory and reflection in theorem proving: A survey and critique. Technical Report CRC-053, SRI Cambridge, Millers Yard, Cambridge, UK. This report is also available on the Web as `http://www.cl.cam.ac.uk/users/jrh/papers/reflect.dvi.gz`.

Harrison, J. (1997a) Floating point verification in HOL Light: The exponential function. Technical Report 428, University of Cambridge Computer Laboratory, New Museums Site, Pembroke Street, Cambridge, CB2 3QG, UK.

Harrison, J. (1997b) Proof style. Technical Report 410, University of Cambridge Computer Laboratory, New Museums Site, Pembroke Street, Cambridge, CB2 3QG, UK. To appear in the proceedings of TYPES'96, Lecture Notes in Computer Science, Springer-Verlag 1998. Also available on the Web as `http://www.cl.cam.ac.uk/users/jrh/papers/style.html`.

Harrison, J. (1997c) Verifying the accuracy of polynomial approximations in HOL. In Gunter, E. L. and Felty, A. (eds.), *Theorem Proving in Higher Order Logics: 10th International Conference, TPHOLs'97*, Volume 1275 of *Lecture Notes in Computer Science*, Murray Hill, NJ, pp. 137–152. Springer-Verlag.

Harrison, J. and Théry, L. (1993) Extending the HOL theorem prover with a computer algebra system to reason about the reals. See Joyce and Seger (1993), pp. 174–184.

Henkin, L. (1963) A theory of propositional types. *Fundamenta Mathematicae*, **52**, 323–344.

Henstock, R. (1968) A Riemann-type integral of Lebesgue power. *Canadian Journal of Mathematics*, **20**, 79–87.

Henstock, R. (1991) *The General Theory of Integration.* Clarendon Press.

Hilbert, D. and Ackermann, W. (1950) *Principles of Mathematical Logic.* Chelsea. Translation of 'Grundzüge der theoretischen Logik', 2nd edition (1938; first edition 1928); translated by Lewis M. Hammond, George G. Leckie and F. Steinhardt; edited with notes by Robert E. Luce.

Hobbes, T. (1651) *Leviathan.* Andrew Crooke.

Hodges, W. (1993) *Model Theory*, Volume 42 of *Encyclopedia of Mathematics and its Applications.* Cambridge University Press.

Holmes, R. M. (1998) *Naive Set Theory with a Universal Set*, Volume 10 of *Cahiers du Centre de logique.* Bruylant-Academia, Louvain-la-Neuve.

Hooker, J. N. (1988) A quantitative approach to logical inference. *Decision Support Systems*, **4**, 45–69.

Hoover, D. N. and McCullough, D. (1993) Verifying launch interceptor routines with the asymptotic method. Technical report TM-93-0034, Odyssey Research Associates, 301 Dates Drive, Ithaca NY 14850-1326, USA.

Huet, G. (1975) A unification algorithm for typed λ-calculus. *Theoretical Computer Science*, **1**, 27–57.

Huet, G. and Lang, B. (1978) Proving and applying program transformations expressed with second-order patterns. *Acta Informatica*, **11**, 31–56.

Huet, G. and Saïbi, A. (1994) Constructive category theory. On the Web: `ftp://ftp.inria.fr/INRIA/Projects/coq/Gerard.Huet/Cat.dvi.Z`.

IEEE (1985) Standard for binary floating point arithmetic. ANSI/IEEE Standard 754-1985, The Institute of Electrical and Electronic Engineers, Inc., 345 East 47th Street, New York, NY 10017, USA.

Jacobson, N. (1989) *Basic Algebra I* (2nd ed.). W. H. Freeman.

Johnstone, P. T. (1982) *Stone spaces*, Volume 3 of *Cambridge studies in advanced mathematics.* Cambridge University Press.

Jones, C. (1991) Completing the rationals and metric spaces in LEGO. In Huet, G., Plotkin, G., and Jones, C. (eds.), *Proceedings of the Second Workshop on Logical Frameworks*, pp. 209–222. Available by FTP from `ftp.dcs.ed.ac.uk` as `export/bra/proc91.dvi.Z`.

Joyce, J. J. (1991) More reasons why higher-order logic is a good formalism for specifying and verifying hardware. In Subrahmanyam, P. A. (ed.), *Proceedings of the 1991 International Workshop on Formal Methods in VLSI Design*, Miami.

Joyce, J. J. and Seger, C. (eds.) (1993) *Proceedings of the 1993 International Workshop on the HOL theorem proving system and its applications*, Volume 780 of *Lecture Notes in Computer Science*, UBC, Vancouver, Canada. Springer-Verlag.

Jutting, L. S. van Bentham (1977) *Checking Landau's "Grundlagen" in the AUTOMATH System*. Ph. D. thesis, Eindhoven University of Technology. Useful summary in Nederpelt, Geuvers, and Vrijer (1994), pp. 701–732.

Kajler, N. (1992) CAS/Pi: A portable and extensible interface for computer algebra systems. In Wang, P. S. (ed.), *International Symposium on Symbolic and Algebraic Computation, ISSAC'92*, pp. 376–386. Association for Computing Machinery.

Kantrowitz, M. and Noack, L. M. (1995) Functional verification of a multiple-issue, pipelined, superscalar Alpha processor — the Alpha 21164 CPU chip. *Digital Technical Journal*, **7**, 136–144.

Karmarkar, N. (1984) A new polynomial-time algorithm for linear programming. *Combinatorica*, **4**, 373–395.

Kelley, J. L. (1975) *General topology*, Volume 27 of *Graduate Texts in Mathematics*. Springer-Verlag. First published by D. van Nostrand in 1955.

Khachian, L. G. (1979) A polynomial algorithm in linear programming. *Soviet Mathematics Doklady*, **20**, 191–194.

Knuth, D. E. (1969) *The Art of Computer Programming; Volume 2: Seminumerical Algorithms*. Addison-Wesley Series in Computer Science and Information processing. Addison-Wesley.

Kreisel, G. (1990) Logical aspects of computation: Contributions and distractions. In *Logic and Computer Science*, Volume 31 of *APIC Studies in Data Processing*, pp. 205–278. Academic Press.

Kreisel, G. and Krivine, J.-L. (1971) *Elements of mathematical logic: model theory* (Revised second ed.). Studies in Logic and the Foundations of Mathematics. North-Holland. First edition 1967. Translation of the French 'Eléments de logique mathématique, théorie des modeles' published by Dunod, Paris in 1964.

Kuhn, S. (1991) The derivative à la Carathéodory. *The American Mathematical Monthly*, **98**, 40–44.

Kumar, R., Kropf, T., and Schneider, K. (1991) Integrating a first-order automatic prover in the HOL environment. See Archer, Joyce, Levitt, and Windley (1991), pp. 170–176.

Kurzweil, J. (1958) Generalized ordinary differential equations and continuous dependence on a parameter. *Czechoslovak Mathematics Journal*, **82**, 418–446.

Lakatos, I. (1976) *Proofs and Refutations: the Logic of Mathematical Discovery*. Cambridge University Press. Edited by John Worrall and Elie Zahar. Derived from Lakatos's Cambridge PhD thesis; an earlier version was published in the *British Journal for the Philosophy of Science* vol. 14.

Lambek, J. and Scott, P. J. (1986) *Introduction to higher order categorical logic*, Volume 7 of *Cambridge studies in advanced mathematics*. Cambridge University Press.

Landau, E. (1930) *Grundlagen der Analysis.* Leipzig. English translation by F. Steinhardt: 'Foundations of analysis: the arithmetic of whole, rational, irrational, and complex numbers. A supplement to textbooks on the differential and integral calculus', published by Chelsea; 3rd edition 1966.

Landin, P. J. (1966) The next 700 programming languages. *Communications of the ACM*, **9**, 157–166.

Lang, S. (1994) *Algebra* (3rd ed.). Addison-Wesley.

Lazard, D. (1988) Quantifier elimination: Optimal solution for two classical examples. *Journal of Symbolic Computation*, **5**, 261–266.

Leonard, T. (1993) The HOL numeral library. Distributed with HOL system.

Levelt, A. H. M. (ed.) (1995) *International Symposium on Symbolic and Algebraic Computation, ISSAC'95*, Montreal. Association for Computing Machinery.

Libes, D. (1995) *Exploring Expect: a Tcl-based toolkit for automating interactive programs.* O'Reilly.

Lightstone, A. H. (1965) *Symbolic Logic and the Real Number System.* Harper and Row.

Lindemann, F. (1882) Über die Zahl π. *Mathematische Annalen*, **120**, 213–225.

Łojasiewicz, S. (1964) Triangulations of semi-analytic sets. *Annali della Scuola Normale Superiore di Pisa, ser. 3*, **18**, 449–474.

Loos, R. and Weispfenning, V. (1993) Applying linear quantifier elimination. *The Computer Journal*, **36**, 450–462.

Mahler, K. (1953) On the approximation of logarithms of algebraic numbers. *Philosophical Transactions of the Royal Society of London, Series A*, **245**, 371–398.

McCune, W. (1997) Solution of the Robbins problem. *Journal of Automated Reasoning*, **19**, 263–276.

McShane, E. J. (1973) A unified theory of integration. *The American Mathematical Monthly*, **80**, 349–357.

Megill, N. D. (1996) Metamath: A computer language for pure mathematics. On the Web: `ftp://ftp.shore.net/members/ndm/metamath.ps.gz`.

Mehlhorn, K. et al. (1996) Checking geometric programs or verification of geometric structures. In *Proceedings of the 12th Annual Symposium on Computational Geometry (FCRC'96)*, Philadelphia, pp. 159–165. Association for Computing Machinery.

Melham, T. F. (1992) The HOL logic extended with quantification over type variables. See Claesen and Gordon (1992), pp. 3–18.

Melham, T. F. (1993) *Higher Order Logic and Hardware Verification*, Volume 31 of *Cambridge Tracts in Theoretical Computer Science.* Cambridge University Press. A revision of the author's PhD thesis.

Ménissier-Morain, V. (1994) *Arithmétique exacte, conception, algorithmique et performances d'une implémentation informatique en précision arbitraire.* Thèse, Université Paris 7.

Meray, C. (1869) Remarques sur la nature des quantités définies par la condition de servir de limites à des variables données. *Revue des Sociétés savantes, Sciences mathématiques, physiques et naturelles (2nd series)*, **4**.

Milner, R. (1978) A theory of type polymorphism in programming. *Journal of Computer and Systems Sciences*, **17**, 348–375.

Miner, P. S. (1995) Defining the IEEE-854 floating-point standard in PVS. Technical memorandum 110167, NASA Langley Research Center, Hampton, VA 23681-0001, USA.

Moore, J S., Lynch, T., and Kaufmann, M. (1996) A mechanically checked proof of the correctness of the kernel of the $AMD5_K86$ floating-point division algorithm. Unpublished technical report; available on the Web as `http://devil.ece.utexas.edu:80/~lynch/divide/divide.html`.

Moskowski, B. C. (1986) *Executing Temporal Logic Programs*. Cambridge University Press.

Nederpelt, R. P., Geuvers, J. H., and Vrijer, R. C. de (eds.) (1994) *Selected Papers on Automath*, Volume 133 of *Studies in Logic and the Foundations of Mathematics*. North-Holland.

Negri, S. and Soravia, D. (1995) The continuum as a formal space. Rapporto Interno 17-7-95, Dipartimento di Matematica Pura e Applicata, Università di Padova.

Nesi, M. (1993) Value-passing CCS in HOL. See Joyce and Seger (1993), pp. 352–365.

Ng, K. C. (1992) Argument reduction for huge arguments: Good to the last bit. Unpublished draft, available from the author (`kwok.ng@eng.sun.com`).

Norrish, M. (1997) An abstract dynamic semantics for C. Technical Report 421, University of Cambridge Computer Laboratory, New Museums Site, Pembroke Street, Cambridge, CB2 3QG, UK.

O'Leary, J., Leeser, M., Hickey, J., and Aagaard, M. (1994) Non-restoring integer square root: A case study in design by principled optimization. In Kropf, T. and Kumar, R. (eds.), *Proceedings of the Second International Conference on Theorem Provers in Circuit Design (TPCD94): Theory, Practice and Experience*, Volume 901 of *Lecture Notes in Computer Science*, Bad Herrenalb (Black Forest), Germany, pp. 52–71. Springer-Verlag.

Owre, S., Rushby, J. M., and Shankar, N. (1992) PVS: A prototype verification system. In Kapur, D. (ed.), *11th International Conference on Automated Deduction*, Volume 607 of *Lecture Notes in Computer Science*, Saratoga, NY, pp. 748–752. Springer-Verlag.

Page, I. (1996) Constructing hardware-software systems from a single description. *Journal of VLSI Signal Processing*, **12**, 87–107.

Parker, F. D. (1966) *The Structure of Number Systems*. Teachers' Mathematics Reference series. Prentice-Hall.

Paulson, L. C. (1987) *Logic and computation: interactive proof with Cambridge LCF*, Volume 2 of *Cambridge Tracts in Theoretical Computer Science*. Cambridge University Press.

Paulson, L. C. (1994) *Isabelle: a generic theorem prover*, Volume 828 of *Lecture Notes in Computer Science.* Springer-Verlag. With contributions by Tobias Nipkow.

Payne, M. and Hanek, R. (1983) Radian reduction for trigonometric functions. *SIGNUM Newsletter*, **18**(1), 19–24.

Perron, O. (1914) Über den Integralbegriff. *Heidelberg Akademie, Wissenschaftlich Abteilung A*, **16**, 1–16.

Pesin, I. N. (1970) *Classical and modern integration theories.* Academic Press.

Pomerance, C. (1987) Very short primality proofs. *Mathematics of Computation*, **48**, 315–322.

Pratt, V. (1975) Every prime has a succinct certificate. *SIAM Journal of Computing*, **4**, 214–220.

Pratt, V. R. (1995) Anatomy of the Pentium bug. In Mosses, P. D., Nielsen, M., and Schwartzbach, M. I. (eds.), *Proceedings of the 5th International Joint Conference on the theory and practice of software development (TAPSOFT'95)*, Volume 915 of *Lecture Notes in Computer Science*, Aarhus, Denmark, pp. 97–107. Springer-Verlag.

Prawitz, D. (1965) *Natural deduction; a proof-theoretical study*, Volume 3 of *Stockholm Studies in Philosophy.* Almqvist and Wiksells.

Presburger, M. (1930) Über die Vollständigkeit eines gewissen Systems der Arithmetik ganzer Zahlen, in welchem die Addition als einzige Operation hervortritt. In *Sprawozdanie z I Kongresu metematyków slowiańskich, Warszawa 1929*, pp. 92–101, 395. Warsaw. Annotated English version by Stansifer (1984).

Rabin, M. O. (1991) Decidable theories. In Barwise, J. and Keisler, H. (eds.), *Handbook of mathematical logic*, Volume 90 of *Studies in Logic and the Foundations of Mathematics*, pp. 595–629. North-Holland.

Remes, M. E. (1934) Sur le calcul effectif des polynomes d'approximation de Tchebichef. *Comptes Rendus Hebdomadaires des Séances de l'Académie des Sciences*, **199**, 337–340.

Richmond, D. E. (1985) An elementary proof of a theorem in calculus. *The American Mathematical Monthly*, **92**, 589–590.

Roberts, J. B. (1962) *The Real Number System in an Algebraic Setting.* W. H. Freeman and Company.

Robinson, A. (1956) *Complete Theories.* Studies in Logic and the Foundations of Mathematics. North-Holland.

Robinson, A. (1963) *Introduction to model theory and to the metamathematics of algebra.* Studies in Logic and the Foundations of Mathematics. North-Holland.

Robinson, A. (1966) *Non-standard Analysis.* Studies in Logic and the Foundations of Mathematics. North-Holland.

Robinson, J. (1949) Definability and decision problems in arithmetic. *Journal of Symbolic Logic*, **14**, 98–114. Author's PhD thesis.

Rudin, W. (1976) *Principles of Mathematical Analysis* (3rd ed.). McGraw-Hill.

Rushby, J. (1991) Design choices in specification languages and verification systems. See Archer, Joyce, Levitt, and Windley (1991), pp. 194–204.

Russell, B. (1919) *Introduction to mathematical philosophy.* Allen & Unwin.

Sambin, G. (1987) Intuitionistic formal spaces — a first communication. In Skordev, D. G. (ed.), *Mathematical Logic and its Applications: Proceedings of an Advanced International Summer School in honor of the 80th anniversary of Kurt Gödel's birth*, Druzhba, Bulgaria, pp. 187–204. Plenum Press.

Seger, C. and Joyce, J. J. (1991) A two-level formal verification methodology using HOL and COSMOS. Technical Report 91-10, Department of Computer Science, University of British Columbia, 2366 Main Mall, University of British Columbia, Vancouver, B.C, Canada V6T 1Z4.

Seger, C.-J. H. and Bryant, R. E. (1995) Formal verification by symbolic evaluation of partially-ordered trajectories. *Formal Methods in System Design*, **6**, 147–189.

Seidenberg, A. (1954) A new decision method for elementary algebra. *Annals of Mathematics*, **60**, 365–374.

Siekmann, J. and Wrightson, G. (eds.) (1983) *Automation of Reasoning — Classical Papers on Computational Logic, Vol. I (1957-1966).* Springer-Verlag.

Slind, K. (1991) An implementation of higher order logic. Technical Report 91-419-03, University of Calgary Computer Science Department, 2500 University Drive N. W., Calgary, Alberta, Canada, TN2 1N4. Author's Masters thesis.

Spivey, J. M. (1988) *Understanding Z: a specification language and its formal semantics*, Volume 3 of *Cambridge Tracts in Theoretical Computer Science.* Cambridge University Press.

Stålmarck, G. (1994) System for determining propositional logic theorems by applying values and rules to triplets that are generated from Boolean formula. United States Patent number 5,276,897; see also Swedish Patent 467 076.

Stansifer, R. (1984) Presburger's article on integer arithmetic: Remarks and translation. Technical Report CORNELLCS:TR84-639, Cornell University Computer Science Department.

Stoll, R. R. (1979) *Set theory and logic.* Dover Publications. Originally published by W.H. Freeman in 1963.

Sutherland, D. (1984) Formal verification of mathematical software. Technical Report CR 172407, NASA Langley Research Center, Hampton, VA, 23665, USA.

Szczerba, L. W. (1989) The use of Mizar MSE in a course in foundations of geometry. In Srzednicki, J. (ed.), *Initiatives in logic*, Volume 2 of *Reason and argument series.* M. Nijhoff.

Tang, P. T. P. (1989) Table-driven implementation of the exponential function in IEEE floating-point arithmetic. *ACM Transactions on Mathematical Software*, **15**, 144–157.

Tarski, A. (1936) Der Wahrheitsbegriff in den formalisierten Sprachen. *Studia Philosophica*, **1**, 261–405. English translation, 'The Concept of Truth in Formalized Languages', in Tarski (1956), pp. 152–278.

Tarski, A. (1938) Über unerreichbare Kardinalzahlen. *Fundamenta Mathematicae*, **30**, 176–183.

Tarski, A. (1951) *A Decision Method for Elementary Algebra and Geometry*. University of California Press. Previous version published as a technical report by the RAND Corporation, 1948; prepared for publication by J. C. C. McKinsey.

Tarski, A. (ed.) (1956) *Logic, Semantics and Metamathematics*. Clarendon Press.

Théry, L. (1997) Proving and computing: a certified version of the Buchberger's algorithm. Research report RR-3275, INRIA Sophia Antipolis.

Thompson, H. B. (1989) Taylor's theorem using the generalized Riemann integral. *The American Mathematical Monthly*, **97**, 346–350.

Thurston, H. A. (1956) *The number system*. Blackie.

Trybulec, A. (1978) The Mizar-QC/6000 logic information language. *ALLC Bulletin (Association for Literary and Linguistic Computing)*, **6**, 136–140.

Turing, A. M. (1936) On computable numbers, with an application to the Entscheidungsproblem. *Proceedings of the London Mathematical Society (2)*, **42**, 230–265.

Van Tassel, J. P. (1993) Femto-VHDL: The semantics of a subset of VHDL and its embedding in the HOL proof assistant. Technical Report 317, University of Cambridge Computer Laboratory, New Museums Site, Pembroke Street, Cambridge, CB2 3QG, UK. Author's PhD thesis.

Verkest, D., Claesen, L., and Man, H. D. (1994) A proof of the nonrestoring division algorithm and its implementation on an ALU. *Formal Methods in System Design*, **4**, 5–31.

Volder, J. (1959) The CORDIC trigonometric computing technique. *IRE Transactions on Electronic Computers*, **8**, 330–334.

Vorobjov, N. N. (1990) Deciding consistency of systems of polynomial in exponent inequalities in subexponential time. In Mora, T. and Traverso, C. (eds.), *Proceedings of the MEGA-90 Symposium on Effective Methods in Algebraic Geometry*, Volume 94 of *Progress in Mathematics*, Castiglioncello, Livorno, Italy, pp. 491–500. Birkhäuser.

Walters, H. R. and Zantema, H. (1995) Rewrite systems for integer arithmetic. In Hsiang, J. (ed.), *Rewriting techniques and applications: 6th international conference, RTA'95*, Volume 914 of *Lecture Notes in Computer Science*, Kaiserslautern, Germany, pp. 324–338. Springer-Verlag.

Walther, J. S. (1971) A unified algorithm for elementary functions. In *Proceedings of the AFIPS Spring Joint Computer Conference*, pp. 379–385.

Weispfenning, V. and Becker, T. (1993) *Groebner bases: a computational approach to commutative algebra.* Graduate Texts in Mathematics. Springer-Verlag.

Whitehead, A. N. and Russell, B. (1910) *Principia Mathematica (3 vols).* Cambridge University Press.

Wichmann, B. A. (1989) Towards a formal specification of floating point. *The Computer Journal*, **32**, 432–436.

Wilkie, A. J. (1996) Model completeness results for expansions of the ordered field of reals by restricted Pfaffian functions and the exponential function. *Journal of the American Mathematical Society*, **9**, 1051–1094.

Wilkinson, J. H. (1963) *Rounding Errors in Algebraic Processes*, Volume 32 of *National Physical Laboratory Notes on Applied Science.* Her Majesty's Stationery Office (HMSO), London.

von Wright, J. (1991) Mechanising the Temporal Logic of Actions in HOL. See Archer, Joyce, Levitt, and Windley (1991), pp. 155–159.

von Wright, J., Hekanaho, J., Luostarinen, P., and Långbacka, T. (1993) Mechanizing some advanced refinement concepts. *Formal Methods in System Design*, **3**, 49–82.

Index

MIX
Papier aus verantwortungsvollen Quellen
Paper from responsible sources
FSC® C105338
FSC
www.fsc.org

If you have any concerns about our products,
you can contact us on
ProductSafety@springernature.com

In case Publisher is established outside the EU,
the EU authorized representative is:
Springer Nature Customer Service Center GmbH
Europaplatz 3, 69115 Heidelberg, Germany

Printed by Libri Plureos GmbH
in Hamburg, Germany